Central Bank Digital Currency

Leo Kriese

Central Bank Digital Currency

A Technical, Legal and Economic Analysis

Springer

Leo Kriese
Frankfurt am Main, Germany

ISBN 978-3-031-44737-2 ISBN 978-3-031-44738-9 (eBook)
https://doi.org/10.1007/978-3-031-44738-9

This Springer imprint is published by the registered company Springer Nature Switzerland AG
The registered company address is: Gewerbestrasse 11, 6330 Cham, Switzerland

Preface

This book is based on my dissertation which was accepted by the Faculty of Law of the Friedrich-Schiller-University of Jena in spring of 2023. The dissertation was written during my work as a research assistant at the Chair of Public Law, European Law, Public International Law and International Economic Law.

I would like to thank my esteemed doctoral supervisor, Prof. Dr. Christoph Ohler, LL.M., for the excellent supervision of the thesis. He was instrumental in bringing the thesis about this topic into being. I am extremely grateful for the trust he has placed in me, his valuable support and the academic freedom he has granted me. I am indebted to Prof. Dr. Christian Alexander for the rapid preparation of the second opinion and his valuable advice on the civil law part of this book.

I am greatly indebted to Jan Ceyssens and Laszlo Butt from the European Commission's DG FISMA. They gave me the opportunity to gain an insight into the practical handling of my topic during a research stay in Brussels in late summer of 2022. I am extremely grateful for that extraordinary opportunity and the valuable support I received.

My sincere thanks go to all those who have accompanied and supported me in the creative process in very different ways, especially my former colleagues at the European Commission. I am particularly grateful towards Jérôme Deslandes, Julio Baquero-Cruz, Marine Puel, Ulrich Clemens, Geneviève Janssens, Raphael Lemahieu and Anton Jevcak for their infinite patience in answering my many questions and their valuable advice.

Finally, special thanks are due to my mother. It is also thanks to her that this book was able to come into being in this form. Her constant encouragement and support in the course of writing the manuscript has strengthened my resolve to complete the work in this short period of time.

Frankfurt am Main, Germany
Summer 2023

Leo Kriese

Contents

Abbreviations

AML	Anti-Money Laundering
BGB	German Civil Code
BGBl.	German Federal Law Gazette
BGH	German Federal Supreme Court of Justice
BVerfG	German Federal Constitutional Court
CASP	Crypto-asset service provider
CBDC	Central Bank Digital Currency
cf.	Compare
CFR	Charter of Fundamental Rights of the European Union
CFT	Countering the Financing of Terrorism
DLT	Distributed ledger technology
EBA	European Banking Authority
ECB	European Central Bank
ECJ	European Court of Justice
ECtHR	European Court of Human Rights
ed	Editor(s)
edn.	Edition
EIOPA	European Insurance and Occupational Pensions Authority
ELB	Effective Lower Bound
ELTEG	EURO Legal Tender Expert Group
EMU	Economic and Monetary Union
ESCB	European System of Central Banks
ESMA	European Securities and Markets Authority
ESRB	European Systemic Risk Board
f.n.	Footnote
FATF	Financial Action Task Force
ff.	And the following
GDP	Gross domestic product
HBI	Hardware-based bearer-instrument
i.e.	That is
LCR	Liquidity Coverage Ratio

lit.	Litera
MFI	Monetary financial institution
MiCA	Markets in Crypto-Assets
MRO	Main refinancing operation
MRR	Minimum Reserve Requirements
NBFI	Non-bank financial intermediary
NFC	Non-financial corporation
NIM	Net interest margin
NSFR	Net Stable Funding Ratio
para.	Paragraph/marginal number
PET	Privacy-enhancing techniques
PSD	Payment Services Directive
PSP	Payment service provider
RoE	Return on equity
SEPA	Single Euro Payments Area
SSM	Single Supervisory Mechanism
TEU	Treaty on European Union
TFEU	Treaty on the Functioning of the European Union
TIPS	TARGET Instant Payment Settlement
ZLB	Zero Lower Bound
ZPO	German Code of Civil Procedure

Part I
Understanding the Notion of Central Bank Digital Currency

Chapter 1
Terminology and Motives for Central Bank Digital Currency

Abstract This chapter introduces the notion of central bank digital currency (CBDC) and the motives for its establishment. It presents an overview to the current situation of digital currencies worldwide. It also presents the main legal, technical and economic questions related to CBDC and the structure the work will follow in order to answer these questions. The existing forms of electronic and digital money as well as the most commonly named motives will be revealed and discussed in more detail.

Looking at the title of this book, one might think that it deals with a futuristic-looking invention that is often portrayed ambivalently in science fiction films. In fact, central bank digital currency (CBDC) has been subject to international discussion for some time. For example, a study published by the Bank for International Settlements at the beginning of 2019 shows that almost 70% out of 63 central banks surveyed worldwide were already considering the introduction of central bank digital currency in 2018.[1] About half of them were examining both a retail model (for households and businesses) and a model for monetary financial institutions (MFIs)[2] only (the so-called wholesale model). Only three years later, in 2021, the number of central banks surveyed rose to 81, 90% of which are involved with central bank digital currency.[3] According to this study, almost 68% of the central banks surveyed even consider it possible to introduce central bank digital currency in the next three to six years.[4] First countries have already introduced a digital currency, such as the Commonwealth of The Bahamas, the Federal Republic of Nigeria and the People's Republic of China.[5] So central bank digital currency is by no means a futuristic phenomenon that is unlikely to be implemented in our lifetime. But what

[1]Barontini and Holden (2019), p. 7 graphic 3.

[2]Commercial banks and other financial institutions.

[3]Kosse and Mattei (2022), pp. 3 and 4 graphic 1.

[4]Kosse and Mattei (2022), p. 9 graphic 6.

[5]Soderberg (2022), p. 2. For an overview see https://www.atlanticcouncil.org/cbdctracker/. For the Nigerian eNaira see https://enaira.gov.ng/.

L. Kriese, *Central Bank Digital Currency*,
https://doi.org/10.1007/978-3-031-44738-9_1

exactly is meant by central bank digital currency and what legal and economic problems are associated with it? To answer that, in particular the project of a digital euro, which has been in existence since mid-2020,[6] will be taken as a basis. This book will explore the central questions of central bank digital currency: What models and technical designs can central bank digital currency be based on? How should it be introduced into the monetary cycle? What economic aspects need to be considered? However, the book will mainly focus on the legal issues, in particular the question of competence and the status as legal tender. But civil law and constitutional law aspects will also be examined. To address the aforementioned aspects, the book is structured as follows: An introductory part shows a first notion of the concept of CBDC, including the technical background. To understand how CBDC could work technically is a necessary basis for the legal analysis in part three. Examining the legal foundations is crucial for establishing innovative technologies because they determine what the participants involved are empowered to do under what conditions.[7] Hence, the legal analysis forms the main part of this book. Part four studies the economic dimension of CBDC. The book is then supplemented with an appendix that contains a draft proposal for a regulation on the digital euro as a way of summarising and vividly demonstrating the main findings of the book.

1.1 Terminology and Delimitations

Central bank digital currency is commonly understood as the digital representation of a monetary unit that is of equal rank as existing forms of central bank money.[8] The ECB understands the digital euro to be a liability of the Eurosystem denominated in euro and recorded in digital form.[9] This understanding raises the question of how central bank digital currency is to be distinguished from other, in particular electronic and existing digital forms of money.

1.1.1 Scriptural Money

Next to cash, the most familiar and commonly used manifestation of money is book money. Book money is the non-physical form of a sum of money that used to be recorded in (analogue) books, but is today usually recorded on electronic data

---

[6] See ECB (2020a).

[7] Cf. Muscheler and Hunt (2021), p. 9.

[8] Strobel (2021), p. 556; Hanl and Michaelis (2019), p. 2; Bitkom (2020), p. 7.

[9] ECB (2020a), p. 6.

carriers.[10] Legally, it is a claim, usually on a credit institution.[11] The most common manifestation of these claims are sight deposits on the current account, which is why book money is also called scriptural money.[12] These demand deposits, so-called overnight deposits,[13] are in their legal nature a claim of the customer on his bank from irregular custody according to Sections 700 (1), first sentence, 488 (1), second sentence, of the German Civil Code (BGB), directed to the payout of the account balance (so-called credit balance surplus[14]) in cash.[15] In legal terms, sight deposits are to be strictly distinguished from the current account in which they are booked. In terms of its legal nature, the current account is a current account agreement within the meaning of Section 355 of the German Commercial Code (HGB), which itself only serves to process cashless payment transactions.[16] Due to its booking and transfer, scriptural money can be regarded as a hybrid of traditional and digital format.[17] Scriptural money is used by means of bank transfers, direct debits and payment cards (giro card or debit card and credit card).[18] Especially the payment cards thereby function as the 'key to the money'.[19] However, the decisive difference between book money and central bank digital currency is not their legal nature, their accounting or transfer, but rather the way they are created. In both cases, the money is a liability of a bank or a claim on a bank.[20] However, book money is created by (private) commercial banks through account bookings, e.g. cash deposits and the granting of loans, whereas central bank digital currency is issued by a central bank.[21] Moreover, according to Article 128 (1), third sentence, TFEU and Article 10 Regulation 947/98,[22] book money is not legal tender.[23] In contrast, the introduction of the digital euro as legal tender is at least favoured.[24]

---

[10] Hahn and Häde (2010), para. 23; Cf. Balz (2021), p. 18.

[11] Grundmann (2022), para. 6; Omlor (2014), p. 104; Haug (2022), para. 52.

[12] Cf. Hahn and Häde (2010), para. 23.

[13] Van Look (2014a), para. 2.

[14] BGH, 08.07.1982 – I ZR 148/80, juris para. 11.

[15] BGH, 08.07.1982 – I ZR 148/80, juris para. 11; Canaris (1981), para. 1165; Henssler (2023), para. 1; Read and Schäfer (2020), p. 15.

[16] BGH, 08.07.1982 – I ZR 148/80, juris para. 11; Leyens (2023), para. 4; Lehmann (2016), para. 208 ff.; Van Look (2014a), para. 2.

[17] Milkau (2020), p. 26; Read and Schäfer (2020), p. 15; Balz et al. (2020), p. 10.

[18] Grundmann (2022), para. 9; Schmieder (2022), para. 1; Ellenberger (2022), para. 37.

[19] Omlor (2014), p. 133.

[20] Omlor and Birne (2020), p. 7.

[21] Kirchhartz (2014), para. 18.

[22] Council Regulation (EC) 974/98 of 3 May 1998 on the introduction of the euro (11 May 1998) OJ L 139/1, lastly amended by Council Regulation (EU) 2022/1207 (12 July 2022) OJ L 187/16.

[23] Cf. Omlor and Birne (2020), p. 7 who describe central bank digital currency as 'book money plus'.

[24] ECB (2020a), pp. 24, 25 and 33.

1.1.2 E-Money

An already existing form of digital money is the so-called e-money. According to Article 2 No. 2 EMD,[25] e-money means electronically, including magnetically, stored monetary value as represented by a claim on the issuer which is issued on receipt of funds for the purpose of making payment transactions as defined in Article 4 No. 5 PSD2,[26] and which is accepted by a natural or legal person other than the electronic money issuer. The best-known use cases of e-money are the cash card and PayPal.[27] At first glance, central bank digital currency could well fall within the scope of Article 2 No. 2 EMD. The term monetary value means any kind of means of payment, i.e. legal means of payment as well as means of exchange recognised in accordance with public perception of the market.[28] The digital euro can easily be recognised as a monetary value when introduced as legal tender. The concept of electronic storage of this value is to be understood broadly, whereby the type and location of the storage medium are irrelevant.[29] When using Blockchain or other forms of the distributed ledger technology (DLT),[30] the storage of information on ownership and transfer of the digital euro in the respective data blocks should be sufficient.[31] The use of the digital euro for payment transactions within the meaning of Article 4 No. 5 PSD2 is not problematic. The criterion of third-party acceptance will also not cause any difficulties when introduced as a legal means of payment. More problematic is the recognition as 'claim against the issuer' and 'issuance against payment of a sum of money'. A classification of the digital euro proves to be difficult insofar as the concrete design of the digital euro has not yet been completely clarified on the part of the ECB. Depending on the model chosen,[32] either the ECB itself or a financial intermediary will be regarded as the e-money issuer.[33] In addition, the claim within the meaning of Article 2 No. 2 EMD consists of a claim for the re-exchange of the e-money into legal tender, cf. Article 11 No. 2 EMD.[34] However, if the digital euro is introduced as legal tender, the content of the

[25]Directive 2009/110/EC of the European Parliament and of the Council of 16 September 2009 on the taking up, pursuit and prudential supervision of the business of electronic money institutions amending Directives 2005/60/EC and 2006/48/EC and repealing Directive 2000/46/EC (10 October 2009) OJ L 267/7, lastly amended by Directive (EU) 2015/2366 (23 December 2015) OJ L 337/35.

[26]Directive (EU) 2015/2366 of the European Parliament and of the Council of 25 November 2015 on payment services in the internal market, amending Directives 2002/65/EC, 2009/110/EC and 2013/36/EU and Regulation (EU) No 1093/2010, and repealing Directive 2007/64/EC (23 December 2015) OJ L 337/35.

[27]Van Look (2014b), para. 74; Omlor (2020), para. 7.

[28]BaFin (2011), No. 4 lit. a. aa.

[29]Wettlaufer and Patz (2020), para. 17; Terlau (2022), para. 16, 18; Casper et al. (2023), para. 230.

[30]See in more detail Sect. 2.2.1.

[31]Cf. Auffenberg (2019), p. 343; Terlau (2021), para. 49; Omlor and Birne (2020), p. 8.

[32]For this see Sect. 2.1.

[33]Cf. Omlor and Birne (2020), p. 7.

[34]Cf. Auffenberg (2019), p. 343.

claim on the e-money issuer can at most be a claim for exchange into other forms of legal tender. In addition, the e-money unit must be issued against the payment of an amount of money from legal tender.[35] However, it is not yet clear whether the digital euro will only be generated if the future holder offers an equivalent share of cash or book money in return. Moreover, the digital euro itself is to be legal tender, so that the purpose pursued with this element of the definition, the linking of e-money to legal tender,[36] does not need to be implemented separately.

Lastly and most important, e-money and central bank digital currency differ in the personal scope of application of the EMD. The ECB is only to be regarded as an issuer of electronic money insofar as it issues electronic money outside its capacity as a monetary authority, cf. Article 1 (1) lit. d EMD. Therefore, a model in which the ECB is the only issuer of the digital euro cannot be classified as an issuance of e-money without a change in the law.[37]

1.1.3 Crypto Token

However, due to progressive technological development, e-money has largely been overtaken by the use of so-called token in the financial sector. A precise definition of this term is difficult. There is agreement that tokens are the generic term for digital representations of a value in the form of individualised database entries.[38] Article 3 (1) No. 2 of the proposal for the MiCA-Regulation[39] agrees with this, but refers to tokens as 'crypto-assets' and defines these as a digital representation of value or rights which may be transferred and stored electronically, using distributed ledger technology or similar technology. They aim to provide a tamper-proof verification of the legal ownership of the value or right.[40] Tokens are usually subdivided according to their economic function, although the designation is not uniform. For example, there are currency or payment tokens, utility tokens and investment or security tokens.[41] Payment tokens are particularly relevant for distinguishing crypto tokens from central bank digital currency. These function as a means of exchange and payment and, as so-called 'tokenised money', they represent the main application of

[35] Wettlaufer and Patz (2020), para. 25; Terlau (2021), para. 39; German parliamentary paper 17/3023, p. 40.

[36] BaFin (2011), No. 4 lit. a. aa.

[37] Omlor and Birne (2020), p. 7.

[38] Langenbucher et al. (2020), para. 2; Matzke (2021), para. 1; Fromberger and Zimmermann (2020), para. 68; Varmaz et al. (2021), para. 35, 37, 53.

[39] Proposal for a Regulation of the European Parliament and of the Council on Markets in Crypto-assets, and amending Directive (EU) 2019/1937, COM/2020/593 final.

[40] Matzke (2021), para. 5.

[41] Langenbucher et al. (2020), para. 9; Kaulartz (2021), para. 26; Varmaz et al. (2021), para. 39.

the token-technology in the financial sector.[42] Prominent examples of these payment tokens are the misleadingly named cryptocurrencies[43] such as Bitcoin, Ether or Libra.

A subtype of payment tokens are so-called asset-referenced tokens or value-backed tokens.[44] These are tokens that are linked to a real object with its own value, such as a state fiat currency (e.g. euro, dollar, etc.), commodities or precious metals.[45] So-called stablecoins, i.e. digital images whose reference objects are fiat currencies, are becoming increasingly important.[46] The use of fiat currencies as reference objects aims at avoiding the high volatility of cryptocurrencies and instead maintain a stable value.[47] A prominent example is Tether, which is a representation of the US dollar.[48]

Both payment tokens and central bank digital currency digitally represent a value using DLT, which can function as a means of payment.[49] One important difference, however, is that payment tokens are created by private actors, whereas central bank digital currency is sovereignly issued by central banks.[50] Furthermore, due to the mere digital representation of a value, tokens do not have their own (intrinsic) value, as metals do. Since they are not issued by a sovereign, the principle of nominal value under monetary law does not apply to them neither.[51] According to the principle of nominal value, the payment value of the currency unit is no longer determined by its intrinsic value, but by the sovereignly determined nominal value (face value, 'a euro is a euro').[52] In contrast to the theory of valorism,[53] changes in the economic value of the currency unit are therefore not taken into account for the fulfilment of a monetary debt (so-called nominalism under monetary debt law) and are assigned to the creditor's area of risk.[54] As a result, cryptocurrencies form their value only on the

---

[42] Matzke (2021), para. 44; Varmaz et al. (2021), para. 42; Langenbucher et al. (2020), para. 10.

[43] Since they are not issued by a public authority they cannot be seen as a currency, cf. Omlor (2021), para. 12; Gschnaidtner (2020), para. 60; other opinion is Hofert (2018), p. 5.

[44] See Article 3 (1) No. 3 MiCA-Regulation proposal.

[45] Fromberger and Zimmermann (2020), para. 75.

[46] Fromberger and Zimmermann (2020), para. 76; Kaulartz (2021), para. 61; cf. Article 3 (1) No. 4 MiCA-Regulation proposal.

[47] Langenbucher et al. (2020), para. 13; cf. Article 3 (1) No. 4 MiCA-Regulation proposal.

[48] Matzke (2021), para. 10.

[49] Cf. Varmaz et al. (2021), para. 53; Fromberger and Zimmermann (2020), para. 70.

[50] Hanl and Michaelis (2019), p. 2; Varmaz et al. (2021), para. 53; Langenbucher et al. (2020), para. 13 ff.

[51] Cf. Ohler (2021), pp. 111 and 112; Grothe (1999), p. 73; Bossu et al. (2020), p. 29 No. 57.

[52] BVerwG, 03.10.1972 – I C 36.68, juris para. 24; Ohler (2021), p. 111; Grothe (1999), pp. 71 and 72; see also No. 1 lit. b of the Commission Recommendation of 22 March 2010 on the scope and effects of legal tender of euro banknotes and coins (30 March 2010) OJ L 83/70.

[53] On this see Proctor (2012), para 9.07 and 9.08 (with further references).

[54] BVerwG, 03.10.1972 – I C 36.68, juris para. 24; BGH 08.01.1981 – VI ZR 128/79, juris para. 16; BFH, 27.07.1967 – IV 300/64, juris para. 53; Ohler (2021), p. 112; Mann (1992), p. 90; Grothe (1999), pp. 70 and 71.

basis of supply and demand and are thus exposed to strong price fluctuations.[55] This volatility is absorbed by stablecoins, but in contrast to the central bank, private actors cannot guarantee sufficient coverage of the tokens with fiat currency.[56]

1.1.4 Central Bank Money

Finally, central bank digital currency needs to be distinguished from existing forms of central bank money. In addition to cash (banknotes and coins), central bank money also includes the deposits of certain financial institutions at the central banks, the so-called reserves.[57] Both together form the monetary base M0 of an economy.[58] It is true that reserves also represent a digital form of central bank money.[59] However, in contrast to the digital euro, this form of money is only available to certain financial institutions, whereas the use of the digital euro by everyone is intended.[60]

1.2 Motives for Introducing Central Bank Digital Currency

After the notion of central bank digital currency has been roughly characterised and CBDC has been distinguished from other forms of money, the question arises as to why the introduction of a digital euro is necessary at all. In the academic literature and on the part of the central banks a whole bundle of motives can be found.[61]

1.2.1 Dwindling Usage of Cash

The motive often cited first for the introduction of central bank digital currency is the allegedly dwindling use of cash in payment transactions.[62] At first glance, this

[55] ECB (2020a), appendix 2; Varmaz et al. (2021), para. 53; Brunnermeier et al. (2021), p. 24.

[56] Fromberger and Zimmermann (2020), para. 76; Panetta (2018), p. 2; Balz et al. (2020), p. 10; cf. also Brunnermeier and Landau (2022), p. 22.

[57] Hanl and Michaelis (2019), p. 2; Read and Schäfer (2020), p. 15.

[58] Ohler (2021), pp. 81 ff.; Thiele (2019), pp. 99 and 100.

[59] Thiele (2019), p. 84; Read and Schäfer (2020), p. 15.

[60] Balz (2021), p. 19. For this see also Chap. 2.

[61] For an overview see Bindseil (2020), p. 5; Bitkom (2020), p. 10; ECB (2020a), p. 9; Soderberg (2022), p. 7.

[62] ECB (2020a), p. 9; Balz (2021), p. 19; Bindseil (2020), p. 6; Vollmer (2020), p. 30; Utzig (2020), p. 20; Panetta (2022).

motive may seem quite comprehensible, especially if you consider how often you yourself use cash for payments. The declining use of cash can also be proven empirically. According to a survey conducted by the Bundesbank, the share of cash payments in Germany fell from 74% in 2017 to around 60% in 2020, with cashless payments clearly predominating, especially for higher amounts (EUR 50 and above).[63] This trend can also be seen at the European level. According to two studies conducted by the ECB, the share of cash payments in all payment transactions in the euro area totalled 79% in 2016,[64] compared to 73% in 2019.[65] In Sweden, which is commonly known for its high share of cashless payment transactions, the share of cash payments in the most recent payment transaction made by the respondents was still around 40% in 2010, but only 13% in 2018.[66] And in Latvia, according to a recent study conducted by the Latvian central bank in August 2022, the share of cashless payments (71%) clearly outweighs the share of cash payments (29%).[67]

However, despite this discernible downward trend, it should not be forgotten that cash is still of considerable importance, especially in the euro area, and cash is still highly used.[68] For example, in Italy and Spain more than 80% of all payment transactions are still made with cash.[69] Also, about 70% of respondents of all ages in Germany see no need for alternative digital payment methods.[70] Even in Norway, where the share of cash use was below 5% in autumn 2020,[71] there is 'no acute need to introduce central bank digital currency'[72] according to *Ida Wolden Bache*, deputy governor of the Norwegian central bank. The considerable importance of cash in the euro area is even recognised by the ECB, but it notes that a change of role may occur, especially in extreme situations such as the COVID-19 pandemic.[73] However, detached from such extreme situations the introduction of central bank digital currency does not appear to be compelling with regard to the extent cash is used.[74]

---

[63] Deutsche Bundesbank (2021), pp. 3 and 21.

[64] ECB (2017), p. 19.

[65] ECB (2020b), p. 19.

[66] Sveriges Riksbank (2018), p. 6.

[67] Latvijas Banka (2022).

[68] Cf. Cœuré (2018).

[69] ECB (2020b), pp. 121 and 106.

[70] Deutsche Bundesbank (2021), pp. 26 and 27.

[71] Wolden Bache (2020), charts p. 3.

[72] Wolden Bache (2020).

[73] ECB (2020a), p. 10.

[74] Like here also Strobel (2021), p. 557.

1.2.2 Technological Change and Innovation

Another motive cited almost as frequently is the technological change in payment transactions.[75] Innovations such as contactless payment, mobile payment, cryptocurrencies and stablecoins are changing the digital payment landscape, to which central banks want to adapt to with central bank digital currency.[76] In his function as deputy governor of the Bank of Italy, *Panetta* speaks of central bank digital currency as a 'natural consequence of the digitalisation process of the financial system',[77] and Governor *Brainard* of the US Federal Reserve of the 'payment system of the future'.[78] To justify this openness to technology, Article 127 (2), fourth indent, TFEU could be used. According to this provision, it is the fundamental task of the ESCB[79] to promote the smooth functioning of payment systems. When conducting this task, the ESCB should also be guided by users' needs because payment systems have a prominent position in the economy.[80] If, as a result of general technological developments, the expectations of payers and payees with regard to payment transactions change, it is not harmful to consider the introduction of central bank digital currency in view of the ESCB's obligation to promote.

In this context, especially in the economic literature, supporting the digitisation of the economy is also cited as a reason to introduce central bank digital currency.[81] This refers to terms such as 'Industry 4.0', 'Smart Economy' or 'Internet of Things'. Central bank digital currency shall enable the end-users to pay with 'programmable money'[82] in automated processes.[83] This refers to processes in which payment transactions are carried out automatically upon the fulfilment of conditions previously defined in a 'smart contract', such as the immediate and automatic triggering of a payment transaction upon the transfer of goods.[84] However, this does not necessarily require central bank digital currency; rather, the technical design of the payment systems, which can also be operated by private individuals, is decisive.[85] Moreover, it is questionable whether issuing central bank digital currency with the aim to foster the economy still falls within the remit of the ESCB or the European

[75] Balz (2021), p. 18; BIS (2021), p. 1.

[76] Wolden Bache (2020).

[77] Panetta (2018), p. 2.

[78] Brainard (2022).

[79] European System of Central Banks, consisting of the ECB and the central banks of the Member States, cf. Article 282 (1), first sentence, TFEU.

[80] Freimuth (2013), para. 30; Selmayr (2015), Art. 127 AEUV para. 28.

[81] Balz (2021), p. 19; ECB (2020a), p. 9.

[82] Critical to this term Milkau (2020), p. 26.

[83] Bitkom (2020), p. 11; Utzig (2020), p. 20; Balz et al. (2020), p. 11. For use cases of digital currencies see in more detail Bechtel et al. (2022), para. 74 ff.

[84] Balz et al. (2020), p. 12; Brühl (2017), p. 142.

[85] Strobel (2021), p. 557; critical also Milkau (2020), p. 27.

Union. Economic policy is divided between the Union and the Member States, Article 119 (1) TFEU. The Member States are responsible for general and cross-sectoral economic policy.[86] Fostering the digitisation of the economy can be such a general and cross-cutting matter of economic policy and thus fall within the competence of the Member States. On the other hand, digitisation is also a driver in the competition of payment transactions.[87] This could address the competition competence of the European Union according to Article 3 (1) lit. b TFEU. In order to maintain the efficiency of payment transactions, the ESCB could act in a supporting role and at the same time in its own capacity when introducing central bank digital currency, Article 127 (1), second sentence, and (2), fourth indent, TFEU.

Irrespective of individual legal issues, adaptation to technological change in both payment transactions and the economy does not necessarily need to be cited as a motive for the introduction of central bank digital currency.

1.2.3 Situations of Oligopoly in the Digital Payments Sector

Closely linked to the technological change in payment transactions is the protection of users from oligopolies in the digital payments sector, which is often cited as a further motive. Payment transactions, especially in their digital form, are particularly strongly dominated by private players who, due to their market strength, possess dominant market positions.[88] Examples include Apple Pay, Google Pay, Amazon Pay, WeChat and Alipay in China and M-Pesa in Africa.[89] The dangers arising from this high market concentration are complex. For example, there is a risk of stunted competition in the payments sector.[90] However, European economic policy is based on the principle of an open market economy with free competition, Article 119 (1) TFEU. It is therefore primarily the task of private actors to increase competition through innovation.[91] Furthermore, with the provisions of the competition and antitrust law there already exist sovereign mechanisms to enhance competition. Hence, central bank digital currency is not necessarily required in this regard.[92]

However, oligopolies are often accompanied by the risk of abuse or arbitrary restriction of individuals.[93] For example, private providers may mix the exchange and payment function of money with functions that are usually separated, such as

[86] Häde (2022), para. 4; Kempen (2018), para. 12.

[87] Milkau (2020), p. 23.

[88] Bindseil (2020), p. 6; Brainard (2022).

[89] Brunnermeier et al. (2021), p. 2; Wolden Bache (2020).

[90] Soderberg (2022), p. 7; Cf. Panetta (2018), p. 3.

[91] Brainard (2022).

[92] Panetta (2018), p. 3; critical also Strobel (2021), p. 557.

[93] Wolden Bache (2020); Panetta (2022).

data collection and social networking via social networking sites.[94] In this case there is a risk that the few strong market players with many users will commercially exploit the payment data obtained in this way, for example with personalised advertising, so that the privacy of users is particularly affected.[95]

Additionally, in highly concentrated markets, special attention must be paid to the consequences of a failure of individual players.[96] Especially in the case of newly arising payment technologies such as cryptocurrencies and stablecoins, there often does not exist a comprehensive regulatory framework yet,[97] so that users regularly do not receive compensation for their losses if a private player fails.

Particularly in view of the last two risks mentioned, a state-issued digital currency can inspire more trust among users in the digital payment landscape and serve as a public complement to private-sector offerings.[98]

1.2.4 Sovereignty

One more politically shaped motive for the introduction of central bank digital currency is the preservation of monetary sovereignty.[99] Through the digitisation of the payment landscape, more and more private providers but also foreign states have contributed to the emergence of new digital forms of money.[100] The increasing attractiveness of these alternative means of payment and their rising use within the population leads to the risk that the own currency will be substituted by these digital private money or foreign currency forms.[101] As a result, there is the threat of so-called 'digital dollarisation'.[102] The substitution of foreign currencies or stablecoins for the central bank's own currency may also impair classical tasks of central banks, namely the monetary policy transmission mechanism.[103] Closely linked to monetary policy is also the possibility of analysing its effectiveness by means of the transaction data in payment transactions, i.e. financial flows and money

94 Brunnermeier et al. (2021), p. 2.

95 Brunnermeier et al. (2021), p. 16; Balz (2021), p. 20; Panetta (2022); Lagarde (2022); Nagel (2022).

96 Soderberg (2022), p. 6; Bitkom (2020), p. 11; Cf. ECB (2020a), pp. 9 and 13.

97 For the EU see the revolutionary Commission proposal for a Regulation of the European Parliament and of the Council on Markets in Crypto-assets, and amending Directive (EU) 2019/1937, COM/2020/593 final.

98 Brainard (2022); Panetta (2022).

99 Milkau (2020), p. 24; Panetta (2022).

100 Balz (2021), p. 20; Milkau (2020), p. 24.

101 ECB (2020a), p. 11; Panetta (2022); Herrmann (2010), p. 178.

102 Brunnermeier et al. (2021), p. 2.

103 Soderberg (2022), p. 7; ECB (2020a), p. 12; Brunnermeier and Landau (2022), p. 16.

distribution.[104] This data sovereignty would be jeopardised if the central bank's own money were to be overlaid with cryptocurrencies or stablecoins or foreign central bank digital currency and would impair its own sovereignty in the critical infrastructure of payment transactions.[105]

Furthermore, the issuance of CBDC also affects the desire of many states for political independence.[106] The combination of a highly concentrated payment landscape dominated by private players and competitive pressure from foreign central bank digital currency leads to the fact that states which cannot keep pace with this technological development in the financial sector are exposed to the political agenda of the more technically innovative states.[107] The euro area in particular seems predestined for this, as non-European payment systems and service providers (Visa, Mastercard, American Express) are already largely used for traditional cashless payment transactions.[108] The risk of this political dependence of payment transactions was particularly evident in the Russia-Ukraine war. Due to Russia's military intervention in Ukraine, many states imposed financial sanctions. As a result, the US credit card companies Visa and Mastercard discontinued their business in Russia.[109] Major crypto platforms whose operators are based in the United States also excluded Iranian and Venezuelan users from their services due to the US sanctions.[110] This political agenda, mediated more indirectly by private actors, is in contrast with the direct political influence exerted by foreign central bank digital currencies. Some states have already introduced central bank digital currency,[111] most notably the E-CNY of the People's Republic of China and the Sand Dollar of the Bahamas. These states not only have a competitive advantage in the struggle for the place of a world reserve currency.[112] They can also merge with politically like-minded states[113] and, due to the almost unlimited financial power of the state, gain

---

[104] Bitkom (2020), p. 14.

[105] Bitkom (2020), p. 14; Balz (2021), p. 20; cf. ECB (2020a), p. 10; Brunnermeier and Landau (2022), p. 34.

[106] Cf. ECB (2020a), p. 10; Opinion of Advocate General Pitruzella case C-422/19 *Hessischer Rundfunk* ECLI:EU:C:2020:756, para. 82 fn. 43.

[107] Cf. Nagel (2022).

[108] Lagarde (2022). Therefore, ECB's decision to select the US group Amazon for a pilot in the digital euro project caused a stir, https://www.derstandard.de/story/2000139231884/digitaler-euro-ezb-holt-sich-amazon-als-partner. Accessed 31 July 2023.

[109] Tagesschau broadcast on 06.03.2022, https://www.tagesschau.de/wirtschaft/weltwirtschaft/russland-visa-mastercard-101.html. Accessed 31 July 2023.

[110] Forbes Magazin 03.03.2022, https://www.forbes.com/sites/stevenehrlich/2022/03/03/iranian-venezuela-users-abruptly-dropped-from-major-crypto-platforms-as-russian-sanctions-grow/?sh=3ec05aef70b0&utm_source=instagram&utm_medium=social&utm_campaign=forbes. Accessed 31 July 2023.

[111] See for an overview Soderberg (2022), p. 2.

[112] Read and Schäfer (2020), p. 17; Brunnermeier et al. (2021), pp. 21 and 22; Bitkom (2020), p. 14.

[113] For example, China, Thailand, Hong Kong and United Arab Emirates, cf. CNBC 24.02.2021, https://www.cnbc.com/2021/02/24/chinas-pboc-joins-cross-border-digital-currency-project.html. Accessed 31 July 2023.

supremacy in cross-border payments—with all the possibilities of international political influence.[114]

1.2.5 Miscellaneous Motives

There are further motives that are often cited for the need of central bank digital currency, although these depend in part on regional characteristics.

On the one hand, the financial inclusion of broad sections of the population is cited as a keyword. Central bank digital currency is intended to reach all those who do not have access to cashless payment transactions because they do not have a bank account.[115] However, the lack of financial inclusion has many causes. It is a common phenomenon in areas with low-income and low-educated households, as well as in regions that are not profitable for commercial private payment service providers or where geographical disparities lead to difficulties of money supply.[116] The motive of financial inclusion is therefore only a regional feature and cannot justify the introduction of central bank digital currency alone, especially in highly industrialised countries.[117]

Furthermore, central bank digital currency shall also often aim at reducing costs. On the one hand, it should reduce the costs of cash (production, transport and distribution, disposal).[118] On the other hand, the costs of international payment transactions, which on a global average currently amount to just around 7% of the transaction volume,[119] shall also be reduced.[120] However, before there is a noticeable reduction in costs, users will perhaps still have to pay for the technical usability of central bank digital currency, especially the costs for hardware and software.[121]

Another, albeit less frequently mentioned motive is the use of central bank digital currency as a tool of monetary policy. In this case, a new channel of monetary policy transmission with direct influence on households and companies is to be created via the possibility to remunerate central bank digital currency.[122] However, this strongly depends on the model chosen as the basis for the issuance of the digital euro.[123]

---

[114]For example, China's debt-trap-diplomacy, cf. Financial Express 14.09.2022, https://www.financialexpress.com/world-news/how-chinas-debt-trap-diplomacy-will-use-cbdcs-to-replace-the-swift-banking-system/2667020/. Accessed 31 July 2023.

[115]Vollmer (2020), p. 31; Soderberg (2022), p. 5.

[116]Soderberg (2022), p. 4; Panetta (2018), p. 3.

[117]Cf. Strobel (2021), p. 557; Brainard (2022).

[118]Panetta (2018), pp. 3 and 4; ECB (2020a), p. 10 fn. 12; Wolden Bache (2020).

[119]World Bank (2020).

[120]Bitkom (2020), p. 11; Soderberg (2022), pp. 5 and 6.

[121]Panetta (2018), pp. 3 and 4.

[122]ECB (2020a), p. 12; Bitkom (2020), p. 13.

[123]See in more detail Sects. 2.1 and 4.2.

References

Auffenberg L (2019) E-Geld auf Blockchainbasis. BKR 2019:341–345

BaFin (2011) Leaflet to the ZAG. 22.12.2011 (revised on 29.11.2017)

Balz B (2021) Digitales Zentralbankgeld – Gehen Notenbanken neue Wege? Kreditwesen 74(21): 18–21

Balz B, Diehl M, Winter H (2020) Digitales Geld. Kreditwesen 73(24):10–14

Barontini C, Holden H (2019) Proceeding with caution – a survey on central bank digital currency. BIS Papers No. 101. https://www.bis.org/publ/bppdf/bispap101.pdf. Accessed 31 July 2023

Bechtel et al (2022) Die Zukunft des Zahlungsverkehrs in einer DLTbasierten europäischen Wirtschaft. In: Kunschke D, Spitz M, Pohle J (eds) FinTech, 2nd edn. ESV, Berlin. https://doi.org/10.37307/b.978-3-503-20689-6.09

Bindseil U (2020) Tiered CBDC and the financial system. ECB Working Paper Series No. 2351. https://www.ecb.europa.eu/pub/pdf/scpwps/ecb.wp2351~c8c18bbd60.en.pdf. Accessed 31 July 2023

BIS (2021) Central bank digital currency: executive summary. https://www.bis.org/publ/othp42.pdf. Accessed 31 July 2023

Bitkom (2020) Infopapier digitaler Euro auf der Blockchain. https://www.bitkom.org/sites/main/files/2020-04/200423_infopapier_digitaler-euro-auf-der-blockchain.pdf. Accessed 31 July 2023

Bossu W et al (2020) Legal aspects of central bank digital currency: central bank and monetary law considerations. IMF Working Paper WP/20/254. https://www.imf.org/en/Publications/WP/Issues/2020/11/20/Legal-Aspects-of-Central-Bank-Digital-Currency-Central-Bank-and-Monetary-Law-Considerations-49827. Accessed 31 July 2023

Brainard L (2022) Preparing for the financial system of the future. Speech at the US Monetary Policy Forum, 18.02.2022. https://www.federalreserve.gov/newsevents/speech/brainard20220218a.htm. Accessed 31 July 2023

Brühl V (2017) Bitcoins, blockchain und distributed ledgers. Wirtschaftsdienst 97(2):135–142. https://doi.org/10.1007/s10273-017-2096-3

Brunnermeier M, Landau J-P (2022) The digital euro: policy implications and perspectives. https://www.europarl.europa.eu/RegData/etudes/STUD/2022/703337/IPOL_STU(2022)703337_EN.pdf. Accessed 31 July 2023

Brunnermeier M et al (2021) The digitalization of money. BIS Working Papers No. 941. https://www.bis.org/publ/work941.pdf. Accessed 31 July 2023

Canaris C-W (1981) Bankvertragsrecht, 2nd edn. De Gruyter, Berlin/New York

Casper et al (2023) § 1. In: Casper M, Terlau M (eds) Zahlungsdiensteaufsichtsgesetz, 3rd edn. Beck, München

Cœuré B (2018) The future of central bank money. Speech at the International Center for Monetary and Banking Studies Geneva, 14.05.2018. https://www.ecb.europa.eu/press/key/date/2018/html/ecb.sp180514_4.en.html. Accessed 31 July 2023

Deutsche Bundesbank (2021) Statistik zum Zahlungsverhalten 2020. http://www.bundesbank.de/resource/blob/855642/cabf0971e0f0697d688dcc57c0cb65d3/mL/zahlungsverhalten-in-deutschland-2020-data.pdf. Accessed 31 July 2023

ECB (2017) The use of cash by households in the euro area. Occasional Paper Series No. 201. https://www.ecb.europa.eu/pub/pdf/scpops/ecb.op201.en.pdf. Accessed 31 July 2023

ECB (2020a) Report on a digital euro. https://www.ecb.europa.eu/pub/pdf/other/Report_on_a_digital_euro~4d7268b458.en.pdf. Accessed 31 July 2023

ECB (2020b) Study on the payment attitudes of consumers in the euro area. https://www.ecb.europa.eu/pub/pdf/other/ecb.spacereport202012~bb2038bbb6.en.pdf. Accessed 31 July 2023

Ellenberger (2022) § 36. In: Ellenberger J, Bunte H (eds) Bankrechtshandbuch, 6th edn. Beck, München

Freimuth (2013) Art. 128 AEUV. In: Siekmann H (ed) Kommentar zur Europäischen Währungsunion. Mohr Siebeck, Tübingen

Fromberger, Zimmermann (2020) § 1. In: Maume P, Maute L (eds) Rechtshandbuch Kryptowerte. Beck, München
Grothe H (1999) Fremdwährungsverbindlichkeiten. De Gruyter, Berlin/New York
Grundmann (2022) § 245. In: Säcker F et al (eds) Münchener Kommentar zum BGB, vol 2, 9th edn. Beck, München
Gschnaidtner (2020) § 2. In: Maume P, Maute L (eds) Rechtshandbuch Kryptowerte. Beck, München
Häde (2022) Art. 119 AEUV. In: Calliess C, Ruffert M (eds) EUV/AEUV Kommentar, 6th edn. Beck, München
Hahn H, Häde U (2010) Währungsrecht - § 3, 2nd edn. Beck, München
Hanl A, Michaelis J (2019) Digitales Zentralbankgeld als neues Instrument der Geldpolitik, MAGKS Joint Discussion Paper Series in Economics, No. 09-2019
Haug (2022) § 106. In: Ellenberger J, Bunte H (eds) Bankrechtshandbuch, 6th edn. Beck, München
Henssler (2023) § 700. In: Säcker F et al (eds) Münchener Kommentar zum BGB, vol 6, 9th edn. Beck, München
Herrmann C (2010) Währungshoheit, Währungsverfassung und subjektive Rechte. Mohr Siebeck, Tübingen
Hofert E (2018) Regulierung der Blockchains. Mohr Siebeck, Tübingen
Kaulartz (2021) § 5. In: Omlor S, Möslein F (eds) FinTech-Handbuch, 2nd edn. Beck, München
Kempen (2018) Art. 119 AEUV. In: Streinz R (ed) Beck'scher Kurzkommentar EUV/AEUV, 3rd edn. Beck, München
Kirchhartz (2014) § 1. In: Erne R (ed) Claussen, Bank- und Börsenrecht, 5th edn. Beck, München
Kosse A, Mattei I (2022) Gaining momentum – results of the 2021 BIS survey on central bank digital currencies. BIS Papers No. 125. https://www.bis.org/publ/bppdf/bispap125.pdf. Accessed 31 July 2023
Lagarde C (2022) Interview mit Redaktionsnetzwerk Deutschland. https://www.rnd.de/wirtschaft/christine-lagarde-im-interview-ezb-chefin-fuer-neugestaltung-der-euro-banknoten-USXKKEOBN5C4NDVU4XXR6S54E4.html. Accessed 31 July 2023
Langenbucher et al (2020) Chapter 11. In: Langenbucher K, Bliesener D, Spindler G (eds) Bankrechts-Kommentar, 3rd edn. Beck, München
Latvijas Banka (2022) Payment radar. https://www.bank.lv/en/operational-areas/payment-systems/payment-radar. Accessed 31 July 2023
Lehmann M (2016) Grundriss des Bank- und Kapitalmarktrechts. C.F. Müller, Heidelberg
Leyens (2023) § 355. In: Baumbach A, Hopt K (eds) Handelsgesetzbuch, 42nd edn. Beck, München
Mann F (1992) The legal aspect of money, 5th edn. Oxford University Press, Oxford
Matzke (2021) § 10. In: Omlor S, Möslein F (eds) FinTech-Handbuch, 2nd edn. Beck, München
Milkau U (2020) Automatisiertes Bezahlen als Lackmustest für einen Digital Euro. Kreditwesen 73(24):23–28
Muscheler K, Hunt C (2021) Recent legal developments in the area of crypto-assets and a digital euro. Institute for Law and Finance Working Paper Series No. 164. https://www.ilf-frankfurt.de/fileadmin/user_upload/ILF_WP164.pdf. Accessed 31 July 2023
Nagel J (2022) Digitaler Euro – Chancen und Risiken? https://www.imfs-frankfurt.de/news-medien/details/news/digitales-zentralbankgeld-zugaenglich-machen-vortrag-von-bundesbankpraesident-dr-joachim-nagel-im-video.html. Accessed 31 July 2023
Ohler C (2021) Unkonventionelle Geldpolitik. Mohr Siebeck, Tübingen
Omlor S (2014) Geldprivatrecht. Mohr Siebeck, Tübingen
Omlor S (2020) § 675c. In: Staudinger Kommentar zum BGB, online-version via juris
Omlor (2021) § 33. In: Omlor S, Möslein F (eds) FinTech-Handbuch, 2nd edn. Beck, München
Omlor S, Birne A (2020) Digitales Zentralbankgeld im Euroraum. RDi 2020:1–10
Panetta F (2018) 21st century cash: central banking, technological innovation and digital currencies. SUERF Policy Note No. 40. https://www.suerf.org/policynotes/3251/21st-century-cash-central-banking-technological-innovation-and-digital-currencies. Accessed 31 July 2023

Panetta F (2022) Central bank digital currencies: defining the problems, designing the solutions. Contribution to a panel discussion at the US Monetary Policy Forum, 18.02.2022. https://www.ecb.europa.eu/press/key/date/2022/html/ecb.sp220218_1~938e881b13.en.html. Accessed 31 July 2023

Proctor C (2012) Mann on the legal aspect of money, 7th edn. Oxford University Press, Oxford

Read O, Schäfer S (2020) Digitales Zentralbankgeld – pro und contra. Kreditwesen 73(24):15–18

Schmieder (2022) § 27. In: Ellenberger J, Bunte H (eds) Bankrechtshandbuch, 6th edn. Beck, München

Selmayr (2015) Art. 127 AEUV. In: Groeben H, Schwarze J, Hatje A (eds) Europäisches Unionsrecht, 7th edn. Nomos, Baden-Baden

Soderberg G (2022) Behind the scenes of central bank digital currency. IMF FinTech Notes No. 2022/004. https://www.imf.org/en/Publications/fintech-notes/Issues/2022/02/07/Behind-the-Scenes-of-Central-Bank-Digital-Currency-512174. Accessed 31 July 2023

Strobel B (2021) Digitaler Euro? – Ein Überblick über die rechtlichen und wirtschaftlichen Fragen. BKR 2021:556–561

Sveriges Riksbank (2018) Payment patterns in Sweden. https://www.riksbank.se/globalassets/media/statistik/betalningsstatistik/2018/payments-patterns-in-sweden-2018.pdf. Accessed 31 July 2023

Terlau (2021) § 34. In: Omlor S, Möslein F (eds) FinTech-Handbuch, 2nd edn. Beck, München

Terlau (2022) § 35. In: Ellenberger J, Bunte H (eds) Bankrechtshandbuch, 6th edn. Beck, München

Thiele A (2019) Die europäische Zentralbank. Mohr Siebeck, Tübingen

Utzig S (2020) Redaktionsgespräch. Kreditwesen 73(24):20–22

Van Look (2014a) § 2. In: Erne R (ed) Claussen, Bank- und Börsenrecht, 5th edn. Beck, München

Van Look (2014b) § 4. In: Erne R (ed) Claussen, Bank- und Börsenrecht, 5th edn. Beck, München

Varmaz et al (2021) Chapter 1. In: Omlor S, Link M (eds) Kryptowährungen und Token. R&W, Frankfurt a.M.

Vollmer U (2020) Digitales Zentralbankgeld und Kryptowährungen. WiSt 49(2–3):29–35. https://doi.org/10.15358/0340-1650-2020-2-3-29

Wettlaufer, Patz (2020) § 13. In: Maume P, Maute L (eds) Rechtshandbuch Kryptowerte. Beck, München

Wolden Bache I (2020) Central bank digital currency and real-time payments. Speech at Finance Norway's Payments Conference, 05.11.2020. https://www.norges-bank.no/en/news-events/news-publications/Speeches/2020/2020-11-05-bache/. (speech) and https://www.norges-bank.no/contentassets/6999efbb3fb044069c1a84a510b5975c/finance-norway-5-november-2020.pdf?v=11/05/2020104025&ft=.pdf. (slides) Accessed 31 July 2023

World Bank (2020) Remittance prices worldwide, vol 33. https://remittanceprices.worldbank.org/sites/default/files/rpw_report_march_2020.pdf. Accessed 31 July 2023

Chapter 2
Technical Design

Abstract This chapter examines the basis for the legal analysis—the technical design of central bank digital currency. It sets out the target group of the digital currency and explains concepts discussed in academia and in practice as to how CBDC can be issued and put into circulation. Furthermore, it examines the innovative and conventional technologies that could underlie these models such as Corda, Blockchain or TIPS. The chapter illustrates possible forms of a payment system with CBDC such as account-based and token-based. Finally, it presents the ECB's current experiments on the technical design of a digital currency.

One important question is who should be the users of central bank digital currency? In this regard, a distinction is made in the discussion so far between restricted and unrestricted access to the CBDC. The former is referred to as the wholesale model, in which there is only a narrowly defined group of users.[1] Those are usually credit institutions that already hold accounts at the central bank, i.e. mainly the commercial banks.[2] This understanding of the term wholesale, which is common in the discussion about central bank digital currency, differs from the understanding of the term in payment transaction theory. There, the term wholesale usually describes major customers with high transaction volumes or large-value payments.[3] However, central bank digital currency in the wholesale variant is hardly interesting for academia, as it does not fundamentally differ from the current reserves[4] as a form of central bank money and, compared to the retail model, barely influences the existing financial structure.[5] In contrast, the retail or general-purpose model does not restrict the circle of users.[6] All economic entities, especially households and firms, shall

[1] Balz et al. (2020), p. 13; Diehl (2021), para. 43.

[2] Diehl (2021), para. 43.

[3] Kahn and Roberds (2009), p. 4; Diehl (2021), para. 46.

[4] See above Sect. 1.1.4.

[5] Bindseil (2020), p. 4; Read and Schäfer (2020), p. 16; Diehl (2021), para. 44.

[6] Diehl (2021), para. 43.

L. Kriese, *Central Bank Digital Currency*,
https://doi.org/10.1007/978-3-031-44738-9_2

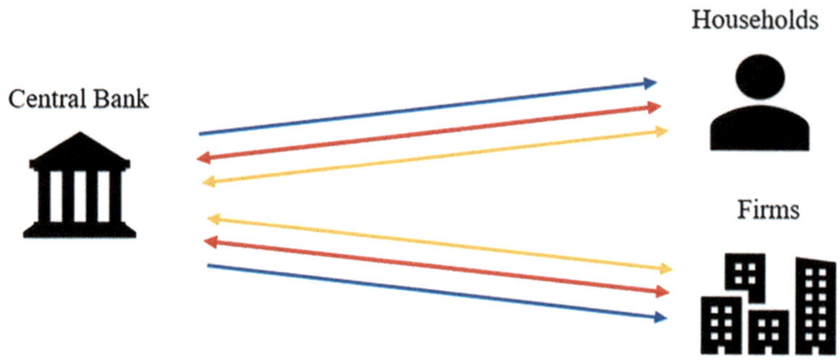

Fig. 2.1 Direct model (inspired by Auer and Böhme 2021)

have access to a digital form of central bank money.[7] Due to this innovative basic structure, the retail model is often at the centre of academic discourse and the considerations of the ECB[8] and will be discussed in this book more closely.

2.1 Issuance and Circulation

The question of who issues central bank digital currency and how it can be put into circulation is discussed in the literature in various models, which vary in detail in their terminology and specific design.[9]

2.1.1 Direct Model

One possible design option is often referred to as the direct or one-sided model. It operates in the following manner (see Fig. 2.1).

The central bank digital currency is issued by the central bank and is recorded as its liability item in the central bank balance sheet (blue arrows). The end-users, i.e. households and firms, hold an account with the central bank and have a direct legal or contractual relationship with it (red arrows).[10] In this model, the central bank not only issues and distributes the central bank digital currency, it also settles all payments between households and firms itself, excluding the financial intermediaries that have been active up to now (yellow arrows).[11]

[7]Diehl (2021), para. 49.

[8]ECB (2020), p. 3.

[9]For an overview see Terlau (2021), para. 4; Diehl (2021), para. 62.

[10]ECB (2020), p. 38; Soderberg (2022), p. 8.

[11]Auer and Böhme (2020), p. 90.

However, this model is hardly favoured because of its enormously high operational requirements for central banks.[12] In addition, if this model were to be chosen, the central bank would have to guarantee the requirements for combating money laundering and terrorism financing according to Article 2 (1) No. 1, Article 3 No. 1 AMLD[13] and would thus enter unfamiliar territory for central banks.[14]

2.1.2 *Hybrid and Intermediated Model*

For these reasons, the predominant view in the discussion so far has favoured a hybrid model or an intermediated model, each with the use of intermediaries. Both models are almost identical in their basic structure and only differ in detail. Common to both is a two-tier structure in which the central banks hold the issuing monopoly on central bank digital currency on the first tier, whereby they are not necessarily dependent on their own technical infrastructures, but could also use those of private companies.[15] On the second tier, the other tasks associated with a payment, such as verification and settlement of the transaction as well as end-user interactions (anti-money laundering, data protection, customer service) are assigned to the intermediaries.[16] Due to this two-tier structure and unlike in the direct model, the intermediaries are no longer bypassed by the central bank's activities but are actively involved in the distribution process, which can open up new business areas for them. For this reason, both models are very popular in the practical considerations of those central banks that have already experimented with pilot projects of central bank digital currency. Sweden, for example, used the hybrid model for its e-krona pilot project.[17] The E-CNY of the People's Republic of China also has a two-tier design.[18] The ECB as well experimented with a two-tier model in an early phase and also prefers this in its project report.[19]

Just like in the direct model, central bank digital currency represents a liability item of the central bank in the hybrid model (see Fig. 2.2) as well.[20] However, the

---

[12] ECB (2020), p. 38; Auer and Böhme (2020), p. 90.

[13] Directive (EU) 2015/849 of the European Parliament and of the Council of 20 May 2015 on the prevention of the use of the financial system for the purposes of money laundering or terrorist financing, amending Regulation (EU) No 648/2012 of the European Parliament and of the Council, and repealing Directive 2005/60/EC of the European Parliament and of the Council and Commission Directive 2006/70/EC (5 June 2015) OJ L 141/73, lastly amended by Directive (EU) 2019/2177 (27 December 2019) OJ L 334/155.

[14] Cf. Omlor and Birne (2020), p. 3.

[15] Soderberg (2022), p. 10; ECB (2019), p. 4.

[16] Soderberg (2022), pp. 10 and 11.

[17] Armelius et al. (2020), p. 87; Auer et al. (2020), p. 24.

[18] PBoC (2021), p. 3; Auer et al. (2020), p. 22.

[19] ECB (2019) and ECB (2020), p. 26. Clearer also ECB (2022a).

[20] Terlau (2021), para. 4; Diehl (2021), para. 62; Omlor and Birne (2020), p. 3.

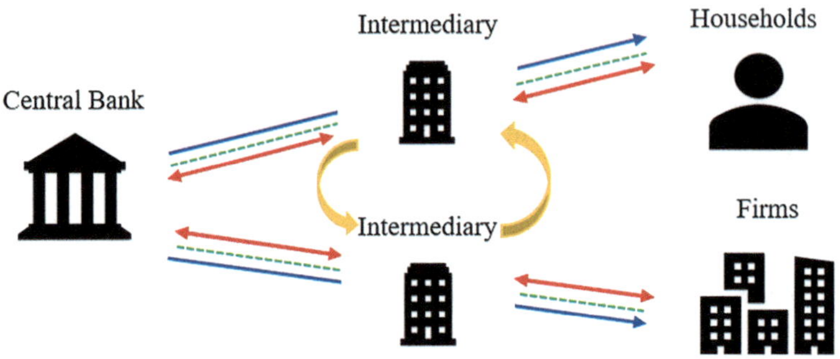

Fig. 2.2 Hybrid model (inspired by Auer and Böhme 2021)

end-users no longer have a direct legal or contractual relationship with the central bank, but rather a contractual relationship with the financial intermediaries.[21] These can be commercial banks but also other payment service providers. These intermediaries settle the transactions between the end-users (retail payments) exclusively among themselves in the name of the respective users and assert the end-users' claim against the central bank for the issuance of the CBDC on a fiduciary basis by means of an account held with the central bank.[22] The distribution of central bank digital currency shall take place in the following manner:[23] The end-user approaches its respective financial intermediary with a request to issue units of central bank digital currency in a certain amount. The intermediary then approaches the central bank on behalf of its user and reduces its deposits with the central bank by the nominal value of the requested units of CBDC. The central bank then debits the intermediary's reserve account and authorises the issuance of the currency units.

Unlike in the direct model, the end-users have only intermediated access to central bank digital currency.[24] Nevertheless, the CBDC is still a liability item of the central bank, so it is not allocated to the intermediaries on their balance sheet.[25] This has the advantage that the insolvency of an intermediary does not affect the end-user.[26] In the hybrid model, the central bank also periodically receives copies of all data records relating to retail payments (green dashed lines in Fig. 2.2).[27] If an intermediary fails, the central bank can use the backup copies to reconstruct the ownership of the individual units of CBDC and the transactions and restore them if

[21] Omlor and Birne (2020), p. 3.

[22] ECB (2020), p. 26; ECB (2019), p. 7; Omlor and Birne (2020), p. 3; Auer and Böhme (2020), p. 90.

[23] See for the following ECB (2019), p. 6.

[24] Soderberg (2022), p. 8.

[25] Auer and Böhme (2020), p. 90.

[26] Auer and Böhme (2021); Auer and Böhme (2020), p. 90.

[27] Auer and Böhme (2020), p. 91.

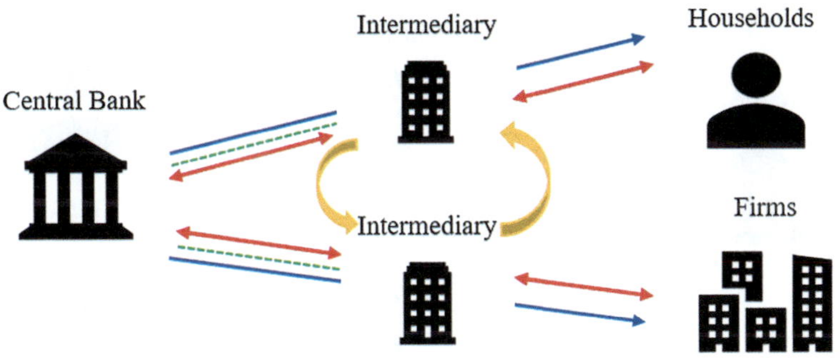

Fig. 2.3 Intermediated model (inspired by Auer and Böhme 2021)

necessary.[28] However, a disadvantage of the hybrid model is the huge amount of data that accumulates when retail payments are recorded and is stored by the central bank's technical infrastructure.[29] In addition, the central bank must be able to take sufficient account of data protection and data security requirements.[30]

Therefore, in the intermediated model (see Fig. 2.3) only the data records of transactions between the intermediaries are periodically recorded by the central bank (so-called wholesale payments, green dashed lines).

However, the advantage of this data reduction is offset by the disadvantage that the central bank must rely on the diligence of intermediaries in recording retail payments in order not to inadvertently satisfy unjustified claims by end-users for the issuance of currency units of central bank digital currency to which they are not entitled (anymore).[31]

2.1.3 Indirect Model

To further emphasise the role and importance of intermediaries, *Adrian and Mancini-Griffoli* developed the indirect model (also called synthetic-CBDC).[32]

According to this model (see Fig. 2.4), central bank digital currency is a liability of commercial banks towards their customers that is backed by original central bank digital currency.[33] The commercial banks issue digital tokens denominated in euro to their customers and secure each token at a ratio of 1:1 with deposits in the form of

[28] Auer and Böhme (2021).

[29] Auer and Böhme (2021).

[30] Auer and Böhme (2021).

[31] Auer and Böhme (2021).

[32] Adrian and Mancini-Griffoli (2019), p. 14.

[33] Omlor and Birne (2020), p. 3.

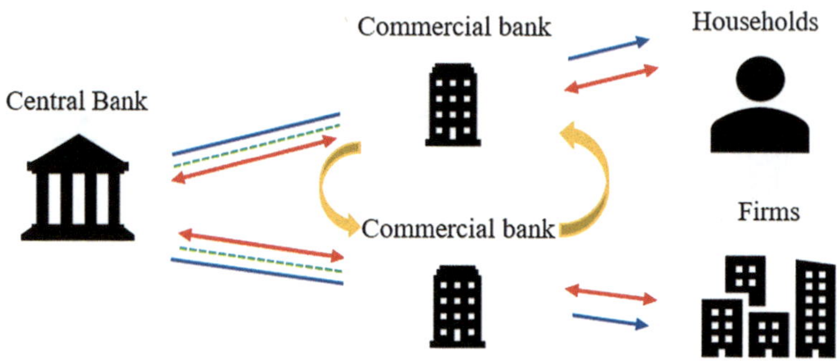

Fig. 2.4 Indirect model (inspired by Auer and Böhme 2021)

central bank digital currency through accounts held with the central bank.[34] They also process the payment transactions among the end-users.[35] The central bank, on the other hand, only issues original central bank digital currency to the commercial banks and handles their inter-bank transactions (green dashed lines).[36] Hence, this model represents a public-private partnership in the financial sector and thus strengthens the role of the commercial banks.[37]

The special feature of this model is that central bank digital currency accessible to end-users is not a liability of the central bank, but a liability of the commercial banks, which is only collateralised with deposits in the form of original central bank digital currency.[38] According to the predominant view, in the absence of a central bank liability it can therefore not be considered as true central bank digital currency, but rather as a form of stablecoins or e-money.[39] Only the Hong Kong Monetary Authority favours this model of digital 'central bank currency'.[40] In addition, unlike in the hybrid model, end-users are now again confronted with the default and insolvency risk of commercial banks because there is no separation in the balance sheets in this model.

[34] Read and Schäfer (2020), p. 18.

[35] Auer and Böhme (2020), p. 88.

[36] Auer and Böhme (2020), p. 88.

[37] Adrian and Mancini-Griffoli (2019), p. 14.

[38] Auer and Böhme (2020), p. 88.

[39] Soderberg (2022), p. 8; Auer and Böhme (2020), p. 88; cf. also the ECB's understanding of a digital euro in ECB (2020), p. 6.

[40] Hong Kong Monetary Authority (2021), p. 20.

2.2 Technical Infrastructure

To understand the concept of central bank digital currency more deeply, it is helpful to enquire the technical infrastructure that perhaps may underlie it. In the context of cryptocurrencies, the focus is often on decentralised technologies, mainly the distributed ledger technology (DLT) and one of its subtypes, the Blockchain technology. But the use of DLT for central bank digital currency is not necessarily a key feature.[41] It is predominantly preferred for decentralised distribution systems.[42] Central bank digital currency can also be distributed using centrally controlled conventional data technologies.[43] Ultimately, centralised and decentralised technology can also be combined.[44] In its experiments to date, the ECB has tested central bank digital currency using both decentralised technologies in the form of Corda and Blockchain as well as a combination of the centralised TIPS system with decentralised DLT systems.[45] Although the underlying technology is not yet clear, some official statements by the ECB point towards the use of Blockchain and distributed ledger technology.[46] Therefore, the following section will address the concepts of DLT, Corda, Blockchain and TIPS.

2.2.1 *Distributed Ledger Technology*

According to Article 3 (1) No. 1 of the MiCA-Regulation draft, distributed ledger is a technology that supports the distributed recording of encrypted data.[47] This addresses two central characteristics of DLT: The distributed recording of information and the use of cryptographic methods. Thus, the ledger is a database, or more precisely a general register, in which, just as in a company, business transactions are stored as data records, but here in the form of transactions between the network participants.[48] The difference between conventional databases and DLT is that the recording does not take place on centrally controlled, albeit physically distributed, nodes, but on all computers of the users participating in the network.[49] This is

[41] ECB (2020), p. 29 fn. 52; Hanl and Michaelis (2019), p. 6.

[42] ECB (2020), pp. 39 and 40; Soderberg (2022), p. 17; Hong Kong Monetary Authority (2021), p. 21.

[43] Auer and Böhme (2020), p. 91.

[44] See for e.g. the *E-CNY*, cf. PBoC (2021), p. 10.

[45] ECB (2019); ECB (2021). See in more detail Sect. 2.4.

[46] ECB Appendix (2021), p. 2: '(. . .) we are testing how to shape different elements of a blockchain prototype (. . .)'; Panetta (2022b): 'In particular, we are assessing the potential of DLT and the extent to which it could improve our services'.

[47] Data in the form of state informations, cf. Hanl and Michaelis (2019), p. 4.

[48] Varmaz et al. (2021), para. 22; Brühl (2017), p. 135.

[49] Auer and Böhme (2020), p. 92.

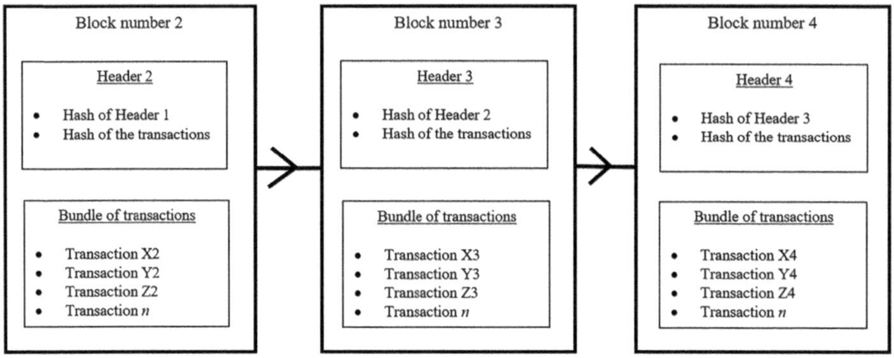

Fig. 2.5 Simplified illustration of the Blockchain (inspired by Frommberger and Zimmermann 2020, para 13)

roughly comparable to a constellation in which all bank transfers are recorded directly on the computers of the bank customers of all banks in a system.[50] Regular updates of the ledger are required to ensure that every user is up to date with regard to the data records. Since, by definition, in decentralised systems this cannot be done by a central authority, it requires a consensus mechanism between the network participants.[51] However, due to time delays of the updates and the asynchronous nature of the transaction and the information about the transaction, in the case of distributed recording of transactions with digital units there is always a risk that one or more users will have access to the units more than once (so-called double-spending).[52] The manifold forms of DLT have developed various mechanisms to prevent this (see below). Furthermore, access to the DLT network is either granted to anyone with the respective software (permissionless) or only to a firmly defined user group (permissioned).[53]

2.2.2 *Blockchain*

The Blockchain technology underlying Bitcoin is a use case of DLT.[54] The title 'Blockchain' stems from the fact that the individual transactions made and confirmed by the network participants are periodically bundled and recorded together with a header in a data block (see Fig. 2.5).[55] The header contains, among other

[50] González-Meneses et al. (2021), para. 39.

[51] Hanl and Michaelis (2019), p. 4; Auer and Böhme (2020), p. 92.

[52] Hofert (2018), p. 4; Kaulartz (2021), para. 9. Cf. also Schmieder (2022), para. 15.

[53] Brühl (2017), p. 140; Geiling (2016), p. 30.

[54] Siegel (2021), Chapter 3 para. 105; Brühl (2017), p. 140.

[55] Cf. Omlor (2019), p. 289.

things, the so-called hash of the respective preceding block.[56] The hash is an alphanumeric representation of the bundled transactions and functions as a kind of digital fingerprint.[57] By referencing to the predecessor block, the header connects the individual data blocks to an inseparable 'chain' (Blockchain).[58]

The individual Bitcoin itself only represents a digital unit in the meaning of a data record that is assigned to a specific network address in the blockchain network.[59] In a transaction, only the assignment subject, i.e. the network address, changes, while the assignment object, the Bitcoin record, remains unaffected in this respect.[60] For a transaction, the parties to the transaction each need a pair of keys consisting of a public and a private key.[61] Only the private key, not the Bitcoin unit, is stored in a so-called wallet.[62] The person initiating the transaction generates a data bundle consisting of the recipient's public key, the transaction amount, the transaction history and his own public key and encrypts this data bundle using his private key.[63] The recipient's public key serves as the receiving address; it is comparable to an account number in banking transactions, the sender's private key is accordingly comparable to the PIN or TAN.[64] The transaction history records all transactions that make the initiating party appear as the subject to which the amount to be transferred is assigned to.[65] The initiating party's public key is used by the recipient to decrypt the data bundle, as it necessarily corresponds with the initiating party's private key.[66] Because of this, the recipient can check whether the initiating party is the 'authorised owner' of the amount and can also verify the identity because only the owner of the private key could authorise this transaction.[67] However, the recipient cannot check whether the bitcoin unit to be transferred has already been transferred elsewhere at the same time (double-spending).[68] Therefore, the transaction is bundled in parallel in a transaction pool and periodically checked by all network participants (so-called nodes[69]).[70] The nodes then solve complex mathematical algorithms (so-called

[56] Terlau (2022), para. 187.

[57] Frommberger and Zimmermann (2020), para. 14; Schrey and Thalhofer (2017), p. 1432; Kaulartz (2021), para. 13 and 14.

[58] Langenbucher et al. (2020), para. 3; Brühl (2017), p. 137.

[59] Beck (2015), p. 581; Terlau (2022), para. 183; Langenbucher et al. (2020), para. 4.

[60] Frommberger and Zimmermann (2020), para. 19; Hofert (2018), p. 3.

[61] Beck (2015), p. 581; Kaulartz (2021), para. 27.

[62] Frommberger and Zimmermann (2020), para. 25; Spindler and Bille (2014), p. 1358.

[63] Brühl (2017), p. 136; Terlau (2022), para. 185.

[64] Spindler and Bille (2014), p. 1358; Kaulartz (2021), para. 33; Frommberger and Zimmermann (2020), para. 16 and 17.

[65] Brühl (2017), p. 136.

[66] Schrey and Thalhofer (2017), p. 1432; Brühl (2017), p. 136.

[67] Terlau (2022), para. 186; Kaulartz (2021), para. 31; Brühl (2017), p. 136.

[68] Geiling (2016), p. 29.

[69] Frommberger and Zimmermann (2020), para. 7.

[70] Brühl (2017), pp. 136 and 137.

proof-of-work) using enormous computing power, validate the transaction and then combine the verified transactions into the blocks described above.[71] For verification, the nodes use the previous Blockchain and check the complete transaction history of the individual Bitcoin unit against the ledger, so that a double-spending would be noticed and the transaction would not be validated.[72]

2.2.3 *Corda*

Corda is also a DLT use case and is operated by the international banking consortium R3.[73] Unlike the Blockchain, the nodes do not have to reach a consensus on the state of the ledger, but on the state of a so-called state object.[74] This is a digital document that records the existence, content and current status of an agreement between the transaction parties and is recorded in the Corda ledger.[75] Unlike the Blockchain, the Corda ledger is not visible to every network participant, but only to the respective transaction parties.[76] A transaction takes place through a consensus of the transaction parties on a new state of the state object, which offsets the previous state and thus forms a chain of origin.[77] For the consensus, the parties also use cryptographic methods.[78] By continuously agreeing on new states that offset old states, Corda, unlike the Blockchain, does not require the storage of continuous data blocks.[79] To avoid the double-spending problem, so-called notary nodes are used.[80] These are network participants with special access rights determined by the operator of the system, who use the ledger to check whether a state of the state object that is to be offset by the current transaction has already been offset by a previous transaction.[81]

---

[71] Terlau (2021), para. 11; Langenbucher et al. (2020), para. 3; Spindler and Bille (2014), p. 1358; Brühl (2017), p. 136.

[72] Spindler and Bille (2014), p. 1358; Terlau (2022), para. 186; Geiling (2016), p. 29; Frommberger and Zimmermann (2020), para. 5, 23.

[73] Siegel (2021), para. 127; Geiling (2016), p. 32.

[74] Brown (2018), p. 8.

[75] Brown (2018), p. 8.

[76] Brown (2018), p. 8.

[77] Brown (2018), p. 9.

[78] Brown (2018), p. 8.

[79] Siegel (2021), para. 106; Brown (2018), p. 8.

[80] ECB (2019), p. 5.

[81] Hearn and Brown (2019), p. 37; Brown (2018), p. 10; ECB (2019), p. 5.

2.2.4 TIPS

The letters TIPS stand for TARGET Instant Payment Settlement. TARGET is an acronym for Trans-European Automated Real-time Gross Settlement Express Transfer. TARGET is the generic term for TARGET2, TARGET2-Securities and TIPS.[82] These systems act as clearing houses for credit transfers. On the one hand, clearing can take place by immediately booking each individual payment transaction (so-called gross system).[83] On the other hand, it is also possible to bundle the mutual payment flows for each participant in the payment system (netting) and establish a balance, which is then settled by means of a single payment (so-called net system).[84] TARGET2 is a real-time gross settlement system for large-value euro interbank payments only, whereas TIPS acts as a clearing system for small-value payments between households and businesses.[85] TIPS is centrally operated by the Eurosystem,[86] more precisely by the Deutsche Bundesbank, the Banca d'Italia, the Banco de España and the Banque de France.[87] It works as follows:[88] The individual customer initiates a payment order with his payment service provider (PSP), usually a commercial bank. The PSP transmits this order to TIPS. TIPS verifies the instant payment order and blocks the respective transfer amount on the central bank account of the instructing PSP. When the payment order is accepted by the recipient's PSP, TIPS releases the amount, debits it from the payer's PSP and credits it to the central bank account of the recipient's PSP. TIPS then informs the recipient's and payer's PSPs of the successful transaction. The whole process takes less than five seconds.[89] TIPS thus has three characteristics. First, participation requires an account at a national central bank.[90] Secondly, payment orders are settled exclusively by booking the PSPs' claims against the central bank, i.e. by central bank money in the form of reserves.[91] Thirdly, the group of participants is strongly limited to holders of central bank accounts (so-called participants) and institutions (so-called reachable parties)

---

[82] Renzetti et al. (2021), p. 12 fn. 14.

[83] Schmieder (2022), para. 9.

[84] Schmieder (2022), para. 10.

[85] Arcese et al. (2021), pp. 7 and 8; Herresthal (2019), p. 899.

[86] For a definition see Article 282 (1), second sentence, TFEU.

[87] Renzetti et al. (2021), p. 27; cf. Article 2 No. 77 of the Guideline of the European Central Bank of 5 December 2012 on a Trans-European Automated Real-time Gross Settlement Express Transfer system (TARGET2) (ECB/2012/27) (30 January 2013) OJ L 030/1, lastly amended by Guideline (EU) 2022/688 (29 April 2022), OJ L 126/25.

[88] See Renzetti et al. (2021), p. 17 and ECB (2023).

[89] Renzetti et al. (2021), p. 24.

[90] ECB (2023); Herresthal (2019), p. 899.

[91] ECB (2023).

who have a separate legal/contractual relationship with the participants on the basis of which payments by the institutions are made via the participants' account.[92]

2.3 Design of the Payment System

How central bank digital currency can be transferred between users as means of payment depends largely on the way the payment system is designed, i.e. which functionalities it offers. There are usually two design options/functionalities, but they are not always referred to uniformly.[93]

2.3.1 Account-Based or Claim-Based or Online Functionality

Firstly, there is the possibility of designing payment systems based on accounts. In these systems, the payment medium records a claim on an account balance against a third party, hence this system is also called a claim-based system.[94] Transactions with the payment medium take place by transferring these claims.[95] To do this, all parties involved in the transaction are required to hold an account with one or more third parties, who post the transactions to the accounts.[96] Today's system of transferring scriptural money forms a classic example of an account-based payment system.[97] The validation of payment transactions in account-based systems thus depends on the identity and solvency of the payer, who must identify himself as the holder of the account initiating the payment.[98] In addition, it is necessary to update the account balances of the payer and the payee after each transaction.[99] As this system often requires the connection to a network, one can also label it as the 'online functionality' of the means of payment.

However, a purely account-based system of central bank digital currency has some disadvantages. Since it is not commercial bank money, but a liability item of the central bank, transactions must ultimately pass through and be recorded in some

[92]Deutscher Sparkassen- und Giroverband e.V. (2017); Herresthal (2019), p. 899; Renzetti et al. (2021), pp. 15 and 16.

[93]On this see fundamentally Kahn and Roberds (2009).

[94]Armelius et al. (2020), p. 87; Adrian and Mancini-Griffoli (2019), p. 2.

[95]Mancini-Griffoli et al. (2018), p. 8; Adrian and Mancini-Griffoli (2019), p. 2.

[96]Cf. Read and Schäfer (2020), p. 16.

[97]ECB (2020), pp. 29 and 30; Bindseil (2020), p. 4.

[98]Brunnermeier et al. (2021), p. 4; Hanl and Michaelis (2019), p. 4; Adrian and Mancini-Griffoli (2019), p. 2; Kahn and Roberds (2009), p. 6; Vollmer (2020), p. 30.

[99]BIS (2021), p. 4.

form of central bank-owned accounts.[100] This entails enormous operational costs.[101] In addition, the risks in the account-based system, such as fraudulent actions by the account holder, false transaction records etc., affect the account provider and thus ultimately the central bank.[102] Furthermore, account-based systems do not allow for offline use of the means of payment, which would exclude many potential users.[103]

2.3.2 Bearer-Instrument or Value-Based or Token-Based or Offline Functionality

For the second way of designing a payment system it is hard to find a unified terminology. Some refer to it as a store-of-value-system (value-based system),[104] others as a token-system (token-based system)[105] and still others as a bearer-instrument.[106] What all these terms have in common is that such a system consists of a payment medium that usually must be handed over in order to carry out the transaction.[107] Classic examples from the analogue world are cash and coins made of precious metal.[108] With these, the holder of the medium in circulation is also considered to be the holder of the associated value, hence the payee does not check the identity of the payer but rather if the medium is authentic and genuine.[109] Usually, no third party is needed for this check, but the payee always bears the risk of counterfeiting.[110] As in this system payments are usually initiated in proximity of payer and payee and are validated on a peer-to-peer basis, one can also label it the 'offline functionality' of the means of payment.

Central bank digital currency in this form would therefore be considered as a digital data record that is exchanged between users in a cash-like manner.[111] However, unlike physical objects such as coins, digital data sets face the risk that

---

[100] Cf. Kahn et al. (2018), p. 2.

[101] Like here Bindseil (2020), p. 4 and Kahn et al. (2018), p. 10.

[102] Kahn et al. (2018), p. 8.

[103] Cf. ECB (2020), p. 30.

[104] Kahn and Roberds (2009), p. 6; Vollmer (2020), p. 30.

[105] Instead of many see: Brunnermeier et al. (2021), p. 4; Adrian and Mancini-Griffoli (2019), p. 2; Read and Schäfer (2020), p. 16. Critical to this terminology: BIS (2021), p. 4 and Brunnermeier and Landau (2022), p. 32.

[106] ECB (2020), p. 30.

[107] Read and Schäfer (2020), p. 16; Brunnermeier and Landau (2022), p. 13; Adrian and Mancini-Griffoli (2019), p. 2.

[108] Kahn and Roberds (2009), p. 6; Vollmer (2020), p. 30.

[109] Berentsen and Schär (2018), pp. 97 and 98; Kahn and Roberds (2009), p. 6; Brunnermeier et al. (2021), p. 4.

[110] ECB (2020), p. 30; Hanl and Michaelis (2019), p. 4; Kahn et al. (2018), p. 8.

[111] Thießen (2021), p. 27; Diehl (2021), para. 42; Armelius et al. (2020), p. 87; Mancini-Griffoli et al. (2018), p. 8.

they are easy to copy and can therefore be used several times at once.[112] In order to prevent this double-spending, the central bank digital currency would also have to be registered somehow in one place in a register.[113]

2.3.3 *Terminology for the Digital Euro*

The traditional payment system of today is a hybrid system of account-based and bearer-instrument. This is due to the authorship and manifestation of the forms of money that are available to the public. Public money, created by central banks, is cash and thus a system with a bearer-instrument. Private money, mainly created by commercial banks, is scriptural money and thus an account-based system. This hybrid form of today's payment system is therefore essentially based on the fact that there are two forms of money issued by different emitters. These manifestations also limit their usability. Since scriptural money conceptually is not physical, it can only be used for online payments. Cash, on the other hand, is physical and can therefore never be used for online payments, but only for offline payments. The digital euro has the special feature that there is only one issuer and thus only *one* form of money, *the* digital euro. However, it shall be equipped with various functionalities that enable a broad usability.[114] It should be noted that the terms for these functionalities have not yet been clearly defined.

On the one hand, the digital euro shall be used for online payments.[115] According to the ECB's glossary, online payments are payments whose settlement requires either the payer or the payee to be connected to a network.[116] In this case, it is an account-based payment system. Hence, in the further course of this book, this functionality will be referred to as the account-based digital euro.

On the other hand, the digital euro shall also be used for offline payments.[117] According to the ECB's glossary, offline payments are payments whose settlement takes place directly between the payer and the payee without the need for a network connection at the time of this interaction.[118] Since no third party is required for the settlement, it is a payment system based on a bearer-instrument. Hence, in the further course of this book, this functionality will be referred to as the digital euro as a bearer-instrument. However, it should be noted at this point that this manifestation of the digital euro appears to be extremely problematic. It is questionable how offline payments are made with regard to data protection and combating money laundering

[112] Hanl and Michaelis (2019), p. 4.

[113] Armelius et al. (2020), p. 87. Similar also BIS (2021), p. 4 and Kahn et al. (2018), p. 12.

[114] Garratt et al. (2020); ECB (2020), p. 41 and ECB (2021).

[115] ECB (2020), p. 34.

[116] ECB (2022b).

[117] ECB (2020), p. 34.

[118] ECB (2022b).

and terrorism financing.[119] In addition, the scope and implementation of the settlement between the parties appears questionable.[120]

2.4 Models of the European Central Bank

In its technical trials the European Central Bank has experimented with a total of four different workstreams.

2.4.1 Centralised Approach

The first workstream experimented with central bank digital currency that is account-based.[121] The Eurosystem solely issued and distributed the digital units, thus it completely dispenses with the involvement of intermediaries. Hence, this can be classified as the direct model with an account-based payment system. Technically, it is based on the centrally managed TIPS system with interfaces to already existing payment systems.

2.4.2 Combined Approach

In the second workstream, the Eurosystem combines a centrally managed ledger with platforms that operate on a DLT basis.[122]

In the first sub-model (so-called 'flat approach'), the central banks only act as liquidity exchanges. A ledger centrally managed by the Eurosystem based on the TIPS system is connected to two different distributed ledger technologies. The first DLT is a network of payment channels in which central bank digital currency is created. For that, the end-users open a payment channel with a financial intermediary. In this channel, the end-users can transfer central bank digital currency among themselves without this being recorded in the central ledger of the Eurosystem. For the settlement of their payment orders the financial intermediaries hold central bank accounts.[123] With the second DLT, the intermediaries create smart contracts[124] that are recorded in the Eurosystem's ledger. End-users then receive or send funds to

[119] See Sect. 3.4.

[120] See Sect. 3.2.2.

[121] For this and the following see ECB (2021), p. 1.

[122] For this and the following see ECB (2021), p. 2.

[123] Thießen (2021), p. 28.

[124] For the terminology see Brühl (2017), p. 142.

each other by executing the smart contracts. At first glance, this model may seem similar to the account-based intermediated model. However, central bank digital currency is not issued by the Eurosystem, but is generated in the payment channels between the end-user and the financial intermediary. In substance, it is therefore more alike to the indirect model described above and is thus not 'central bank' digital currency.[125]

The second sub-model is different, with the ECB taking a tiered approach. Tier one consists of the central ledger based on the TIPS system and controlled by the Eurosystem. Tier two consists of platforms operated by private market participants. The Eurosystem issues central bank digital currency on tier one. The distribution is carried out on tier two by selected financial intermediaries who own a central bank account and distribute the central bank digital currency obtained to the end-users via various platforms, whether DLT-based or based on conventional technology. This model can be classified as an account-based hybrid or intermediated model with a clear division of tasks between central banks and the private sector.[126]

2.4.3 *Blockchain Approach*

With the third workstream, the ECB is pursuing a new approach in technical terms.[127] It tested a platform based on the Blockchain for the issuance and distribution of central bank digital currency. The central bank digital currency is to be stored as a digital representation of an asset with a fixed value as a data set on the Blockchain. The Blockchain has several ledgers, a central ledger with all transactions that take place and a separate ledger for each unit of central bank digital currency with the particular transaction history of this unit. The issuance of the central bank money is carried out by the Eurosystem, the payment transactions take place directly between the end-users based on the Blockchain. For transactions, the end-users use cryptographic key pairs that are kept in a separate portable device. The end-users gain access to the Blockchain via the (private) provider of a wallet, on which (contradictory to the usual technical functioning[128]) not the keys but the particular units of central bank digital currency shall be stored. In conclusion, this is a hybrid model payment system with a bearer-instrument.

[125] See also the doubts expressed by the ECB (2021), p. 5.

[126] Schaaf (2022) speaks of 'some kind of public-private-partnership'.

[127] For this and the following see ECB (2021), pp. 2 and 3.

[128] Typically, in the context of the Blockchain, only the private key is stored on a wallet and the value-representing records are not transferred, see Sect. 2.2.2. Also, according to the ECB '(. . .) the units of the digital euro simply change ownership', see ECB (2021), p. 3.

2.4.4 *Offline Approach*

Finally, the ECB tested a hardware-based bearer-instrument (HBI) for offline payments.[129] With the help of the HBI, transactions are to be processed directly between users without the need for an intermediary.[130] The HBI could take various mobile forms, such as a smartphone, a smart card, a dongle or a wristband with screen function,[131] as long as a software can be stored on this device and as long as there is a standard interface (Bluetooth, near-field communication).[132] The technical core of the HBI is the software, which is described in the experiments as a 'secure element' (SE). The SE is used to store cryptographic information on it and it should help to prevent double-spending or to implement transaction limits.[133] The digital euro accessible with the HBI could take on three possible forms:[134] First, it can be regarded as an 'indivisible token', i.e. a data record that is digitally signed by the central bank and represents a fixed value, similar to today's notes and coins. Secondly, it can be designed as a 'divisible token', which does not represent a fixed value but rather the exact value that is needed for the respective transaction (e.g. EUR 6.36). Last but not least, it can also be designed as a balance that increases or decreases depending on the transaction. However, the HBIs tested in this way faced a variety of problems.[135] To solve the double-spending problem, a connection to the Eurosystem's online ledger is needed on a regular basis to reconcile the balances and the transactions made.[136] Therefore, the technologies tested so far have not been capable to enable the end-users to perform an indefinite number of consecutive offline transactions.[137] Instead, these transactions would have to be recorded and stored locally on the HBI, so that the transaction speed is reduced with an increasing number of transactions and the number of possible offline transactions is limited by the storage capacity of the HBI.[138] As a result, it can be said that the similarity to cash aimed at[139] with the HBI can only be guaranteed to a very limited extent, if at all.[140]

---

[129] ECB (2021), p. 3.

[130] Deutsche Bundesbank (2021), p. 4.

[131] Kiff et al. (2020), p. 32 mention further forms such as payment cards, QR-code based prepaid cards or with a smart chip equipped banknote.

[132] Deutsche Bundesbank (2021), pp. 4 and 8.

[133] Deutsche Bundesbank (2021), p. 5.

[134] See Deutsche Bundesbank (2021), p. 5.

[135] See the summary of the ECB (2021), p. 5.

[136] Deutsche Bundesbank (2021), p. 5.

[137] Deutsche Bundesbank (2021), p. 6.

[138] Deutsche Bundesbank (2021), p. 6.

[139] Deutsche Bundesbank (2021), p. 4.

[140] Deutsche Bundesbank (2021), p. 7.

2.5 Summary

As a technical starting point for the legal analysis, the previous section results in the following: Predominantly, the ECB seems to prefer two-tier models in which financial intermediaries are involved in some form, be it for distributing the central bank digital currency or only for granting access to it, while at the same time preserving the Eurosystem's monopoly on the issuance of CBDC.[141] In addition, a mixed form of account-based and bearer-based payment system seems conceivable. Whether the specific technical infrastructure is managed centrally or decentrally, by means of conventional or innovative technologies, is not necessarily decisive for the legal assessment.[142]

References

Adrian T, Mancini-Griffoli T (2019) The rise of digital money. IMF FinTech Notes No. 19/01. https://www.imf.org/-/media/Files/Publications/FTN063/2019/English/FTNEA2019001.ashx. Accessed 31 July 2023

Arcese M et al (2021) Real-time gross settlement systems – breaking the wall of scalability and high availability. Banca D'Italia Markets, Infrastructures, Payment Systems No. 2. https://www.bancaditalia.it/pubblicazioni/mercati-infrastrutture-e-sistemi-di-pagamento/approfondimenti/2021-002/N.2-MISP.pdf?language_id=1. Accessed 31 July 2023

Armelius H et al (2020) E-krona design models: pros, cons and trade-offs. Sveriges Riksbank Econ Rev 1:80–96. https://www.riksbank.se/globalassets/media/rapporter/pov/artiklar/engelska/2020/200618/2020_2-e-krona-design-models-pros-cons-and-trade-offs.pdf. Accessed 31 July 2023

Auer R, Böhme R (2020) The technology of retail central bank digital currency. BIS Q Rev:85–100. https://www.bis.org/publ/qtrpdf/r_qt2003j.pdf. Accessed 31 July 2023

Auer R, Böhme R (2021) Central bank digital currency: the quest for minimally invasive technology. BIS Working Papers No. 984. https://www.bis.org/publ/work948.pdf. Accessed 31 July 2023

Auer R et al (2020) Rise of the central bank digital currencies: drivers, approaches and technologies. BIS Working Papers No. 880. https://www.bis.org/publ/work880.pdf. Accessed 31 July 2023

Balz B, Diehl M, Winter H (2020) Digitales Geld. Kreditwesen 73(24):10–14

Beck B (2015) Bitcoins als Geld im Rechtssinne. NJW 2015:580–586

Berentsen A, Schär F (2018) The case for central bank electronic money and the non-case for central bank cryptocurrencies. Federal Reserve Bank of St. Louis Review, Second Quarter 2018, 100(2):97–106. https://doi.org/10.20955/r.2018.97-106

Bindseil U (2020) Tiered CBDC and the financial system. ECB Working Paper Series No. 2351. https://www.ecb.europa.eu/pub/pdf/scpwps/ecb.wp2351~c8c18bbd60.en.pdf. Accessed 31 July 2023

BIS (2021) Central bank digital currencies: system design and interoperability. https://www.bis.org/publ/othp42_system_design.pdf. Accessed 31 July 2023

Bossu W et al (2020) Legal aspects of central bank digital currency: central bank and monetary law considerations. IMF Working Paper WP/20/254. https://www.imf.org/en/Publications/WP/

[141] Cf. especially Panetta (2022a).

[142] Cf. Bossu et al. (2020), p. 10 no. 17 and 18.

Issues/2020/11/20/Legal-Aspects-of-Central-Bank-Digital-Currency-Central-Bank-and-Monetary-Law-Considerations-49827. Accessed 31 July 2023

Brown R (2018) The Corda platform: an introduction. https://www.corda.net/content/corda-platform-whitepaper.pdf. Accessed 31 July 2023

Brühl V (2017) Bitcoins, Blockchain und Distributed Ledgers. Wirtschaftsdienst 97(2):135–142. https://doi.org/10.1007/s10273-017-2096-3

Brunnermeier M, Landau J-P (2022) The digital euro: policy implications and perspectives. https://www.europarl.europa.eu/RegData/etudes/STUD/2022/703337/IPOL_STU(2022)703337_EN.pdf. Accessed 31 July 2023

Brunnermeier M et al (2021) The digitalization of money. BIS Working Papers No. 941. https://www.bis.org/publ/work941.pdf. Accessed 31 July 2023

Deutsche Bundesbank (2021) Eurosystem experimentation regarding a digital euro – research workstream on hardware bearer instrument. https://www.ecb.europa.eu/paym/digital_euro/investigation/profuse/shared/files/deexp/ecb.deexp211011_2.en.pdf?33e4ca807a0c37e6fbfac8c447748501. Accessed 31 July 2023

Deutscher Sparkassen- und Giroverband e.V. (2017) EZB startet Geldtransfer in Echtzeit. Betriebswirtschaftliche Blätter 30 June 2017

Diehl (2021) Chapter 2. In: Omlor S, Link M (eds) Kryptowährungen und Token. R&W, Frankfurt a.M.

ECB (2019) Exploring anonymity in central bank digital currencies. In Focus Series No. 4. https://www.ecb.europa.eu/paym/intro/publications/pdf/ecb.mipinfocus191217.en.pdf. Accessed 31 July 2023

ECB (2020) Report on a digital euro. https://www.ecb.europa.eu/pub/pdf/other/Report_on_a_digital_euro~4d7268b458.en.pdf. Accessed 31 July 2023

ECB (2021) Digital euro experimentation scope and key learnings. https://www.ecb.europa.eu/pub/pdf/other/ecb.digitaleuroscopekeylearnings202107~564d89045e.en.pdf. Accessed 31 July 2023

ECB (2022a) Civil Society Seminar: shaping the digital euro. https://www.ecb.europa.eu/pub/conferences/html/ecb_civilsoc.en.html. (speech) and https://www.ecb.europa.eu/pub/conferences/shared/pdf/shaping_the_digital_euro.pdf. (slides) Accessed 31 July 2023

ECB (2022b) Digital euro glossary. https://www.ecb.europa.eu/paym/digital_euro/investigation/profuse/shared/files/dedocs/ecb.dedocs220420.en.pdf?cc6c5408f1ffdaf2e367a9121bc07eba. Accessed 31 July 2023

ECB (2023) What is TARGET Instant Payment Settlement System (TIPS)? https://www.ecb.europa.eu/paym/target/tips/html/index.en.html. Accessed 31 July 2023

ECB Appendix (2021) The Eurosystem's analysis of privacy-enhancing techniques in central bank digital currencies. https://www.ecb.europa.eu/pub/pdf/annex/ecb.sp210414_1_annex~43eee6196e.en.pdf?ed992ba1ebc6915fe12bf5d57013ae549. Accessed 31 July 2023

Frommberger, Zimmermann (2020) § 1. In: Maume P, Maute L (eds) Rechtshandbuch Kryptowerte. Beck, München

Garratt R et al (2020) Token- or account-based? A digital currency can be both. Federal Reserve Bank of New York Liberty Street Economics. https://libertystreeteconomics.newyorkfed.org/2020/08/token-or-account-based-a-digital-currency-can-be-both/. Accessed 31 July 2023

Geiling L (2016) Distributed Ledger – Die Technologie hinter den virtuellen Währungen am Beispiel der Blockchain. BaFinJournal, pp 28–32. https://www.bafin.de/SharedDocs/Downloads/DE/BaFinJournal/2016/bj_1602.html. Accessed 31 July 2023

González-Meneses et al (2021) § 6. In: Omlor S, Möslein F (eds) FinTech-Handbuch, 2nd edn. Beck, München

Hanl A, Michaelis J (2019) Digitales Zentralbankgeld als neues Instrument der Geldpolitik, MAGKS Joint Discussion Paper Series in Economics, No. 09-2019

Hearn M, Brown R (2019) Corda: a distributed ledger. https://www.corda.net/wp-content/uploads/2019/08/corda-technical-whitepaper-August-29-2019.pdf. Accessed 31 July 2023

Herresthal C (2019) Die SEPA Instant-Überweisung (SCT Inst). ZIP 2019:895–907

Hofert E (2018) Regulierung der Blockchains. Mohr Siebeck, Tübingen
Hong Kong Monetary Authority (2021) e-HKD: a technical perspective, technical whitepaper on retail central bank digital currency. https://www.hkma.gov.hk/media/eng/doc/key-functions/financial-infrastructure/e-HKD_A_technical_perspective.pdf. Accessed 31 July 2023
Kahn C, Roberds W (2009) Why pay? An introduction to payments economics. J Financ Intermediation 18(1):1–23
Kahn C et al (2018) Should the central bank issue e-money? https://www.atlantafed.org/-/media/documents/news/conferences/2018/1018-financial-stability-implications-of-new-technology/papers/rivadeneyra_should_the_central_bank_issue_emoney.pdf. Accessed 31 July 2023
Kaulartz (2021) § 5. In: Omlor S, Möslein F (eds) FinTech-Handbuch, 2nd edn. Beck, München
Kiff J et al (2020) A survey of research on retail central bank digital currency. IMF Working Papers WP/20/104. https://www.imf.org/-/media/Files/Publications/WP/2020/English/wpiea2020104-print-pdf.ashx. Accessed 31 July 2023
Langenbucher et al (2020) Chapter 11. In: Langenbucher K, Bliesener D, Spindler G (eds) Bankrechts-Kommentar, 3rd edn. Beck, München
Mancini-Griffoli T et al (2018) Casting light on central bank digital currency. Staff Discussion Note No. 18/08. https://www.imf.org/en/Publications/Staff-Discussion-Notes/Issues/2018/11/13/Casting-Light-on-Central-Bank-Digital-Currencies-46233. Accessed 31 July 2023
Omlor S (2019) Digitaler Zahlungsverkehr. JuS 2019:289–294
Omlor S, Birne A (2020) Digitales Zentralbankgeld im Euroraum. RDi 2020:1–10
Panetta F (2022a) A digital euro that serves the needs of the public: striking the right balance. Introductory statement at the Committee on Economic and Monetary Affairs of the European Parliament, 30.03.2022. https://www.ecb.europa.eu/press/key/date/2022/html/ecb.sp220330_1~f9fa9a6137.en.html. Accessed 31 July 2023
Panetta F (2022b) Demystifying wholesale central bank digital currency. Speech at the Symposium on "Payments and Securities Settlement in Europe – today and tomorrow", 26.09.2022. https://www.ecb.europa.eu/press/key/date/2022/html/ecb.sp220926~5f9b85685a.en.html. Accessed 31 July 2023
PBoC (2021) Progress on Research and Development of E-CNY in China. http://www.pbc.gov.cn/en/3688110/3688172/4157443/4293696/2021071614584691871.pdf. Accessed 31 July 2023
Read O, Schäfer S (2020) Digitales Zentralbankgeld – pro und contra. Kreditwesen 73(24):15–18
Renzetti M et al (2021) TIPS - The Pan-European Infrastructure for the Settlement of Instant Payment. Banca D'Italia Markets, Infrastructures, Payment Systems No. 1. https://www.bancaditalia.it/pubblicazioni/mercati-infrastrutture-e-sistemi-di-pagamento/questioni-istituzionali/2021-001/en-MIS-20210129.pdf?language_id=1. Accessed 31 July 2023
Schaaf J (2022) In: ECB Civil Society Seminar: shaping the digital euro. https://www.ecb.europa.eu/pub/conferences/html/ecb_civilsoc.en.html. Accessed 31 July 2023
Schmieder (2022) § 25. In: Ellenberger J, Bunte H (eds) Bankrechtshandbuch, 6th edn. Beck, München
Schrey J, Thalhofer T (2017) Rechtliche Aspekte der Blockchain. NJW 2017:1431–1436
Siegel (2021) Chapter 3. In: Omlor S, Link M (eds) Kryptowährungen und Token. R&W, Frankfurt a.M.
Soderberg G (2022) Behind the scenes of central bank digital currency. IMF FinTech Notes No. 2022/004. https://www.imf.org/en/Publications/fintech-notes/Issues/2022/02/07/Behind-the-Scenes-of-Central-Bank-Digital-Currency-512174. Accessed 31 July 2023
Spindler G, Bille M (2014) Rechtsprobleme von Bitcoins als virtuelle Währung. WM 2014:1357–1369
Terlau (2021) § 34. In: Omlor S, Möslein F (eds) FinTech-Handbuch, 2nd edn. Beck, München
Terlau (2022) § 35. In: Ellenberger J, Bunte H (eds) Bankrechtshandbuch, 6th edn. Beck, München

Thießen F (2021) Der Digitale Euro – Stand der Entwicklung und Lücken in den Zielen. Kreditwesen 74(24):27–31

Varmaz et al (2021) Chapter 1. In: Omlor S, Link M (eds) Kryptowährungen und Token. R&W, Frankfurt a.M.

Vollmer U (2020) Digitales Zentralbankgeld und Kryptowährungen. WiSt 49(2–3):29–35. https://doi.org/10.15358/0340-1650-2020-2-3-29

Part II
Analysing the Legal Aspects of Central Bank Digital Currency

Chapter 3
Monetary Constitutional Law

Abstract This chapter focuses on monetary constitutional law. It examines the monetary constitution of the European Union with focus on the rules regulating the currency. The main focus of this chapter is to outline the responsible institution for establishing the digital euro. For that, the chapter analyses various legal bases of the European Central Bank. Furthermore, it studies the role of the European co-legislators when it comes to adjusting the payments environment to changed expectations of economic operators.

3.1 European Union's Competence

The term currency is usually understood to mean both the state-created monetary constitution (monetary order) of a certain area and the concrete monetary unit of that area, such as the euro, dollar or yen.[1] Monetary law includes all provisions on monetary symbols as well as on the distribution of competences.[2] Currency, money and coinage have traditionally been the responsibility of the state,[3] so in German national constitutional law Article 73 (1) No. 4 of the German Constitution grants the Federation exclusive competence in monetary matters. However, with respect to the competences of the European Union (EU) one has to bear in mind Germany's membership in this international organisation as well as in the Economic and Monetary Union (EMU). For the EMU, Article 3 (1) lit. c TFEU grants the EU the exclusive competence for monetary policy in relation to the participating Member States. Thus, legislative activities of the Member States in this area are only possible to a very limited extent, cf. Article 2 (1) TFEU.[4] This means that the EU bears in principle the competence for monetary policy and monetary sovereignty.[5]

[1] Schaal (1998), p. 51; Hahn and Häde (2010), para. 2; Wildmann (2015), p. 202; cf. also joined cases C-422/19 and C-423/19 *Hessischer Rundfunk* ECLI:EU:C:2021:63, para. 46.

[2] Hahn and Häde (2010), para. 5.

[3] See for the history Uhle (2022), para. 76.

[4] Cf. Herrmann (2008), III. 1.

[5] Cf. Siekmann (2013), para. 94; Häde (2022b), para. 10.

L. Kriese, *Central Bank Digital Currency*,
https://doi.org/10.1007/978-3-031-44738-9_3

The question of whether the digitisation of a currency unit is part of monetary policy is one that has often received little attention in the academic discourse to date,[6] but nevertheless needs to be clarified. This follows from the fact that the TFEU does not contain any definition of monetary policy within the meaning of Article 3 (1) lit. c TFEU.[7] Rather, only the objectives and measures of monetary policy are set for those institutions carrying out monetary policy.[8] Pursuant to Article 282 (1), second sentence, TFEU the European Central Bank, together with the national central banks of the Member States whose currency is the euro, constitute the Eurosystem and shall conduct the monetary policy of the Union. However, monetary policy is not equal to the tasks assigned to these institutions.[9] Pursuant to Article 119 (2) TFEU monetary policy consists of internal monetary policy and external monetary policy (exchange rate policy).[10] The latter is not (entirely) entrusted to the ECB or the Eurosystem, cf. Article 138, 219 TFEU.[11] Regardless, the Eurosystem is the bearer of internal monetary policy and from an overall view of the corresponding provisions on competences laid out in Articles 127 ff. TFEU, it can be concluded which areas, among others, are to be assigned to monetary policy.[12] Therefore, monetary policy includes, for example, monetary policy in a narrow sense, i.e. the safeguarding of the intrinsic value of the currency, the provision of payment systems, cf. Article 127 (2) TFEU, the determination of a monetary unit, its nominal value and its denomination, the issuance of money and the designation as legal tender, cf. Article 119 (2), 128 (1) TFEU.[13]

According to the case-law of the European Court of Justice (ECJ), whether a measure, in this case the digitisation of the currency, is part of monetary policy is determined by the objectives pursued with it by the institution taking the measure.[14] However, the (especially judicial) examination should not stop there. Indeed, it is true that in highly complex economic processes, there is often a 'functional limit'[15] of the judiciary, so that the institutions implementing the measure have a broad discretion.[16] But, bearing in mind the principle of conferral,[17] when determining

---

[6] Cf. for e.g. Groß (2020), pp. 71 ff.

[7] Case C-370/12 *Pringle* ECLI:EU:C:2012 :756, para. 53.

[8] Case C-370/12 *Pringle* ECLI:EU:C:2012 :756, para. 53; case C-62/14 *Gauweiler* ECLI:EU:C:2015:400, para. 42; Obwexer (2015), para. 18.

[9] Siekmann (2013), para. 23 fn. 30; Herrmann (2010), pp. 119 and 120; other opinion is Nettesheim (2023a), para. 16.

[10] Ohler (2015), para. 2; Hahn and Häde (2010), para. 4; Rodi (2018a), para. 5; Khan and Richter (2023a), para. 10.

[11] Siekmann (2013), para. 23 fn. 30.

[12] Case C-62/14 *Gauweiler* ECLI:EU:C:2015:400, para. 36 and 37; Lenski (2013), para. 12; Weiß (2002), p. 171; Cf. also Zilioli and Selmayr (2000), p. 628.

[13] Cf. Herrmann (2010), pp. 50, 115 and 116; Martha (1993), p. 752.

[14] Case C-62/14 *Gauweiler* ECLI:EU:C:2015:400, para. 46.

[15] Classen (2016), p. 540.

[16] Case C-62/14 *Gauweiler* ECLI:EU:C:2015:400, para. 46. Also Classen (2016), p. 540.

[17] See Article 5 (1), first sentence, (2) TEU.

competence limits their opinion should not be adopted uncritically. Rather, their objectives should be checked for plausibility, at least in their approach, and then included in an overall consideration of the measure.[18]

The ECB is pursuing the following objectives with the digitisation of the euro:[19] Supporting the digitisation of the economy, strengthening the strategic independence of the EU, preventing the dwindling use of cash, avoiding digital 'dollarisation',[20] monetary policy transmission, strengthening the international role of the euro and improving the cost structure in the money and payments system. The objective of monetary policy transmission as well as the improvement of the cost structure can be seen as part of the internal monetary policy.[21] Strengthening the strategic independence of the EU, avoiding digital 'dollarisation' and strengthening the international importance of the euro cannot be linked directly to the wording of the relevant provisions on monetary policy. However, such policy objectives are virtually inherent to monetary policy regardless of a specific written indication.[22] Supporting the digitisation of the economy primarily refers to competition in the market economy. Nonetheless, monetary policy bears an auxiliary function in this regard, cf. Article 127 (1), second and third sentence, Article 119 (2) TFEU. Regarding a possible decline in the use of cash, the issuance of money is a precondition for monetary policy,[23] so that in the absence of demand, declining money issuance also has an impact on monetary policy. However, the level of cash use within the euro area is still quite high in the foreseeable medium term,[24] so that the plausibility of this objective can be doubted. Nevertheless, when taking an overall view, a monetary policy objective of the digitisation of the euro can clearly be identified, so that the introduction of a digital currency lies within the monetary policy that is exclusively the responsibility of the Union within the meaning of Article 3 (1) lit. c TFEU.[25]

3.2 European Central Bank's Competence

If the competence for the introduction of a digital euro is assigned to the EU, the question arises as to which institution alone or in cooperation with other institutions within the EU is responsible for establishing the digital euro. For determining

[18] BVerfG, 21.06.2016 – 2 BvE 13/13 u.a., juris para. 183 ff. Cf. also Frenz (2015), p. 979.

[19] For the following see ECB (2020), p. 9 and in more detail Sect. 1.2.

[20] In the meaning that foreign currencies or private forms of money replace the domestic currency in the daily use.

[21] Cf. in this regard Kempen (2018a), para. 22.

[22] Cf. also Kempen (2018a), para. 22.

[23] Grünewald et al. (2021), p. 1037.

[24] See the explanations in Sect. 1.2.1.

[25] Omlor (2019), p. 339; Omlor (2021), para. 14; cf. also Bossu et al. (2020), p. 34 no. 73.

institutional competences, one has to bear in mind essentially two limitations:[26] First, the principle of conferral[27] needs to be preserved. Secondly, the principle of institutional balance[28] flowing from Article 13 (2) TEU must be considered, which is comparable to the principle of separation of powers in national constitutions.[29] Since there is no explicit provision on digital currencies in neither the TEU nor the TFEU, the competence to establish a digital euro also needs to be embedded in the existing regulatory framework in order to avoid an amendment of the Treaties under Article 48 TEU, which can result to be politically costly.[30]

At first, the competence of the ECB (or the Eurosystem) for establishing the digital euro will be examined because it is the body closest to the subject in monetary matters. As the bases of the ECB's competences are primarily regulated in the TFEU and the ESCB Statute,[31] a digital euro established by the ECB would be based on EU primary law. The following legal analysis separates between an account-based digital euro and a digital euro as a bearer-instrument.

3.2.1 Account-Based Digital Euro

As stated above, the digital euro can be designed as account-based. The legal basis for this could be Article 127 (2) TFEU in conjunction with Article 17 ESCB Statute. Therefore, establishing a CBDC would need to be a basic task of the ESCB within the meaning of Article 127 (2) TFEU. It can be argued that the digital 'dollarisation' by private or foreign cryptocurrencies harms the monetary policy transmission mechanism.[32] This refers to monetary policy within the meaning of Article 127 (2), first indent, TFEU. Furthermore, it can also affect Article 127 (2), fourth indent, TFEU: Due to increasing digitisation, the habits and expectations of economic participants in payment transactions change. A digital currency could meet these changed expectations.[33] Therefore, it can be reasonably argued that issuing a CBDC is part of the ESCB's objectives under Article 127 (2) TFEU.[34]

Next, attention is drawn to Article 17 ESCB Statute. According to this, the ECB and the national central banks may open accounts for credit institutions, public

---

[26] Nabilou (2020), p. 306.

[27] Article 5 (1), first sentence, (2) TEU.

[28] For this see Streinz (2019), para. 276; Nettesheim (2023b), para. 31; Streinz (2018), para. 23.

[29] Cf. de Witte (2020), para. 11.19. Other opinion is Meinel (2022), para. 52.

[30] Pfister (2020), p. 30.

[31] Protocol (No. 4) on the Statute of the European System of Central Banks and the European Central Bank (7 June 2016) *OJ C 202/230*.

[32] See Sect. 1.2.4.

[33] See Sect. 1.2.2.

[34] Like here ECB (2020), p. 24; Pfister (2020), p. 31; Wierts and Boven (2020), pp. 27 and 28; Manger-Nestler (2021a), para. 68; Nabilou (2020), p. 307.

entities and other market participants and accept assets, including book entry securities, as collateral in order to conduct their operations. Of particular interest is the term 'other market participants'. If this would include households and private entities, then Article 17 ESCB Statute (in conjunction with Article 127 (2) TFEU) could be a suitable legal basis for the retail digital euro in the direct model.[35]

Starting with the wording 'market participants', this does not prohibit to include households and private entities, as precisely these actors participate in economic market activities through supply and demand. However, the word 'other' establishes a reference to credit institutions and public entities also mentioned in the provision, which rather advocates a limited access to central bank accounts. Besides the wording, attention should also be paid to the systematic position of Article 17 ESCB Statute in chapter four of the Statute. This chapter is titled with 'Monetary policy tasks and operations of the ESCB' and contains provisions on open market and credit operations (Article 18), minimum reserves (Article 19) and other monetary policy instruments (Article 20). The latter in particular clarifies that opening accounts with central banks needs to correlate with the monetary policy of the ESCB. Traditionally, this was not directly aimed at the general public. This is due to the fact that historically credit institutions held a monopoly in accepting deposits and lending to the economy.[36] Hence, they were to be provided with privileged access to central bank facilities if monetary policy were to unfold its maximum effectiveness.[37] However, that does not necessarily argue against opening central bank accounts with households and private entities. This view is also supported by a comparison to the competences of the Deutsche Bundesbank under Sections 22, 19 No. 2 of the Bundesbank Act (BBankG[38]), according to which the Bundesbank may conduct business with anyone in the form of accepting giro deposits and other deposits.[39] This wording is based on the identical wording of Section 22 BBankG of 1957.[40] According to the explanatory memorandum to this Act, a strict distinction shall be made for the BBankG between the direct lending business and the central bank's giro business with commercial enterprises and private individuals.[41] The justification for doing business with anyone should thereby arise from monetary policy tasks.[42] Since the direct lending business was perceived not only as dispensable but rather disruptive to central bank's monetary policy tasks, it was abolished.[43] On the other hand, the central bank's giro business shall not be abolished because

[35] Cf. Wierts and Boven (2020), p. 28.

[36] Cœuré (2018).

[37] Cœuré (2018).

[38] Gesetz über die Deutsche Bundesbank in der Fassung der Bekanntmachung v. 22.10.1992 (BGBl. I p. 1782), zuletzt geändert am 28.06.2021 (BGBl. I p. 2250) (Federal Banking Act).

[39] Manger-Nestler (2021b), p. 5.

[40] BGBl. I p. 745.

[41] German parliamentary paper 02/2781, pp. 30, 40.

[42] German parliamentary paper 02/2781, p. 30.

[43] German parliamentary paper 02/2781, p. 30.

'(...) at least certain, albeit not very substantial, funds are tied up in a way that is desirable from a monetary policy point of view'.[44] Admittedly, this only concerns the national central bank law. However, the economic notion underlying these provisions seems quite transferable.[45] Therefore, in the case it is necessary for monetary policy to intervene directly in the private sector, the ESCB must be able to do so in order to fulfil its mandate and a past practice must be disregarded when assessing the scope of a competence.

However, most authors categorically rule out including households and corporations in Article 17 ESCB Statute, either without any justification,[46] with reference to the ECB's previous practice[47] or with reference to the systematical position of the provision.[48] Accommodating to this point of view, Article 17 ESCB Statute would not be a suitable legal basis for an account-based digital euro in the direct model, but without a doubt for the hybrid or intermediated model.[49] Moreover, Article 17 ESCB Statute could also be amended accordingly (in the view expressed here merely by way of clarification) using the simple legislative procedure pursuant to Article 129 (3) TFEU if direct monetary policy influence on the private sector by means of central bank accounts is required from the ESCB's point of view.[50]

In conclusion, both ways of interpreting Article 17 ESCB Statute result in a suitable legal basis for establishing an account-based digital euro, but according to the predominant interpretation only in the hybrid or intermediated model. The authorised financial intermediaries would then need to act on behalf of their customers, i.e. households and firms.

3.2.2 Digital Euro as a Bearer-Instrument

The legal situation with regard to establishing a digital euro as a bearer-instrument by the ECB is more challenging. Therefore, the academic discussion refers to various legal bases.

---

[44] German parliamentary paper 02/2781, p. 40.

[45] Other opinion on this is Administrative Court Frankfurt, 11.02.2010 – 1 K 2319/09.F, juris para. 34.

[46] Pfister (2020), p. 31; Groß (2020), p. 76.

[47] Weenink (2015a), para. 8.

[48] Muscheler and Hunt (2021), p. 9. Similar see also Administrative Court Frankfurt, 11.02.2010 – 1 K 2319/09.F, juris para. 34.

[49] Wierts and Boven (2020), p. 28; Pfister (2020), p. 31.

[50] Pfister (2020), p. 30.

3.2.2.1 Article 128 (1) TFEU

Primarily, Article 128 (1) TFEU in conjunction with Article 16 ESCB Statute is cited. Pursuant to Article 128 (1), first and second sentence, TFEU the European Central Bank shall have the exclusive right to authorise the issue of euro banknotes within the Union and the European Central Bank and the national central banks may issue such notes. Article 16 (1), first and second sentence, ESCB Statute repeat these provisions with identical wording. Thus, the main legal question is whether a digital representation of the euro can also be understood as a 'banknote' within the meaning of the aforementioned provisions. There are essentially two views on this.

Narrow Understanding of the Wording

First, one can advocate a narrow understanding of the aforementioned wording. Accordingly, banknotes are only media in physical form.[51] Argumentative support for this view is mostly provided by systematic references. Since Article 128 (2) TFEU mentions 'coins', the word 'banknote' in Article 128 (1) TFEU should only refer to the traditional substance quality of currency units.[52] Other authors cite Article 16 (2) ESCB Statute, according to which the ECB shall respect as far as possible existing practices regarding the issue and design of banknotes. Those practices regarding the design of banknotes can only exist with physical media.[53] Still others refer to Article 32.4 (2), first sentence, ESCB Statute. According to this provision, the Governing Council may decide that national central banks shall be indemnified against costs incurred in connection with the issue of banknotes. Those costs should only arise if physical banknotes are issued.[54] Finally, some cite the implementing legal acts[55] based on Article 132 (1), second indent, TFEU, which should be exclusively based on a physical understanding of banknotes.[56]

---

[51] Higher Administrative Court of Hesse, 16.10.2007 – 6 UZ 855/07, juris para. 19; Omlor (2019), p. 338; Terlau (2021), para. 24; Bossu et al. (2020), p. 16 no. 29 and p. 20 no. 37; Siekmann (2020), p. 49; Freimuth (2013), para. 4 and 31; Muscheler and Hunt (2021), p. 3.

[52] Manger-Nestler (2021a), para. 66; Manger-Nestler (2021b), p. 9.

[53] Pfister (2020), p. 31.

[54] Omlor (2021), para. 13.

[55] Decision of the European Central Bank of 19 April 2013 on the denominations, specifications, reproduction, exchange and withdrawal of euro banknotes (ECB/2013/10) (30 April 2013) OJ L 118/37, lastly amended by Decision (EU) 2020/2090 (15 December 2020) OJ L 423/62 and Guideline (EU) 2015/280 of the European Central Bank of 13 November 2014 on the establishment of the Eurosystem Production and Procurement System (ECB/2014/44) (20 February 2015) *OJ L 47/29,* lastly amended by Guideline (EU) 2021/2322 (29 December 2021) OJ L 467/3.

[56] Omlor (2021), para. 13.

Functional Understanding of the Wording

One can also advocate a functional understanding of the word 'banknote' in Article 128 (1) TFEU. Proponents of this view focus on the extent to which the digital euro is comparable in its function to conventional banknotes, so that it appears as a 'functional equivalent'[57] to them.[58] This equivalence is said to be given if the digital euro is accessible by the general public without remuneration, fulfils the classical functions of money[59] and can be transferred without the use of intermediaries.[60] For this functional justification of competence, the proponents advocate a variety of arguments. For example, the word 'issue' in Article 128 (1) TFEU or Article 16 ESCB Statute is only intended to mean that central banks create their own liability by issuing banknotes, but not that banknotes must therefore necessarily be physically issued.[61] Thus, neither the TFEU nor the ESCB Statute should contain an expressive prohibition according to which central banks may not create liabilities in any other form than (physical) banknotes.[62] Additionally, the ECB and the national central banks have a monopoly on issuing euro banknotes (subject to penalties, cf. Section 35 (1) No. 1 BBankG). The purpose of this monopoly should be that the central banks can determine the appearance of the currency units themselves, i.e. that Article 128 (1) TFEU does not positively preclude the issuance of other forms of currency that are not necessarily physical.[63] Furthermore, the ECB's competence to issue banknotes also includes, by implication of the second sentence of Article 128 (2) TFEU, the competence to determine the technical characteristics, format, medium and design of the banknotes.[64] Since, according to some authors, it will merely be a 'design upgrade' of banknotes, this competence could also apply to the digital euro.[65] Finally, bearing in mind the increasing digitisation, to justify the functional approach some authors advocate to not interpret the Treaties statically, but rather in a way that is open to new technologies.[66]

---

[57] Groß (2020), p. 74.

[58] Pfister (2020), p. 31; ECB (2020), pp. 24 and 25; Grünewald et al. (2021), p. 1035; cf. Siekmann (2020), p. 49.

[59] Mean of payment, store of value and unit of account. See in more detail Sect. 7.2.1.1.

[60] Siekmann (2020), p. 50; Groß (2020), p. 73; Pfister (2020), p. 31.

[61] Grünewald et al. (2021), p. 1033; Papaschalis (2015), para. 9.

[62] ECB (2020), p. 25; Bossu et al. (2020), p. 18 no. 34; Grünewald et al. (2021), p. 1033.

[63] Opinion of the Advocate General *Pitruzella*, C-422/19, ECLI:EU:C:2020:756, para. 94 and 96; Omlor (2019), p. 339; Omlor and Birne (2020), p. 4.

[64] Kempen (2018b), para. 3; ECB (2020), p. 25.

[65] Wierts and Boven (2020), p. 28.

[66] Pfister (2020), p. 31; Omlor (2019), p. 339; Grünewald et al. (2021), p. 1035.

Legal Statement

When interpreting Article 128 TFEU and Article 16 ESCB Statute, it should first be noted that at the time the EU Treaties were signed or entered into force, digitisation was far from being comparable with today's state of affairs, so that a historical interpretation with reference to the motives of the Treaties for the question of competence is not helpful.[67] In this regard, *Muscheler and Hunt* rightly point out that 'we cannot interpret the legislator's will in either direction (. . .) – for a digital euro simply was not on anyone's radar'.[68] Secondly, the past practice of the central banks cannot be used neither, as this can perhaps be seen as an indication of the central banks' self-understanding of their competences, but cannot be used to justify or deny a competence or with regard to the scope of a competence.

Furthermore, when interpreting competence titles, the principle of conferral from Article 5 (1), first sentence, (2) TEU must be observed, which prevents a justification of competence at the expense of the Member States. Additionally, the interpretation of Union law must create substantial possibilities for action, which should enable the effective realisation of the policies of the Union.[69] According to the settled case-law of the ECJ, 'among the various possible interpretations of a Community provision, preference must therefore be given to the one which is likely to preserve its effectiveness in practice'.[70]

A functional interpretation of the wording is supported by the fact that the EU Treaties cannot comprehensively regulate the powers required to achieve the Union's objectives because new developments cannot be foreseen.[71] Thus, it is plausible to assume that the Treaties are open to technology, so as not to jeopardise the practical effectiveness of Union law. However, the decisive argument against the functional interpretation is that it completely annuls the distribution of competences set out in Article 128 TFEU. This provision assigns in paragraph 1 the competence regarding the issuance of banknotes to the ECB and the central banks, in paragraph 2 regarding the issuance of coins to the Member States. The digital euro as a value-representing data set is not subject to any denomination in the meaning that it is designed as a 'banknote data set' and a 'coin data set'.[72] A fragmentation of competences in the sense that the Member States are responsible for digital denominations below two euros and the EU for all denominations above that is simply not feasible in view of the considerable technical and organisational requirements of a digital currency. In this case, some authors consider that the competence of the ECB and the central banks must outweigh that of the Member States because the Union has exclusive competence in monetary matters and therefore supersedes the

---

[67] Cf. Pfister (2020), p. 31; Groß (2020), p. 72.

[68] Muscheler and Hunt (2021), p. 4.

[69] Nettesheim (2021), para. 178.

[70] Case C-434/97 *Commission/France* ECLI:EU:C:2000:98, para. 21.

[71] Haratsch et al. (2020), para. 184.

[72] Cf. Pfister (2020), p. 31 and Grünewald et al. (2021), pp. 1038 and 1039.

coin-issuing competence of the Member States.[73] This view clearly contradicts the wording of Article 128 TFEU, which provides for a clear division of competences. Thus, this view is not compatible with the principle of conferral and must therefore be rejected.

Furthermore, the functional interpretation of the wording results in a considerable expansion of the central banks' competences.[74] It would then be possible for the central bank to directly monitor payment transaction data at the expense of data protection, to create payment profiles of households and firms and to directly charge negative interest rates on the digital euro to control the money supply.[75] On the primary law basis of Article 128 (1) TFEU, the digital euro would also immediately be given the status as legal tender, cf. Article 128 (1), third sentence, TFEU. This would result in corresponding mandatory adjustments to economic transactions, such as the creation and maintenance of technical access requirements, which could disadvantage financially weak economic participants in particular.[76] These are consequences that should rather be regulated by the democratically legitimised EU co-legislators.[77] In addition, it appears questionable whether a digital euro could fulfil the functions currently fulfilled by banknotes. In this regard, it can be doubted whether CBDC upholds the same level of privacy[78] and financial inclusion in the meaning of widespread accessability.[79] Moreover, a key function of money, the store-of-value function, may be subject to possible restrictions.[80]

Thus, the functional interpretation of the wording must be rejected. Article 128 (1) TFEU in conjunction with Article 16 ESCB Statute is therefore not a suitable legal basis for establishing a retail digital euro as a bearer-instrument.

3.2.2.2 Article 127 (2) TFEU

Furthermore, Article 127 (2) TFEU in conjunction with Article 20 ESCB Statute could serve as a suitable legal basis for a retail digital euro as a bearer-instrument. According to Article 20 ESCB Statute the Governing Council may, by a majority of two thirds of the votes cast, decide upon the use of other operational methods of monetary control as it sees fit, respecting Article 2. It is thus questionable whether the digital euro can be seen as an 'other operational method' within the meaning of Article 20 ESCB Statute. For this, the digital euro would have to be used by the

---

[73] Grünewald et al. (2021), p. 1039.

[74] Nabilou (2020), p. 307.

[75] Cf. Nabilou (2020), p. 307.

[76] Groß (2020), pp. 73 and 74.

[77] Like here Siekmann (2020), p. 49; Groß (2020), pp. 73 and 74; Panetta (2018), pp. 5 and 6. Cf. also Nabilou (2020), p. 307.

[78] On this see Chap. 6.

[79] Muscheler and Hunt (2021), p. 7.

[80] Muscheler and Hunt (2021), p. 7. See in more detail Chap. 8.

ESCB predominantly for monetary policy.[81] Although it seems conceivable that the ECB retains the use of CBDC for monetary policy purposes,[82] this does not prevail in the bundle of motives (see above). Moreover, Article 20 ESCB Statute is only seen as a fall-back provision for unexpected developments in financial markets in case the more specific monetary policy measures (cf. Articles 18 and 19 ESCB Statute) have been exhausted.[83] If establishing the digital euro also creates obligations for third parties, such as in the hybrid or intermediated model for the intermediaries, an act of secondary law of the Council is also required in accordance with Article 20 (2) ESCB Statute.[84] This would lead to a confusion of EU primary and secondary law that would be detrimental to legal clarity. The ECB also assumes that Article 20 ESCB Statute is more likely to be relevant for the wholesale model.[85] Hence, Article 127 (2) TFEU in conjunction with Article 20 ESCB Statute is not a suitable basis for establishing a retail digital euro as a bearer-instrument.

3.2.2.3 Conclusion

In conclusion, the ECB bears the competence under Article 127 (2) TFEU in conjunction with Article 17 ESCB Statute to issue an account-based retail digital euro, at least in the hybrid or intermediated model, and according to the opinion expressed here also in the direct model. However, according to the opinion expressed here, there is no legal basis that could justify the ECB's competence to establish the digital euro as a bearer-instrument.

3.3 Role of the European Union Co-Legislators

If establishing the digital euro with both design options or functionalities on a primary law basis by the ECB (or the Eurosystem) is not possible, the question arises as to the role of the EU co-legislators, consisting of the European Parliament and the Council.

---

[81] Wierts and Boven (2020), pp. 28 and 29.

[82] For more details on this see Chap. 9.

[83] Weenink (2015b), para. 1; Wierts and Boven (2020), pp. 28 and 29.

[84] Cf. Pfister (2020), p. 31; Wierts and Boven (2020), pp. 28 and 29.

[85] ECB (2020), p. 24.

3.3.1 Legislative Powers

In the field of monetary law, the EU co-legislators bear a comprehensive general legislative power under Article 133 TFEU.[86] According to the first sentence of this provision, without prejudice to the powers of the European Central Bank the European Parliament and the Council, acting in accordance with the ordinary legislative procedure, shall lay down the measures necessary for the use of the euro as the single currency. According to the second sentence, such measures shall be adopted after consultation of the European Central Bank.

Therefore, the measures taken by the EU co-legislators need to be 'necessary for the use of the euro as the single currency'. This covers all provisions that serve to protect the unity and integrity of the euro, as well as all other provisions that aim at the smooth functioning of the single currency.[87] With regard to necessity, the EU co-legislators are granted a broad discretion, in which practical considerations from the economy's point of view also need to be considered.[88] As stated above (cf. Sect. 1.2.4), a possible digital 'dollarisation' by foreign and private cryptocurrencies threatens the integrity of the euro.[89] In addition, the digital euro can be seen as a reaction to the changed expectations of the economic participants as a result of general digitisation, so that practical considerations of the economy also play a role.[90] Hence, the introduction of the digital euro, both in account-based form and as a bearer-instrument, is a measure necessary for the use of the euro as a single currency and so Article 133 TFEU is a suitable legal basis.[91]

However, the decisive question then arises as to how the EU co-legislators' monetary law-making power under Article 133 TFEU relates to the competences of the ECB/ESCB under Article 127 ff. TFEU. The beginning of the sentence 'without prejudice to the powers of the European Central Bank' of Article 133, first sentence, TFEU is the source of the legal debate.

The predominant opinion in the literature states that Article 133, first sentence, TFEU guarantees explicit subsidiarity and that the ECB's competences have a comprehensive blocking effect as *leges speciales*.[92] This is underlined by the fact that the ECB is the body closest to the matter in monetary matters.[93] However, this view leads to the following consequence: The ECB/ESCB lacks the competence for

[86] Khan and Richter (2023b), para. 1; Selmayr (2015a), para. 1.

[87] Selmayr (2015a), para. 7, 12; Kempen (2018c), para. 2.

[88] Selmayr (2015a), para. 8 and 11; Häde (2022a), para. 2; Rodi (2018b), para. 3.

[89] Like here Groß (2020), p. 77.

[90] Cf. Sect. 1.2.2. Like here Groß (2020), p. 77.

[91] Like here also Research Division of the German Parliament (2018), pp. 7 and 9 and Häde (2022a), para. 5.

[92] Zilioli and Selmayr (2007), pp. 374, 380 and 381; Häde (2022a), para. 3; Selmayr (2015a), para. 10; Research Division of the German Parliament (2018), p. 10; Wutscher (2019), para. 6; Groß (2020), p. 78; Rodi (2018b), para. 1; Manger-Nestler (2021b), p. 10.

[93] Selmayr (2015a), para. 16; Zilioli and Selmayr (2007), pp. 380 and 381.

establishing a digital euro as a bearer-instrument. This, in turn, is the responsibility of the EU co-legislators. But, since the ESCB has the competence in this respect and this competence blocks the competence of the EU co-legislators, the latter cannot establish an account-based digital euro. The account-based digital euro would also be based on EU primary law and would thus be hierarchically above the digital euro as a bearer-instrument, which is only introduced under EU secondary law. Hence, there would be two parallel designs of the digital euro with different competence bearers and different norm hierarchical ranks. Considering the enormous technical, legal and operational hurdles, such a fragmentation seems almost absurd. Moreover, the renunciation of one of the manifestations of the digital euro does not appear to be expedient either because for using both functionalities different (technical) preconditions must be fulfilled, which can exclude certain groups from the use of the digital euro in each case.[94]

Therefore, the meaning and purpose of the part in Article 133, first sentence, TFEU that provides for subsidiarity should be examined more closely. The disputed wording grounds on the recommendation of a group of experts, which was later adopted by the European Convention, the Intergovernmental Conference and finally in the Treaty of Lisbon.[95] By means of the wording 'without prejudice' it should be avoided '(. . .) to impair the tasks of the European Central Bank by consolidating the legal basis [Article 133 TFEU]'.[96] These tasks are predominantly related to the areas of monetary policy and banknotes, so that the legislative powers of the EU co-legislators shall not interfere with the competences of the ESCB in this area.[97] It is true that the digital euro can be used as a mean for monetary policy transmission.[98] However, this is not the main purpose of the introduction of the digital euro. Rather, it forms only one motive in a bundle of motives in which political and general economic considerations are also observed.[99] Hence, in accordance with *Muscheler and Hunt*, one needs to ask the question whether it is the purpose of Articles 127 ff. TFEU to empower the Eurosystem to establish an instrument which is intended to serve the requirements set out for money by an evolving economic, social, political and technological environment?[100] Establishing a digital euro that serves these requirements does not concern purely specific areas of central banking law, but rather fundamental issues, some of which are of particular relevance to

---

[94] Cf. Bechtel et al. (2022), para. 7.

[95] See Selmayr (2015a), para. 5.

[96] Report of the Group of Experts appointed by the Legal Services of the European Parliament, the Council and the Commission (2003), p. 4 no. 9 (comments added).

[97] Cf. Opinion of the Advocate General *Jacobs*, C-11/00, ECLI:EU:C:2002:556, para. 137 ff.; Manger-Nestler (2017), para. 1; Wutscher (2019), para. 6; Selmayr (2015a), para. 15 and 16. Similar also Manger-Nestler (2021b), p. 9. Going further are Zilioli and Selmayr (2007), p. 381: 'proper functioning of Economic and Monetary Union'.

[98] See Sects. 3.2.1 and 9.2.1.4.

[99] Cf. ECB (2020), p. 9 and Sect. 1.2.

[100] Muscheler and Hunt (2021), p. 5.

fundamental rights (disintermediation, loss of anonymity[101]). For such far-reaching questions of principle, the EU co-legislators appear to be the preferable bearer of competences due to their democratic legitimacy (cf. Article 10 (1), (2), subpara. 2, TEU).[102] Indeed, the selection of the right legal basis in the Treaties for a measure of the Union institutions may be based on the higher proximity to the matter concerned.[103] However, the European Union has opted for the model of a (representative) democracy, Article 10 (1) TEU. In such a democracy, unlike in a technocracy, fundamental issues of particular relevance to basic rights are decided by the democratically legitimised legislator, not by an independent body that is only legitimised by special expertise.[104] Moreover, the ECJ ruled in the *OLAF* case on the relationship between the EU co-legislators and the ECB that the former must respect the core area of the independent performance of tasks by the latter.[105] This understanding is also supported by the ECB's consultation rights under Articles 127 (4), 282 (5) TFEU for legal acts of the Union in the areas to which the ECB's powers extend. The contracting parties to the Treaties assumed that the Union acts in matters that technically concern the ECB but do not legally fall within its sphere of competence.[106] This is also the situation for establishing the digital euro. It concerns a large number of areas, some of which fall within the technical area of the ECB (monetary policy, functioning of payment systems) and some of which are fundamental issues. Therefore, in order to cope with the very comprehensive subsidiarity clause expressed in Article 133, first sentence, TFEU, it seems more appropriate to reduce this wording by means of a teleological interpretation to the core areas of monetary policy and the issuance of banknotes.[107] Establishing the digital euro does not primarily affect monetary policy aspects or the issuance of banknotes.

Thus, according to the view expressed here, the ECB's competence to establish an account-based digital euro does not have a blocking effect on the EU co-legislators when establishing an account-based digital euro and a digital euro as a bearer-instrument.

---

[101] For more detail see Chaps. 6 and 8.

[102] Like here also the European Commission, https://ec.europa.eu/info/consultations/finance-2022-digital-euro_en (Accessed 31.07.2023): 'For a digital euro to be used as the single currency, concurrently with euro banknotes and coins, it would require a Regulation of the co-legislator, upon a proposal by the Commission, on the basis of Article 133 TFEU'. Cf. also BVerfG, 05.05.2020 – 2 BvR 859/15, juris para. 136 and Selmayr (2015a), para. 16.

[103] Zilioli and Selmayr (2007), p. 380 with regard to the case-law of the ECJ.

[104] Ruffert (2022), para. 2.

[105] Case C-11/00 *OLAF* ECLI:EU:C:2003:395, para. 137 and 138.

[106] Cf. Selmayr (2015b), para. 127, 131; Häde (2008), p. 1029.

[107] Similar for interpretating Article 127 (4) TFEU also the Opinion of Advocate General *Jacobs*, C-11/00, ECLI:EU:C:2002:556, para. 137 ff.

3.3.2 Scope of the Legislative Powers

Next, it needs to be looked at how the EU co-legislators exercise their legislative power. This is of particular relevance because the EU co-legislators, as described above, may not interfere with the basic competences of the ECB. This particularity leads to the fact that, with respect to the distribution of competences in Article 127 (2), first and fourth indent, TFEU and Article 128 (1) TFEU, the EU co-legislators provide the legal framework for establishing the digital euro, while the issuance itself as well as the decision on the issuance remains reserved for the ECB.

The legal framework would have to contain the basic decisions, which in particular affect areas relevant to fundamental rights. Thus, a decision will have to be taken on the model (direct/hybrid) and the role of the intermediaries in this model,[108] as well as the question of legal tender,[109] data protection and the protection of privacy,[110] civil law status[111] and effects on financial stability.[112]

However, it should fall within the ECB's sphere of competence to take a decision on the specific technical design of the digital euro and to apply the specific measures to prevent negative effects on financial stability.

3.4 Conclusion

To conclude, it can be stated that, in the view expressed here, the digital euro should be established by the EU co-legislators because of the far-reaching fundamental issues involved. This is most appropriately done in the legal form of a regulation[113] and can cover both an account-based form and a bearer-instrument.

References

Bechtel et al (2022) Die Zukunft des Zahlungsverkehrs in einer DLTbasierten europäischen Wirtschaft. In: Kunschke D, Spitz M, Pohle J (eds) FinTech, 2nd edn. ESV, Berlin. https://doi.org/10.37307/b.978-3-503-20689-6.09

Bossu W et al (2020) Legal aspects of central bank digital currency: central bank and monetary law considerations. IMF Working Paper WP/20/254. https://www.imf.org/en/Publications/WP/

[108] See Chap. 4.

[109] See Chap. 5.

[110] See Chap. 6.

[111] See Chap. 7.

[112] See Chap. 8.

[113] Selmayr (2015a), para. 11.

Issues/2020/11/20/Legal-Aspects-of-Central-Bank-Digital-Currency-Central-Bank-and-Monetary-Law-Considerations-49827. Accessed 31 July 2023
Classen C (2016) Europäische Rechtsgemeinschaft à l'allemande? Anmerkung zum Urteil des BVerfG vom 21.06.2016, 2 BvR 2728/13. EuR 2016:529–543. https://doi.org/10.5771/0531-2485-2016-5-529
Cœuré B (2018) The future of central bank money. Speech at the International Center for Monetary and Banking Studies Geneva, 14.05.2018. https://www.ecb.europa.eu/press/key/date/2018/html/ecb.sp180514_4.en.html. Accessed 31 July 2023
de Witte (2020) EMU as constitutional law. In: Amtenbrink F, Herrmann C (eds) The EU law of economic and monetary union. Oxford
ECB (2020) Report on a digital euro. https://www.ecb.europa.eu/pub/pdf/other/Report_on_a_digital_euro~4d7268b458.en.pdf. Accessed 31 July 2023
Freimuth (2013) Art. 128 AEUV. In: Siekmann H (ed) Kommentar zur Europäischen Währungsunion. Mohr Siebeck, Tübingen
Frenz W (2015) Anmerkung zu EuGH, Urteil vom 16. Juni 2015 – C-62/14, EZB ist zum Ankauf von Staatsanleihen berechtigt. DVBl 2015:972–980
Groß J (2020) Digitales Geld für alle? HFSt 15:67–79
Grünewald S et al (2021) Digital euro and ECB powers. CMLRev 58:1029–1056. https://doi.org/10.2139/ssrn.3807855
Häde U (2008) Die Pflicht zur Anhörung der Europäischen Zentralbank nach Art. 105 Abs. 4 EGV. In: Gornig G, Schöbener B, Bausback W, Irmscher T (eds) Iustitia et Pax – Gedächtnisschrift für Dieter Blumenwitz, Schriften zum Völkerrecht, vol 176. Berlin
Häde (2022a) Art. 133 AEUV. In: Calliess C, Ruffert M (eds) EUV/AEUV Kommentar, 6th edn. Beck, München
Häde (2022b) § 23. In: Hufeld U, Ohler C (eds) Europäische Wirtschafts- und Währungsunion, vol 9, 1st edn. Nomos, Baden-Baden
Hahn H, Häde U (2010) Währungsrecht - § 2, 2nd edn. Beck, München
Haratsch A et al (2020) Europarecht, 12th edn. Mohr Siebeck, Tübingen
Herrmann (2008) § 11. In: Streinz R, Ohler C, Herrmann C (eds) Der Vertrag von Lissabon zur Reform der EU, 2nd edn. Beck, München
Herrmann C (2010) Währungshoheit, Währungsverfassung und subjektive Rechte. Mohr Siebeck, Tübingen
Kempen (2018a) Art. 119 AEUV. In: Streinz R (ed) Beck'scher Kurzkommentar EUV/AEUV, 3rd edn. Beck, München
Kempen (2018b) Art. 128 AEUV. In: Streinz R (ed) Beck'scher Kurzkommentar EUV/AEUV, 3rd edn. Beck, München
Kempen (2018c) Art. 133 AEUV. In: Streinz R (ed) Beck'scher Kurzkommentar EUV/AEUV, 3rd edn. Beck, München
Khan, Richter (2023a) Art. 119 AEUV. In: Geiger R, Khan D, Kotzur M, Kirchmair L (eds) EUV/AEUV, 7th edn. Beck, München
Khan, Richter (2023b) Art. 133 AEUV. In: Geiger R, Khan D, Kotzur M, Kirchmair L (eds) EUV/AEUV, 7th edn. Beck, München
Lenski (2013) Art. 3 AEUV. In: Lenz C, Borchardt K (eds) EU-Verträge Kommentar, 6th edn. Bundesanzeiger, Köln
Manger-Nestler (2017) Art. 133 AEUV. In: Pechstein M, Nowak C, Häde U (eds) Frankfurter Kommentar EUV/GRC/AEUV. Mohr Siebeck, Tübingen
Manger-Nestler (2021a) Chapter 9. In: Omlor S, Link M (eds) Kryptowährungen und Token. R&W, Frankfurt a.M.
Manger-Nestler C (2021b) Digitales Zentralbankgeld aus währungsrechtlicher Sicht. RdZ 2021:4–11
Martha R (1993) The fund agreement and the surrender of monetary sovereignty to the European Community. CMLRev 30:749–786

Meinel (2022) § 20. In: Hufeld U, Ohler C (eds) Europäische Wirtschafts- und Währungsunion, vol 9, 1st edn. Nomos, Baden-Baden
Muscheler K, Hunt C (2021) Recent legal developments in the area of crypto-assets and a digital euro. Institute for Law and Finance Working Paper Series No. 164. https://www.ilf-frankfurt.de/fileadmin/user_upload/ILF_WP164.pdf. Accessed 31 July 2023
Nabilou H (2020) Testing the waters of the Rubicon: the European Central Bank and central bank digital currencies. J Bank Regul 21(4):299–314. https://doi.org/10.1057/s41261-019-000112-1
Nettesheim (2021) § 9. In: Oppermann T, Classen C, Nettesheim M (eds) Europarecht, 9th edn. Beck, München
Nettesheim (2023a) Art. 3 AEUV. In: Grabitz E, Hilf M, Nettesheim M (eds) Das Recht der Europäischen Union, 78th edn. Beck, München
Nettesheim (2023b) Art. 13 EUV. In: Grabitz E, Hilf M, Nettesheim M (eds) Das Recht der Europäischen Union, 78th edn. Beck, München
Obwexer (2015) Art. 3 AEUV. In: Groeben H, Schwarze J, Hatje A (eds) Europäisches Unionsrecht, 7th edn. Nomos, Baden-Baden
Ohler C (2015) Bankenaufsicht und Geldpolitik in der Währungsunion - § 3. Beck, München
Omlor S (2019) Kryptowährungen im Geldrecht. ZHR 183:294–345
Omlor (2021) § 33. In: Omlor S, Möslein F (eds) FinTech-Handbuch, 2nd edn. Beck, München
Omlor S, Birne A (2020) Digitales Zentralbankgeld im Euroraum. RDi 2020:1–10
Panetta F (2018) 21st century cash: central banking, technological innovation and digital currencies. SUERF Policy Note No. 40. https://www.suerf.org/policynotes/3251/21st-century-cash-central-banking-technological-innovation-and-digital-currencies. Accessed 31 July 2023
Papaschalis (2015) Art. 128 AEUV. In: Groeben H, Schwarze J, Hatje A (eds) Europäisches Unionsrecht, 7th edn. Nomos, Baden-Baden
Pfister C (2020) Central bank digital currency. https://publications.banque-france.fr/en/central-bank-digital-currency. Accessed 31 July 2023
Report of the Group of Experts appointed by the Legal Services of the European Parliament, the Council and the Commission (2003), CONV 618/03, ADD 1
Research Division of the German Parliament (2018) Zur Möglichkeit der Einführung eines digitalen Euro. Ausarbeitung PE 6 – 3000 – 118/18
Rodi (2018a) Art. 119 AEUV. In: Vedder C, Heintschel von Heinegg W (eds) Europäisches Unionsrecht, 2nd edn. Nomos, Baden-Baden
Rodi (2018b) Art. 133 AEUV. In: Vedder C, Heintschel von Heinegg W (eds) Europäisches Unionsrecht, 2nd edn. Nomos, Baden-Baden
Ruffert (2022) Art. 10 EUV. In: Calliess C, Ruffert M (eds) EUV/AEUV Kommentar, 6th edn. Beck, München
Schaal P (1998) Geldtheorie und Geldpolitik, 4th edn. Oldenbourg, München
Selmayr (2015a) Art. 133 AEUV. In: Groeben H, Schwarze J, Hatje A (eds) Europäisches Unionsrecht, 7th edn. Nomos, Baden-Baden
Selmayr (2015b) Art. 282 AEUV. In: Groeben H, Schwarze J, Hatje A (eds) Europäisches Unionsrecht, 7th edn. Nomos, Baden-Baden
Siekmann H (2013) Art. 119 AEUV. In: Siekmann H (ed) Kommentar zur Europäischen Währungsunion. Mohr Siebeck, Tübingen
Siekmann H (2020) Monetary aspects of the euro as single European currency. In: Freitag R, Omlor S (eds) The euro as legal tender. De Gruyter, Berlin and Boston
Streinz R (2018) Art. 13 EUV. In: Streinz R (ed) Beck'scher Kurzkommentar EUV/AEUV, 3rd edn. Beck, München
Streinz R (2019) Europarecht, 11th edn. C.F. Müller, Heidelberg
Terlau (2021) § 34. In: Omlor S, Möslein F (eds) FinTech-Handbuch, 2nd edn. Beck, München
Uhle (2022) Art. 73. In: Dürig G, Herzog R, Scholz R (eds) Grundgesetz Kommentar, 99th edn. Beck, München
Weenink (2015a) Art. 17 Satzung ESZB/EZB. In: Groeben H, Schwarze J, Hatje A (eds) Europäisches Unionsrecht, 7th edn. Nomos, Baden-Baden

Weenink (2015b) Art. 20 Satzung ESZB/EZB. In: Groeben H, Schwarze J, Hatje A (eds) Europäisches Unionsrecht, 7th edn. Nomos, Baden-Baden

Weiß W (2002) Kompetenzverteilung in der Währungspolitik und Außenvertretung des Euro. EuR 2002:165–191

Wierts P, Boven H (2020) Central bank digital currency: objectives, preconditions and design choices. De Nederlandsche Bank Occasional Studies vol 20-01. https://www.dnb.nl/en/publications/publicatieoverzicht/research-publications/occasional-studies/nr-1-2020-central-bank-digital-currency-objectives-preconditions-and-design-choices/. Accessed 31 July 2023

Wildmann L (2015) Makroökonomie, Geld und Währung, vol 2, 3rd edn. De Gruyter, Berlin/Boston

Wutscher (2019) Art. 133 AEUV. In: Becker U, Hatje A, Schoo J, Schwarze J (eds) Schwarze EU-Kommentar, 4th edn. Nomos, Baden-Baden

Zilioli C, Selmayr M (2000) The European Central Bank: an independent specialized organization of Community Law. CMLRev 37:591–643. https://doi.org/10.54648/267439

Zilioli C, Selmayr M (2007) The constitutional status of the European Central Bank. CMLRev 44: 355–399. https://doi.org/10.54648/cola2007030

Chapter 4
Roles of the Parties Involved

Abstract This chapter studies the different roles of the participants involved. In particular, this contains the division of tasks between the private and the public sector, represented by the financial intermediaries and the ECB or Eurosystem. These tasks concern mainly technical aspects such as the end-user services or the settlement of payments with CBDC. However, some legal questions arise as well. For example, the chapter examines whether the EU co-legislators can make the distribution and the provision of core services mandatory for financial intermediaries and whether the ECB could set up a digital euro payments scheme.

4.1 Distribution and Services

As it has been often advocated publicly, it is highly likely that the digital euro will be issued and distributed in a two-tier model with shared competences of the public and private sector. This is similar to the way the issuance and distribution of cash works nowadays. According to *Panetta*, '(. . .) we should aim to replicate this in the digital age'.[1] In this public-private-partnership it is necessary to strictly distinguish between the front-end tasks and the back-end tasks. The front-end contains every task that involves a direct contact with the end-users, whereas the back-end mainly consists of the settlement.[2] Accordingly, front-end tasks are the distribution of the digital euro and the provision of services to the end-users.

For the services provided to the end-users, the ECB envisages a three-layer model. This model consists of core services, optional services and value-added services.[3] The core services are required for the initial release of the digital euro and shall be mandatory to provide for the financial intermediaries.[4] These core services are the following: onboarding and offboarding of end-users, providing

---

[1] Panetta (2022a).

[2] ECB (2022a).

[3] ECB (2022b), slide 6.

[4] ECB (2022b), slides 6 and 9.

L. Kriese, *Central Bank Digital Currency*,
https://doi.org/10.1007/978-3-031-44738-9_4

and maintaining payment instruments, linking digital euro holdings to commercial bank money accounts, funding and defunding of digital euro holdings, installing waterfall-mechanisms,[5] initiating and validating transactions, authenticating the customers and notifying on payment confirmation or rejection.[6]

From a legal point of view, it appears questionable whether the EU co-legislators can make the distribution and the provision of core services mandatory for (certain) financial intermediaries. This could be regarded as a limitation of fundamental rights, especially the right to business according to Article 16 of the Charta of Fundamental Rights of the European Union (CFR).[7] However, it should be noted that a limitation of fundamental rights can be justified, cf. Article 52 (1) CFR. In this regard, Article 133 TFEU can be seen as a legal basis for secondary law which provides for justification of the limitation. As stated above, this provision empowers the EU co-legislators to enact comprehensive general measures in the field of monetary law, provided that they are necessary for the use of the euro as single currency. It has been discussed and most commonly agreed upon, that in a situation where cash supply to the broader part of the population cannot be secured, the legislator may oblige financial intermediaries to offer cash services to consumers.[8] Similar may apply to the situation of central bank digital currency. Here, no technical and sovereign infrastructure for the distribution to the population has been build up yet. To safeguard that the policy objectives the digital euro aims at and which are from general interest will be reached, it appears necessary to include the private sector. Hence, mandatory distribution as well as the provision of core services is necessary for the use of the euro in its digital form.[9] Furthermore, to some extent this will leave room for the financial intermediaries to develop additional business segments and hereby increase their profit. Hence, the limitation of fundamental rights will be alleviated.

The financial intermediaries distributing the digital euro should be chosen in way that ensures widespread usability and a level playing field for financial services. Hence, the circle of chosen intermediaries should be drawn widely. However, to minimize the risks posed by the financial intermediaries (liquidity risk, risk of technical default), the selection should not be discretionary. Rather, it appears expedient to resort to already supervised intermediaries carrying out financial services.[10] For that, choosing PSPs supervised under PSD2 seems reasonable. Furthermore, to use synergetic effects resulting from applying new technologies, it also appears appropriate to use crypto-asset service providers (CASPs) authorised and supervised in accordance with the MiCA-Regulation (-proposal). To do so, this

[5]On this see Sect. 8.3.2.

[6]ECB (2022b), slide 8; Panetta (2022b).

[7]For more detail on the scope of protection see Sect. 8.2.1.

[8]Muscheler and Hunt (2021), pp. 6 and 7 with further references.

[9]Similar Muscheler and Hunt (2021), p. 7.

[10]Cf. ECB (2022b), slide 6; Grünewald (2022), p. 133.

perhaps requires to amend the mentioned regulatory framework accordingly.[11] PSPs are clearly defined institutions, that offer payment services, cf. Article 1 (1) PSD2. Payment services are those business activities that are set out in Annex I of PSD2, cf. Article 4 (3) PSD2. These activities include the transfer of funds. Funds are defined in Article 4 (25) PSD2 as banknotes and coins, scriptural money or electronic money in the meaning of the EMD. Thus, to include PSPs for distributing central bank digital currency, the definition of funds in Article 4 (25) PSD2 must be amended either by adding CBDC in the meaning of the regulation establishing the digital euro or by clarifying that scriptural money also contains CBDC because it is recorded in central banks' balance sheets as a liability item. For CASPs, it is likely that the MiCA-Regulation does not require amendments. According to Article 3 (1) No. (2) MiCA-Regulation-proposal, crypto-assets are defined as a digital representation of value or rights which may be transferred and stored electronically, using distributed ledger technology or similar technology. Hence, depending on the underlying technology used for CBDC, this can be regarded as a crypto-asset within the aforementioned definition.

4.2 Settlement

As set out above, the back-end tasks will mainly consist of the settlement. According to the ECB's glossary, settlement can be understood as the completion of a payment transaction or of its processing with the aim of discharging end-users' obligations through the transfer of funds.[12] From a technical point of view, the settlement consists amongst other of the validation, i.e. checking whether the payer has access to sufficient money that can be transferred, and the recording, i.e. the bookkeeping of the actual transfers of money.[13] Since the digital euro will be a liability item of the Eurosystem, it aims at keeping control of the issuance and the settlement process.[14] For the front-end part of the settlement, the Eurosystem aims at establishing five use cases which are currently under prototyping by private companies.[15] The two most important use cases are the settlement of online and offline transactions, for which the Eurosystems prefers a staggered approach. Desired for the primary issuance is in any case the settlement of online transactions validated by a third-party.[16] Secondly, the Eurosystem also opts for the settlement of offline transactions validated peer-to-

[11] See also Grünewald (2022), p. 133 who rightly points out that this also might require to amend the existing banking prudential system as well as the framework for bank recovery and resolution.

[12] ECB (2023).

[13] Panetta (2022b), fn. 9.

[14] Panetta (2022b); ECB (2022a).

[15] ECB (2022c).

[16] ECB (2022d), p. 6.

peer, i.e. between the end-users' devices.[17] More as experimental work, the Eurosystem furthermore considers the settlement of online transactions validated peer-to-peer.[18]

However, both desired modes of settlement face questions of technical and legal feasibility. Both areas of questionable feasibility ground on the very nature of the settlement process. As laid out, settlement is the completion of a transaction aiming at discharging monetary obligations. Hence, the crucial point of settlement is finality, which is defined as the moment when a payment processed through the payment system is deemed to be complete, even if one of the parties to it has become insolvent after that.[19]

This definition of finality leads to technical issues for the peer-to-peer offline settlement. As set out, according to the ECB's glossary, an offline payment is a payment in which settlement takes place between payer and payee with no need for network connectivity at the time of their interaction. The part of the definition according to which no network connection is required at the time of the interaction suggests that a network connection must take place at least at a later point in time. This should perhaps solve the double-spending problem and serve to update the ledger of the Eurosystem. However, the effects of a faulty transaction appear problematic. If, for example, several offline payments are made in succession and checked for double-spending at a later point in time via a network connection, it seems conceivable that one or even several transactions will not stand up to this check. This may interfere with the understanding of finality and can lead to the question whether the payment processed is 'complete'. Then the question arises as to what extent this affects all other transactions carried out after that erroneous transaction and how a possible reversal is to be carried out technically. Likely, these uncertainties are the reason why the Eurosystem needs to 'further assess' the technical feasibility of the peer-to-peer offline settlement.[20]

But finality is also the crucial point for the online settlement validated by a third party. Since the common understanding of finality raises issues of insolvency, the EU co-legislators enacted the Settlement Finality Directive (SFD)[21] to provide for more legal clarity.[22] However, the SFD only applies to certain participants in a settlement system, Article 1 SFD. Participants are defined as an institution, a central counterparty, a settlement agent, a clearing house or a system operator, Article 2 lit. f

[17] ECB (2022d), p. 6.

[18] ECB (2022d), p. 6.

[19] Athanassiou (2020), para. 24.8.

[20] See ECB (2022d), p. 6.

[21] Directive 98/26/EC of the European Parliament and of the Council of 19 May 1998 on settlement finality in payment and securities settlement systems (11 June 1998) OJ L 166/45.

[22] Athanassiou (2020), para. 24.8.

SFD. An institution is defined as a credit institution,[23] an investment firm[24] or public authorities and publicly guaranteed undertakings. Hence, due to this definition, most PSPs and CASPs were not to be included in the SFD. Since the SFD provides for more legal clarity, excluding most parts of the financial intermediaries that are considered to be subject to mandatory distribution could be detrimental to the success of the digital euro project. Thus, in order to make the online settlement validated by a third party legally feasible, the SFD would need to be revised and amended accordingly.

4.3 Scheme

What has become clear over the course of the previous two sections is that the success of the digital euro in practice will rely on the cooperational work of the public and private sector. To harness the strength of both sectors combined and guide the financial intermediaries when distributing the digital euro and providing core services, the Eurosystem is not weary of emphasising that a 'digital euro scheme rulebook' provided by the Eurosystem is needed.[25] A scheme is a single set of rules, practices and standards for payment transactions with the digital euro.[26] It describes the roles of the participants involved in transfer and settlement and lays down uniform standards for the settlement, such as the identification of the parties and technical standards for the transfer.[27] These technical standards are the basis for the interoperability between PSPs and payments systems.[28] Furthermore, schemes provide for rules on the duration of a transfer, transfer reversal, fees, reachability and settlement of disputes.[29] However, as explicitly laid out in Article 2 (7) of the SEPA Regulation,[30] a payment scheme must be clearly and strictly distinguished from a payment system, which is the technical infrastructure that processes transactions in line with the rules defined in the scheme.[31]

---

[23] As defined in Article 4 (1) No. (1) of Regulation (EU) No 575/2013 of the European Parliament and of the Council of 26 June 2013 on prudential requirements for credit institutions and investment firms and amending Regulation (EU) No 648/2012 (27 June 2013) *OJ L 176/1.*

[24] As defined in Article 4 (1) No. 1 of Directive 2014/65/EU of the European Parliament and of the Council of 15 May 2014 on markets in financial instruments and amending Directive 2002/92/EC and Directive 2011/61/EU (12 June 2014) OJ L 173/349.

[25] ECB (2022b), slide 7; Panetta (2022b); ECB (2022e).

[26] Panetta (2022b); ECB (2022e).

[27] Haug (2022), para. 23.

[28] Haug (2022), para. 23.

[29] Haug (2022), para. 23.

[30] Regulation (EU) No 260/2012 of the European Parliament and of the Council of 14 March 2012 establishing technical and business requirements for credit transfers and direct debits in euro and amending Regulation (EC) No 924/2009 (30 March 2012) OJ L 94/22.

[31] European Payments Council (2023).

The Eurosystem presented three options in this regard.[32] In the 'issuance-model', the Eurosystem would solely be responsible for the issue of the digital euro and would not provide any (back-end) settlement infrastructure. In the 'open-access-model', the Eurosystem would provide the settlement infrastructure and set access rules, so that every undertaking complying with these rules can use the infrastructure in their own way. Alternatively, in the 'end-to-end-model', the Eurosystem would provide a full payment product directly to the end-user, circumventing financial intermediaries. However, what kind of model ultimately will be chosen strongly depends on policy objectives and technical feasibility. Hence, a clear vision of the Eurosystem in this regard cannot be identified at the time being.

However, there are also some legal aspects to the scheme-approach. First, it must be clarified, whether the Eurosystem could set up a digital euro scheme solely based on their own competences as laid out in the Treaties. According to Article 127 (2), fourth indent, TFEU, promoting the smooth operation of payment systems is one of the basic tasks of the ESCB. Additionally, according to Article 22 ESCB Statute, the ECB and national central banks may provide facilities, and the ECB may make regulations, to ensure efficient and sound clearing and payment systems within the Union and with other countries. However, the competence of the ESCB under those articles is mainly focused on coordinating and monitoring payment systems.[33] As laid out, the payment system needs to be strictly distinguished from the payment scheme. This scheme is usually of a private nature. According to Article 2 (a) SFD, a (clearing and settlement) system is a formal arrangement between three or more participants with common rules and standardised arrangements, governed by the law of a Member State chosen by the participants. This definition clearly shows that the system as 'formal arrangement' is a legally binding contract of private law between the participants. Hence, the 'common rules and standardised arrangements' share the same legal nature. If the sovereign wants to prescribe certain rules, it needs to be empowered to do so by law. With regard to the principle of conferral, laid down in Article 5 (1), first sentence, (2) TEU, this is of utmost relevance to the European level as well. And clearly, the wording of Article 127 (2), fourth indent, TFEU solely refers to the payment system, not the scheme. This interpretation is supported by the self-understanding of the Eurosystem. *Panetta* states that '(...) technical standardisation and development of the scheme would ideally be completed before *legislation to mandate its use* is introduced'.[34] This clearly shows that even the Eurosystem does not understands itself as the bearer of competences in this regard. Hence, enacting a digital euro scheme rulebook requires a legislative act of the EU co-legislators.

Regarding the content of this act, there will be some policy considerations to be made. For example, the act needs to set out the roles of the parties involved (owner, manager and operator of the scheme), what basic technical elements the scheme shall

---

[32] On this and the following see Panetta (2022b), fn. 15.

[33] Waldhoff (2022), para. 77.

[34] Panetta (2022b), fn. 14 (emphasis added).

cover and what types of entities shall be able to participate in the scheme.[35] For that, the SEPA Regulation could be used as a blueprint. In Article 3, the SEPA Regulation sets out that certain SEPA schemes (SCT and SDD core) are mandatory for the PSPs providing certain financial services. Article 4 SEPA Regulation sets out common rules for the scheme, scheme operators and owners. Article 5 and the Annex lay down basic technical standards that shall be covered by the scheme. Article 8 generally prohibits the charge of fees for certain financial services but allows for specifically defined exceptions. However, the question of whether the ECB shall be installed as the owner, manager and operator of the digital euro scheme is ultimately based on policy reasoning. Furthermore, the basic technical standards that are to be set out in the regulation strongly depend on the results of the technical investigation phase conducted by the ECB/Eurosystem which is not concluded at the time being.

The last legal concern with regard to the scheme-approach will be the question for the right legal basis. The SEPA Regulation is based on Article 114 TFEU. This is due to the reason that in the past there existed obstacles for the internal market due to different national legal bases for payment transactions across the EU.[36] Hence, the SEPA Regulation relied on aspects of competition and the internal market. In this context, one might question whether Article 133 TFEU could be a suitable legal basis for a digital euro scheme. However, the decisive difference is that the SEPA Regulation laid down provisions for schemes developed by the European Payment Council in order to harmonise payment transactions across the EU in a uniform way. Hence, at the time of their introduction, the SEPA payment scheme(s) aimed at uniformly codifying existing technical standards for payment transactions. For the digital euro, these do not exist yet for the digital euro being a new means of payment. Thus, the scheme-approach does not aim at reducing obstacles for competition and the internal market. It rather aims at safeguarding that (new) public means of payment are distributed in a way that allows end-users to equally and fairly access these means. Although it will have impacts on the competition between PSPs and CASPs as well, the main objective of a digital euro scheme will be to safeguard broad financial inclusion.[37]

4.4 Conclusion

In conclusion, the digital euro will lead to a public-private-partnership between the Eurosystem and the financial intermediaries. While the latter will distribute the digital euro and provide front-end user services, the former will focus on the settlement. Moreover, the Eurosystem is likely to be empowered by the EU

[35] Panetta (2022b), fn. 16.

[36] For the history of the PSD and SEPA Regulation see Haug (2022), para. 3 ff.

[37] Similar Panetta (2022b).

co-legislators to set out a digital euro scheme which contains standardised rules for distribution, transactions and settlement of and with the digital euro. To ensure broad participation, certain amendments to the legal framework will have to be made. However, this chapter is strongly shaped by technical feasibility and policy objectives which cannot be assessed comprehensively at the time being.

References

Athanassiou P (2020) Payment systems. In: Amtenbrink F, Herrmann C (eds) The EU law of economic and monetary union. Oxford

ECB (2022a) The Eurosystem's technical onboarding package for digital euro prototyping. https://www.ecb.europa.eu/paym/digital_euro/investigation/profuse/shared/files/dedocs/ecb.dedocs221207_cover_note_digital_euro_front_end_prototyping_publication_of_technical_onboarding_package.en.pdf?8bccc21f8546c450e8da0eb59732d0a8. Accessed 31 July 2023

ECB (2022b) Euro Retail Payments Board – core, optional and value-added services for the digital euro. https://www.ecb.europa.eu/paym/digital_euro/investigation/governance/shared/files/ecb.degov221206_item3coreandoptionalservices.en.pdf?ce4a9905d51fc7a0f0d8119a911786e7. Accessed 31 July 2023

ECB (2022c) MIP News. 16.09.2022. https://www.ecb.europa.eu/paym/intro/news/html/ecb.mipnews220916.en.html. Accessed 31 July 2023

ECB (2022d) Progress on the investigation phase of a digital euro. https://www.ecb.europa.eu/paym/digital_euro/investigation/governance/shared/files/ecb.degov220929.en.pdf?8eec0678b57e98372a7ae6b59047604b. Accessed 31 July 2023

ECB (2022e) MIP News. 05.12.2022. https://www.ecb.europa.eu/paym/intro/news/html/ecb.mipnews221205.en.html. Accessed 31 July 2023

ECB (2023) Digital euro glossary. 07. March 2023. https://www.ecb.europa.eu/paym/digital_euro/investigation/profuse/shared/files/dedocs/ecb.dedocs220420.en.pdf?cc6c5408f1ffdaf2e367a9121bc07eba. Accessed 31 July 2023

European Payments Council (2023) What is a payment scheme? https://www.europeanpaymentscouncil.eu/what-we-do/sepa-payment-scheme-management/what-payment-scheme. Accessed 31 July 2023

Grünewald S (2022) Legal interoperability of the digital euro: prospects and challenges. In: ESCB Legal Conference 2022. https://www.ecb.europa.eu/pub/pdf/other/ecb.escblegalconferenceproceedings2022~1646d63f3e.en.pdf?08c4311f6b5f39ecf6e6a188cc55c06d. Accessed 31 July 2023

Haug (2022) § 30. In: Ellenberger J, Bunte H (eds) Bankrechtshandbuch, 6th edn. Beck, München

Muscheler K, Hunt C (2021) Recent legal developments in the area of crypto-assets and a digital euro. Institute for Law and Finance Working Paper Series No. 164. https://www.ilf-frankfurt.de/fileadmin/user_upload/ILF_WP164.pdf. Accessed 31 July 2023

Panetta F (2022a) The digital euro and the evolution of the financial system. Introductory statement at the Committee on Economic and Monetary Affairs of the European Parliament, 15.06.2022. https://www.ecb.europa.eu/press/key/date/2022/html/ecb.sp220615~0b859eb8bc.en.html. Accessed 31 July 2023

Panetta F (2022b) Building on our strengths: the role of the public and private sectors in the digital euro ecosystem. Introductory statement at the Committee on Economic and Monetary Affairs of the European Parliament, 29.09.2022. https://www.ecb.europa.eu/press/key/date/2022/html/ecb.sp220929~91a3775a2a.en.html. Accessed 31 July 2023

Waldhoff (2022) Art. 127 TFEU. In: Siekmann H (ed) The European Monetary Union – a commentary on the legal foundations. Bloomsbury Publishing, London

Chapter 5
Status as Legal Tender

Abstract This chapter discusses the status of a digital euro as legal tender. It explains the concept of legal tender and how this status can be acquired. Furthermore, the chapter analyses whether the digital euro can be legal tender in the same way as euro banknotes and euro coins are. In addition, it examines whether such an unrestricted status appears expedient, in particular with regard to mandatory acceptance. To ensure consistency, the chapter also evaluates the status of euro cash as legal tender.

5.1 Concept of Legal Tender

First of all, it needs to be clarified what is meant by the term 'legal tender'. In this context, it is a concept under EU law, which must therefore be determined autonomously.[1] However, neither the TFEU nor the Regulation (EU) 974/98 contain a definition of the term. Moreover, there is also no uniform understanding of the term within the EU at the Member State level.[2] Therefore, a group of experts on the status of the euro as legal tender (ELTEG) has developed three cumulative criteria for the term 'legal tender' on a comparative legal basis, which were adopted by the European Commission in a recommendation[3] (Article 288 (5) TFEU). According to this, legal tender is characterised by (1) a mandatory acceptance, (2) acceptance at full-face value and (3) the effect of discharging of payment obligations.[4] The ECJ also agrees with this when it states that '(. . .) the concept (. . .) signifies, in its ordinary sense, that that means of payment cannot generally be refused in settlement

[1] Joined cases 422/19 and 423/19 *Hessischer Rundfunk* ECLI:EU:C:2021:63, para. 45; Grünewald et al. (2021), p. 1050.

[2] ELTEG (2010), p. 4; Freitag (2020), para. 21.1.

[3] See Article 1 of the Commission Recommendation of 22 March 2010 on the scope and effects of legal tender of euro banknotes and coins (2010/191/EU) (30 March 2010) *OJ L 83/70.*

[4] ELTEG (2010), p. 4. Cf. also Wutscher (2019), para. 5; Siekmann (2018), para. 29.

L. Kriese, *Central Bank Digital Currency*,
https://doi.org/10.1007/978-3-031-44738-9_5

of a debt denominated in the same currency unit, at its full face value, with the effect of discharging the debt'.[5]

5.2 Acquiring Legal Tender Status and Consequences

Next, it is questionable how a medium acquires the status as legal tender (so-called monetarisation[6]) and what consequences result from this.

A medium of exchange acquires the status as legal tender through a sovereign act[7] based on national monetary law.[8] This sovereign act is often referred to as an 'issue' in monetary law, cf. Article 128 (1) TFEU, and comprises the legal act by which the issuer gives the medium a value and thus creates a liability of its own.[9] It is legally disputed whether, for monetarisation, this legal act must still be flanked by a (factual) action that enters the medium into the economic circulation to be used as a means of payment.[10] However, since in the majority of cases the media designated by the central banks as legal tender are always brought into the economic circulation, this dispute is rather of academic nature.

If a medium is monetised accordingly, the defining feature of its status is the sovereign making it mandatory for state authorities and private individuals to accept the medium.[11] However, this obligation does not apply absolutely because it can be restricted on the basis of a contractual agreement.[12] If the obligation to accept is violated without a deviating contractual agreement, this is sanctioned, at least in Germany, only with purely civil law consequences (*mora accipiendi*, Articles 293 ff. BGB).[13] Furthermore, payments with an instrument that is legal tender have a discharging effect on a (monetary) debt (cf. Article 362 (1) BGB).[14]

[5] Joined cases 422/19 and 423/19 *Hessischer Rundfunk* ECLI:EU:C:2021:63, para. 46.

[6] Omlor (2014), p. 120.

[7] Regarding the legal nature of this act see Häde (1991), pp. 62 ff.

[8] Hahn and Häde (2010a), para. 38; Mann (1992), p. 42; Siekmann (2018), para. 7; Freimuth (2013), para. 79; ELTEG (2010), p. 3.

[9] Freimuth (2013), para. 23; ELTEG (2010), p. 4; Weenink (2003), p. 434.

[10] Omlor (2014), p. 120 expressively contrasting the decision of the Higher Administrative Court of Hesse, 16.10.2007 – 6 UZ 855/07, juris para. 25 and 26. For more details on the legal debate see Freimuth (2013), para. 37 ff.

[11] Ohler (2008), p. 321; Arnold (2020), p. 145; Grünewald et al. (2021), pp. 1052 and 1053; Mann (1992), p. 43.

[12] Opinion of the Advocate General *Pitruzella*, C-422/19, ECLI:EU:C:2020:756, para. 108. See also ELTEG (2010), p. 6.

[13] Herrmann (2010), p. 316 fn. 244; Mann (1992), p. 76. For consequences under criminal law in other states see Weenink (2003), p. 438.

[14] Freimuth (2013), para. 81; Herrmann (2010), p. 315.

5.3 Status in the Case of an Introduction Under EU Secondary Law

As the basics of the concept of legal tender have been clarified, the question arises as to whether a digital euro established under EU secondary law on the basis of Article 133 TFEU can acquire this status.

5.3.1 Blocking Effect of the Existing Law

This could be contradicted by the fact that, according to Article 128 (1), third sentence, TFEU and Article 11, second sentence, Regulation (EU) 974/98, banknotes and coins shall be the 'only' such notes and coins with legal tender within the Union.

Some authors infer from this wording that the aforementioned provisions contain an enumerative list of means with legal tender in the euro area and that, in order to introduce the digital euro, the EU primary or secondary law needs to be amended.[15]

However, such an obstructing effect cannot be inferred from the aforementioned provisions.[16] Rather, the wording of the provisions suggests that only the respective media issued by the particular issuer should be the only ones of their kind that are legal tender.[17] Hence, this status is only denied to similar media (banknotes, coins) that do not originate from the listed issuers, such as coins from commercial banks. Since the digital euro is neither a 'coin' nor a 'banknote', the provisions cannot have a blocking effect. If one were to follow the opposing view, Article 11, second sentence, Regulation (EU) 974/98 would have to be contrary to EU primary law, too. This would be because, according to this understanding, Article 128 (1), third sentence, TFEU would already be conclusive and accordingly would preclude to confer the status as legal tender on coins under EU secondary law. However, there are no doubts that the Regulation (EU) 974/98 is compliant with EU primary law, not even on the part of the ECJ.[18]

Hence, in the opinion expressed here, the EU co-legislators can simultaneously establish and confer legal tender status on the digital euro based on Article 133 TFEU, without requiring an amendment of the TFEU nor the Regulation (EU) 974/98.[19]

---

[15] Athanassiou (2018), pp. 204 and 205; Siekmann (2018), para. 33; Omlor (2019), pp. 338 and 339.

[16] Freimuth (2022), para. 76.

[17] Cf. Higher Administrative Court of Hesse, 13.02.2018 – 10 A 2929/16, juris para. 43; Selmayr (2015), para. 10.

[18] Cf. joined cases 422/19 and 423/19 *Hessischer Rundfunk* ECLI:EU:C:2021:63, para. 51.

[19] Similar also ECB (2020), p. 24.

5.3.2 Unilateral Exclusion of Mandatory Acceptance

The status as legal tender is linked to the mandatory acceptance of the corresponding medium (see above). This ensures widespread acceptance and usability of the sovereign payment medium. However, as already explained above, the principle of freedom of contract applies. In the context of payments, it provides that a monetary obligation can be discharged by any means agreed between the parties.[20] This in turn also leads to the fact that the obligation to accept legal tender can be waived by virtue of a private-autonomous agreement between the parties. However, a unilateral exclusion of the mandatory acceptance in general terms and conditions also seems conceivable, for example if companies shy away from the costs possibly associated with the acceptance of the digital euro (initial acquisition costs for technical equipment, transaction costs, maintenance costs etc.). Allowing the practice of individuals to factually abolish mandatory acceptance in large numbers could undermine the concept of legal tender and impair a widespread usability of the digital euro. Therefore, from this point of view, it is questionable whether the EU co-legislators can also provide for a provision in the regulation on establishing the digital euro, which prohibits the unilateral exclusion of mandatory acceptance in general terms and conditions. In addition to possible political considerations, from a legal perspective it seems necessary to clarify whether Article 133 TFEU is also a suitable legal basis for this. Article 133 TFEU is a provision of monetary law that empowers the EU co-legislators to lay down the measures necessary for the use of the euro as the single currency. First and foremost, the provision in the TFEU thus provides for monetary law regulations. However, accepting sovereign means of payment and unilaterally excluding the acceptance in general terms and conditions also touches on the private law aspects of contractual freedom.[21] Hence, it is necessary to examine to what extent Article 133 TFEU also provides for regulating private law aspects related to legal tender.[22] Regarding the aspect of unilaterally excluding mandatory acceptance of legal tender, the experts sent by Germany to the Euro Legal Tender Expert Group (ELTEG) stated that Article 133 TFEU cannot be seen as a suitable legal basis for provisions that go beyond monetary law in a harmonizing matter and concern private law.[23] Instead, the experts hinted at Article 114 TFEU as a possible legal basis. Due to the clear wording, it is true that Article 133 TFEU cannot provide for matters that are of purely private law nature and that are in no way related to monetary law. However, the unilateral exclusion of legal tender by a private party concerns the inner core of the concept of legal tender. As stated above, legal tender is used to discharge of payment obligations. Hence, the provision in questions concerns the settlement of monetary obligations under private law using legal tender. In this regard, the ECJ stated that '(. . .) the European Union's exclusive competence in

[20]Mann (1992), p. 75; Proctor (2012), para. 7.14.

[21]Cf. ELTEG III (2022), p. 2.

[22]For this question with a slightly different focus see also Sect. 7.4.1.

[23]ELTEG III (2022), p. 9 fn. 12.

matters of monetary policy is (. . .) to regulate the procedures for settling pecuniary obligations, whether under public law or private law (. . .)'.[24] Hence, the ECJ does not distinguish private or public law. The key concern is whether the provision in question regulates the procedure for settling pecuniary obligations (using legal tender). As shown, a provision in general terms and conditions that excludes the possibility to pay with certain means of payments that are legal tender concerns the settling of pecuniary obligations. Thus, Article 133 TFEU is a suitable legal basis to prevent the unilateral exclusion of mandatory acceptance in general terms and conditions.

5.4 Exemptions of Mandatory Acceptance

Finally, it is worth discussing whether it seems expedient to provide for exemptions from the mandatory acceptance connected to the status of the digital euro as legal tender.

Some authors consider dispensing with this status altogether and replacing it instead with the central bank's obligation to the holder to exchange the digital euro 1:1 for other forms of central bank money. This is reasoned with the argument that this obligation offers the same security as the sovereignly prescribed mandatory acceptance.[25] Still others consider to limit the addressees of the mandatory acceptance to public institutions and private merchants of a certain size.[26]

Perhaps, all these restrictive considerations are based on aspects of financial inclusion. The practical consequence of the status as legal tender is the full and unconditional usability of the respective medium.[27] This requires to technologically equip the population with a physical device for offline payments and freely accessible[28] wallets for online payments.[29] In addition, end-users need the technical know-how. If a large part of the population would therefore be unable to actually use the digital currency, this would particularly impair the often-cited aspect of financial inclusion and raise doubts about the meaningfulness of the project.[30]

Thus, there are reasonable motives for restricting the mandatory acceptance associated with legal tender status. Moreover, such restrictions are not alien to the current law. For example, Article 11, third sentence, Regulation (EU) 974/98 stipulates that, with the exception of the issuing authority and the persons

[24] Joined cases 422/19 and 423/19 *Hessischer Rundfunk* ECLI:EU:C:2021:63, para. 56.

[25] Pfister (2020), p. 32; Grünewald et al. (2021), p. 1053.

[26] Bossu et al. (2020), pp. 37 and 38 no. 81.

[27] ECB (2020), p. 33.

[28] This does not mean that wallet providers are prohibited to charge fees for their services.

[29] ECB (2020), p. 33.

[30] Cf. Bossu et al. (2020), pp. 37 and 38, Nr. 81; Pfister (2020), p. 32; Bindseil et al. (2021), p. 19.

specifically designated in the national legislation of the issuing Member State, no one is obliged to accept more than fifty coins in a single payment.

In addition, the historical reason for mandatory acceptance of legal tender might no longer be relevant for the digital euro. The mandatory acceptance serves to protect the state's revenue from the creation of money (so-called seigniorage).[31] This seigniorage exists in two forms in the euro area.[32] First, the right of coinage of the Member States. They sell the coins they issue (cf. Article 128 (2) TFEU) to the Eurosystem with their face-value, which generates a profit (so-called coin profit) because the face-value usually surpasses the production costs of the coins.[33] Secondly, government revenue is generated through profit distributions by the Eurosystem. On the one hand, the Eurosystem derives profit from the interest income on central bank assets (lending to commercial banks, government bonds), adjusted for interest expenses for the minimum reserve balances and other expenses (personnel costs, costs in connection with euro banknotes).[34] On the other hand, seigniorage also exists here because the nominal value of the banknotes issued by the Eurosystem exceeds their production costs.[35] But since the digital euro is only a digital record representing a certain value (e.g. EUR 1.227, 32), there are no production costs that are comparable to the classic right of coinage or banknote seigniorage and that could be below the 'face-value'. And as long as there are other forms of central bank money that can be used for lending to commercial banks, the profit distributions of the Eurosystem are not affected by the digital euro in such a way that it would require legal tender status from this point of view.[36] The mandatory acceptance for the digital euro thus may be subject to a 'teleological reduction'.

However, the personal scope of possible exemptions from mandatory acceptance needs to be clarified. Since a certain basic technical equipment and know-how is needed for the use of the digital euro, natural persons should form one use case of the exemptions. One might think of subleasing a room in a student flat-sharing community (with the consent of the landlord). Should the main tenant be forced to open an account in order to receive the sub-rental fee with the digital euro? That should probably not be required. Hence, the very first exemption to be made regards natural persons when these interact with each other on a private (law) basis.

Restricting the mandatory acceptance to public authorities in particular appears to be problematic because precisely these are increasingly evading the already

---

[31] Hahn and Häde (2010b), para. 16.

[32] For more detail see Görgens et al. (2013), pp. 104 ff. and 355 ff.

[33] Görgens et al. (2013), p. 105.

[34] Görgens et al. (2013), p. 106.

[35] Cf. Langner (2020), para. 15.17. See subsequently Eibl (2020), p. 87.

[36] Similar Grünewald et al. (2021), p. 1052 according to whom '[t]he fiscal interest in maintaining the legal tender concept may now be outdated (. . .)'.

applicable mandatory acceptance for cash (cf. for example Section 1 ZahlVGJG,[37] Section 224 (3) AO,[38] Section 17a BBesG,[39] Section 51 (1) BAföG,[40] Section 49 (7) BeamtVG[41]).[42] Since the digital euro can only acquire the status as legal tender by means of a regulation under Article 133 TFEU, for which the ordinary legislative procedure under Article 294 TFEU is prescribed, limiting mandatory acceptance to public bodies without enabling the Member States to deviate from that seems hardly enforceable on a political level.

With regard to merchants and legal entities/partnerships, there is also a risk of overburdening 'smaller' economic participants. This could then be perceived as violating the principle of proportionality, Article 5 (4) TEU. Hence, from a legal point of view this raises the questions which parameters should be used to select those economic participants that might be overburdened by the obligation to accept the digital euro. These criteria need to be calibrated in a way that ensures widespread acceptance on the on hand and prevents overburdening on the other hand. For example, one could examine the expectations of the customers and contracting partners. May they legitimately assume, due to the nature of the service offered or the previous practice in the acceptance of electronic/digital means of payment, that the payment can also be done with the digital euro? If a merchant does not accept cashless payments so far, including him in the scope of mandatory acceptance does not seem convincing. However, there may also be merchants, such as sole proprietors, that accept other electronic means of payments but would nevertheless be overburdened because of their comparatively low turnover. To cover those, another criterion could be (turnover) thresholds above which an overburdening by possible additional costs can be ruled out. But how could one define those thresholds? Since it is hard to estimate the potential costs and possible outweighing benefits for merchants, this may result difficult because the digital euro has not yet been established. It seems more expedient to carry out a public consultation or study, accompanying the evaluation of the digital euro after it has been established. Or it could be left to the Member States to define these thresholds in national law and provide only high-level criteria in the regulation. However, this solution could be detrimental to legal

---

[37] Gesetz über den Zahlungsverkehr mit Gerichten und Justizbehörden v. 22.12.2006 (BGBl. I p. 3416), zuletzt geändert am 31.08.2015 (BGBl. I p. 1474) (German Act on Payment Transactions with Courts and Judicial Authorities).

[38] Abgabenordnung in der Fassung der Bekanntmachung v. 01.10.2002 (BGBl. I p. 3866), zuletzt geändert am 20.12.2022 (BGBl. I p. 2730) (The Fiscal Code of Germany).

[39] Bundesbesoldungsgesetz in der Fassung der Bekanntmachung v. 19.06.2009 (BGBl. I p. 1434), zuletzt geändert am 20.08.2021 (BGBl. I p. 3932) (German Federal Salaries Act).

[40] Bundesgesetz über individuelle Förderung der Ausbildung in der Fassung der Bekanntmachung v. 07.12.2010 (BGBl. I p. 1952), zuletzt geändert am 21.12.2022 (BGBl. I p. 2847) (German Federal Act on individual promotion of education).

[41] Gesetz über die Versorgung der Beamten und Richter des Bundes in der Fassung der Bekanntmachung v. 24.02.2010 (BGBl. I p. 150), zuletzt geändert am 22.11.2021 (BGBl. I p. 4906) (German Act on the Provision of Pensions for Federal Civil Servants and Judges).

[42] Ohler (2008), p. 322.

clarity and certainty. If the Member States were to further define the criteria for exemptions, this could lead to a legal fragmentation. And this would impair the freedom of establishment (Article 49 TFEU) and the freedom to provide services within the Union (Article 56 TFEU). Hence, it seems more convincing to refrain from setting specific thresholds in the regulation for the time being and await the possible impact of the digital euro in more detail.

If the mandatory acceptance of legal tender intends to ensure a widespread use of the digital euro, it also needs to be considered whether any exemptions from mandatory acceptance should be limited in time. In an introductory phase, these exemptions could be implemented for two or three years and, after an evaluation of the digital euro, be adjusted according to the frequency of use and the technical equipment of the population.

5.5 Legal Tender of Euro Cash

If the regulation grants legal tender to the digital euro and defines the concept on the basis of the ECJ ruling, in the follow-up one needs to have a look at the status of euro cash. In the current legal situation there is indeed ECJ case-law on the definition of the term ‘legal tender’ related to cash.[43] However, there is no binding provision in EU secondary law that defines the concept in more detail. It therefore seems worth considering to provide for this in the course of the introduction of a digital euro.[44] For this, three main sources can be useful.

First and foremost, the ECJ ruling *Hessischer Rundfunk*. In this ruling, the ECJ sets out basic principles for the regulation of means of payment with legal tender. As stated above, the Court defines the concept of legal tender.[45] Then it clarifies that Article 133 TFEU empowers the EU co-legislators to specify the legal rules governing the status as legal tender.[46] Furthermore it states that there can be exceptions from mandatory acceptance which are not required to be laid down exhaustively and uniformly in a legislative act.[47] These exceptions may be based on ‘reasons of public interest’ such as security, fighting crime and efficient organisation of payments in society.[48] The Court further stresses two key concerns that all restrictions made have to respect. First, they must respect the principle of proportionality in relation to the objective pursued with the restriction.[49] Secondly, no

[43] Joined cases 422/19 and 423/19 *Hessischer Rundfunk* ECLI:EU:C:2021:63.

[44] ELTEG III (2022), p. 10.

[45] Joined cases 422/19 and 423/19 *Hessischer Rundfunk* ECLI:EU:C:2021:63, para. 46.

[46] Joined cases 422/19 and 423/19 *Hessischer Rundfunk* ECLI:EU:C:2021:63, para. 51.

[47] Joined cases 422/19 and 423/19 *Hessischer Rundfunk* ECLI:EU:C:2021:63, para. 55.

[48] Joined cases 422/19 and 423/19 *Hessischer Rundfunk* ECLI:EU:C:2021:63, para. 66.

[49] Joined cases 422/19 and 423/19 *Hessischer Rundfunk* ECLI:EU:C:2021:63, para. 68.

restriction shall impair the possibility, as a general rule, of discharging a payment obligation in cash.[50]

Secondly, the Commission Recommendation on the scope and effects of legal tender of euro banknotes and coins can be instructive.[51] Besides defining the concept of legal tender (No. 1) it provides for two basic aspects for regulating the legal tender status of cash. Number 2 and 3 of the recommendation lay down the general rule that mandatory acceptance of cash is crucial, but exceptions are possible and lawful if they ground on the 'principle of good faith'. This should for example be the case if the 'retailer has no change available' or 'the face value of the banknote tendered is disproportionate compared to the amount owed to the creditor of the payment'. In addition, number 9 shows that a possible regulation shall be in due respect of specific practices and habits of the Member States.

Last but not least, one needs to consider the final report of the 5th and final meeting of ELTEG III.[52] From this report one can derive legal uncertainty on the scope of legal tender for cash in the Member States, especially regarding the aspects of acceptance and availability, which can be used for justifying legislative action based on Article 133 TFEU. The report showed that there is a broad fragmentation for penalising the unilateral refusal of cash, ranging from a breach of the criminal code to consumer protection acts and the civil code or only classifying it as a breach of contract/incurrence in default of acceptance.[53] Furthermore, according to various studies conducted by the Member States a small percentage (2–3%) of businesses pursues a no-cash policy which is accompanied by a no-cash policy by some public authorities.[54] In addition, access to cash in certain geographical areas in the Member States poses difficulties, mostly due to a low coverage of ATMs or bank branches.[55]

Hence, if the regulation establishing the digital euro also contains provisions on legal tender, in the interest of coherence and better law-making establishing a consistent legal framework for the status of euro cash as legal tender appears necessary.[56] However, since this is a highly debated topic which will ultimately be decided based on political reasoning,[57] this book refrains from giving a specific proposal for the particular provisions. Nevertheless, some key aspects will be presented.

The regulation for the status of euro cash as legal tender would need to contain a provision that defines the concept of legal tender respecting the definition given by

[50] Joined cases 422/19 and 423/19 *Hessischer Rundfunk* ECLI:EU:C:2021:63, para. 55 and 78.

[51] Commission Recommendation of 22 March 2010 on the scope and effects of legal tender of euro banknotes and coins (30 March 2010) OJ L 83/70.

[52] ELTEG III (2022).

[53] ELTEG III (2022), p. 2.

[54] ELTEG III (2022), pp. 3 and 4.

[55] ELTEG III (2022), p. 6.

[56] ELTEG III (2022), pp. 10 and 13.

[57] Cf. ELTEG III (2022), p. 9.

the ECJ and the Commission Recommendation.[58] Furthermore, in line with the discussion for the digital euro, a provision is needed which contains exemptions to the mandatory acceptance. As the ECJ ruled, these exceptions would not need to be laid down exhaustively. Rather, according to Article 2 (1) TFEU the Member States could be empowered to define additional exceptions, being subject to the approval of the Commission and consultation of the ECB (Articles 127 (4), 282 (5) TFEU).[59] Nevertheless, in line with the ECJ ruling, the EU co-legislators could provide for some basic exemptions from mandatory acceptance based on the principle of good faith and reasons of public interest.[60] However, exceptions based on good faith would need to be clearly and precisely defined with the aim to prevent their abuse. Furthermore, the exception stated in Article 11, third sentence, Regulation (EU) 974/98 would need to be included, possibly leading to the amendment of the Regulation (EU) 974/98. In addition, and in parallel to the digital euro, there would need to be a provision that prohibits the unilateral imposition of exclusion.[61] For this, Article 133 TFEU is a suitable legal basis (see above). Last but not least, it might also be worthy to include a provision on safeguarding the access to cash. For example, this could be done by establishing an obligation of the Member States to statutorily act against the reduction of bank branches or to prescribe an ATM coverage ratio for certain areas.[62]

5.6 Conclusion

In summary, it can be stated that the digital euro established on the basis of Article 133 TFEU can also acquire the status as legal tender under this legal basis. However, bearing in mind the aspect of financial inclusion and the principle of proportionality, it seems expedient for the time being to provide for statutorily exemptions from mandatory acceptance for natural persons and merchants that generally do not except cashless payments while at the same time preventing the unilateral exclusion of mandatory acceptance in general terms and conditions.

[58] Cf. ELTEG III (2022), p. 10.
[59] ELTEG III (2022), p. 10.
[60] ELTEG III (2022), p. 10.
[61] ELTEG III (2022), p. 10.
[62] Cf. ELTEG III (2022), p. 10.

References

Arnold (2020) The euro in German (private) law – monetary obligations and the mutual dependence of public and private law. In: Freitag R, Omlor S (eds) The euro as legal tender. De Gruyter, Berlin and Boston

Athanassiou P (2018) Digital innovation in financial services – legal challenges and regulatory policy issues. International Banking and Finance Law Series, vol 34

Bindseil U et al (2021) Central bank digital currency: functional scope, pricing and controls. Occasional Paper Series No. 286. https://www.ecb.europa.eu/pub/pdf/scpops/ecb.op286~9d472374ea.en.pdf. Accessed 31 July 2023

Bossu W et al (2020) Legal aspects of central bank digital currency: central bank and monetary law considerations. IMF Working Paper WP/20/254. https://www.imf.org/en/Publications/WP/Issues/2020/11/20/Legal-Aspects-of-Central-Bank-Digital-Currency-Central-Bank-and-Monetary-Law-Considerations-49827. Accessed 31 July 2023

ECB (2020) Report on a digital euro. https://www.ecb.europa.eu/pub/pdf/other/Report_on_a_digital_euro~4d7268b458.en.pdf. Accessed 31 July 2023

Eibl J (2020) Privatheit durch Bargeld? Mohr Siebeck, Tübingen

ELTEG (2010) Report on the definition, scope and effects of legal tender of euro banknotes and coins. https://ec.europa.eu/economy_finance/articles/euro/documents/elteg_en.pdf. Accessed 31 July 2023

ELTEG III (2022) Final report of the Euro Legal Tender Expert Group. https://ec.europa.eu/transparency/expert-groups-register/screen/meetings/consult?lang=en&meetingId=44035&fromExpertGroups=true. Accessed 31 July 2023

Freimuth (2013) Art. 128 AEUV. In: Siekmann H (ed) Kommentar zur Europäischen Währungsunion. Mohr Siebeck, Tübingen

Freimuth (2022) Art. 128 TFEU. In: Siekmann H (ed) The European Monetary Union – a commentary on the legal foundations. Bloomsbury Publishing, London

Freitag (2020) Euro as legal tender (and banknotes). In: Amtenbrink F, Herrmann C (eds) The EU law of economic and monetary union. Oxford

Görgens E et al (2013) Europäische Geldpolitik, 6th edn. UTB, München

Grünewald S et al (2021) Digital euro and ECB powers. CMLRev 58:1029–1056. https://doi.org/10.2139/ssrn.3807855

Häde U (1991) Geldzeichen im Recht der Bundesrepublik Deutschland. Nomos, Baden-Baden

Hahn H, Häde U (2010a) Währungsrecht - § 23, 2nd edn. Beck, München

Hahn H, Häde U (2010b) Währungsrecht - § 3, 2nd edn. Beck, München

Herrmann C (2010) Währungshoheit, Währungsverfassung und subjektive Rechte. Mohr Siebeck, Tübingen

Langner (2020) ESCB/Eurosystem/National Central Banks. In: Amtenbrink F, Herrmann C (eds) The EU law of economic and monetary union. Oxford

Mann F (1992) The legal aspect of money, 5th edn. Oxford

Ohler C (2008) Die hoheitlichen Grundlagen der Geldordnung. JZ 2008:317–324

Omlor S (2014) Geldprivatrecht. Mohr Siebeck, Tübingen

Omlor S (2019) Kryptowährungen im Geldrecht. ZHR 183:294–345

Pfister C (2020) Central bank digital currency. https://publications.banque-france.fr/en/central-bank-digital-currency. Accessed 31 July 2023

Proctor C (2012) Mann on the legal aspect of money, 7th edn. Oxford

Selmayr (2015) Art. 133 AEUV. In: Groeben H, Schwarze J, Hatje A (eds) Europäisches Unionsrecht, 7th edn. Nomos, Baden-Baden

Siekmann H (2018) Legal tender in the euro area. IMFS Working Paper Series No. 122. https://www.imfs-frankfurt.de/fileadmin/user_upload/IMFS_WP_122.pdf. Accessed 31 July 2023

Weenink H (2003) The legal nature of euro banknotes. J Int Bank Law Regul 18(11):433–439

Wutscher (2019) Art. 128 AEUV. In: Becker U, Hatje A, Schoo J, Schwarze J (eds) Schwarze EU-Kommentar, 4th edn. Nomos, Baden-Baden

Chapter 6
Aspects of Fundamental Rights

Abstract This chapter focuses on fundamental rights of the end-users. In particular, it presents the recurring fear of a loss of anonymity and privacy in the digital payments' environment. Mainly, the chapter discusses the influence of central bank digital currency on the protection of end-users' data. For that, it lays down the legal background of digital payments as well as the legal context of European data protection. In addition, the chapter presents options for a privacy-friendly design of CBDC to dispel the prejudices of 'transparent citizens'.

6.1 Background

For connecting the end-user's fundamental rights[1] to central bank digital currency, the term 'privacy' is mostly used in the debate so far.[2] However, this is not a (pure) legal term in the meaning of a *terminus technicus*.[3] The concept of privacy is characterised by the fact that a matter is exclusively assigned to one person and that this person decides on who is to have access to the matter.[4] In essence the legal discussion on CBDC is about the importance of data protection or the preservation of privacy. In the area of financial transactions, a conceptual distinction must be made between anonymity and privacy. Anonymity means the protection of the identity of the parties to the transaction, rather than the transaction itself.[5] Privacy does not protect the identity of the parties, but determines the conditions and the extent to which the data about the transaction is visible to third parties.[6] For example, the

[1] For the aspects of fundamental rights related to financial intermediaries see Sect. 8.2.1.

[2] For a possible violation of fundamental rights through negative remuneration see Sect. 9.2.2.

[3] Albers (2010), p. 1061.

[4] Eibl (2020), p. 200 with further references.

[5] Brunnermeier and Landau (2022), p. 25.

[6] ECB (2021), p. 18 fn. 9.

L. Kriese, *Central Bank Digital Currency*,
https://doi.org/10.1007/978-3-031-44738-9_6

transaction data may only be visible to all parties in the transaction network when the transaction amounts exceed a certain threshold (so-called selective privacy).[7]

The aspects of anonymity and privacy are highly valued by the end-users. In a public survey conducted by the ECB between October 2020 and January 2021, 43% of the private individuals surveyed stated that the protection of their payment data was their top priority when designing the digital euro.[8] Interestingly, some of the non-private respondents ranked the protection of payment data even higher as the top priority in the design of the digital euro. Thus, among merchants, almost 50% of the respondents opted for the aforementioned prioritisation.[9] If the topic of the 'digital euro' comes across the public discussion, due to concerns on the data protection it is often connoted negatively. In this regard, catchwords such as the 'unlimited surveillance of citizens'[10] or an 'Orwellian dystopia'[11] can be found. But what are these resentments based on?

The currently envisaged design of the digital euro is based on the use of financial intermediaries. These are subject to certain due diligence obligations when establishing a business relationship or executing certain transactions. Due to various legal provisions, this involves the processing of personal data, cf. Article 94 (1) PSD2. In the context of the so-called 'onboarding', these data consist of the first and last name, date and place of birth and residential address of the customers, cf. Article 4 (1) EU Money-Transfer-Regulation.[12] This is the so-called Know-Your-Customer principle (KYC), which is a central principle in the supervision of payment transactions.[13] In addition to identifying customers, financial intermediaries are often obliged to continuously monitor the business relationship with their customers and their transactions, cf. Article 13 (1) lit. d AMLD. Here the intermediaries also collect data, such as information on the parties to the transaction, the transfer amount, date, time and place of the transaction, as well as information on the object of the transfer, including the billing/delivery address, if applicable.[14] These obligations are also to be retained in future regulatory projects.[15] This framework of

---

[7] ECB (2021), p. 18 fn. 9.

[8] ECB (2021), p. 10.

[9] ECB (2021), p. 13.

[10] AfD parliamentary group (2022), p. 1.

[11] Bitkom (2020), p. 17.

[12] Regulation (EU) 2015/847 of the European Parliament and of the Council of 20 May 2015 on information accompanying transfers of funds and repealing Regulation (EC) No 1781/2006 (5 June 2015) *OJ L 141/1*.

[13] Heinson (2019), para. 86; Spoerr (2013), para. 88; Eibl (2020), p. 276.

[14] Cf. Panetta (2022), fn. 25.

[15] Cf. Articles 15 (1), 16 (1) lit. a, 18 (1) lit. a of the proposal for a Regulation of the European Parliament and of the Council establishing the Authority for Anti-Money Laundering and Countering the Financing of Terrorism and amending Regulations (EU) No 1093/2010, (EU) 1094/2010, (EU) 1095/2010, COM/2021/421 final and Proposal for a Regulation of the European Parliament and of the Council on information accompanying transfers of funds and certain crypto-assets, COM/2021/422 final.

collecting data aims at making anonymous payments in cashless payment transactions nearly impossible, as can be seen in recital 3 of the draft for the recast of the EU Money Transfer Regulation[16] and recitals 8 and 9 of the 5th AMLD, the latter now established in Article 10 (1) AMLD.[17] An analysis of these total data volumes allows conclusions to be drawn about the personality structure and the behaviour of the transaction parties.[18] In addition to the creation of payment transaction profiles, information about financial circumstances, social contacts, living conditions, leisure activities, consumer behaviour and, if the location is recorded, movement profiles can be deciphered and created.[19]

Knowing these data is multi-layered, it has advantages but also disadvantages. Knowing the payment habits could allow to predict economic fluctuations, but it can also be abused by the state to socially control individuals.[20] When using the distributed ledger technology, all transactions are stored in the ledger, which, depending on the specific design, is disclosed to the network participants. Hence, for central bank digital currency the dimension of protecting data is fundamentally different to cash, where transactions can be completely anonymous and leave no data traces.[21]

Before conjuring up dystopian conditions, the technical design should be analysed first. For the legal assessment, the question arises as to who is allowed to take note of which data and to what extent. The risks of data leaks on the part of the financial intermediaries also have to be considered.[22] And it must be ensured that the counterparty of the transaction cannot commercially exploit the knowledge gained from the transaction history because otherwise a payment is no longer an exchange of values, but an unintended[23] exchange of data for values.[24]

---

[16]Proposal for a Regulation of the European Parliament and of the Council on information accompanying transfers of funds and certain crypto-assets, COM/2021/422 final.

[17]Heinson (2019), para. 52 and 97.

[18]Cf. Brunnermeier and Landau (2022), p. 24.

[19]In more detail Eibl (2020), pp. 248 ff. See also Panetta (2018), p. 5.

[20]Brunnermeier and Landau (2022), p. 24.

[21]Cf. on this Eibl (2020), p. 125.

[22]Auer and Böhme (2020), p. 94.

[23]For the intended exchange of personal data for values see the Directive (EU) 2019/770 of the European Parliament and of the Council of 20 May 2019 on certain aspects concerning contracts for the supply of digital content and digital services (22 May 2019) OJ L 136/1.

[24]Auer and Böhme (2020), p. 94.

6.2 Legal Context and Principles of European Data Protection

To this end, the following section will examine the legal framework of the European data protection law and highlight some core principles of the data protection law and areas of tension.

6.2.1 Legal Framework of European Data Protection

At the level of EU primary law, the TFEU and the Charter of Fundamental Rights (cf. Article 6 (1), subpara. 1, second clause, TEU) need to be considered first. According to Article 16 (1) TFEU, everyone has the right to the protection of personal data concerning them. It is disputed whether and to what extent this provision provides for a subjective right. According to the prevailing view, Article 16 (1) TFEU guarantees a fundamental right to data protection that is exceptionally reflected in the Treaties.[25] According to another view, the provision solely is an objective-legal guarantee without a dimension of subjective protection, so that only Article 8 CFR is relevant.[26] However, this dispute is likely to be of a purely academic nature because the predominant view also assumes that both provisions are parallel in content but Article 8 CFR is prior for the assessment.[27] Paragraph 1 of Article 8 CFR is identical to Article 16 (1) TFEU. Paragraph 2 sets out the conditions for the data processing. Here it is disputed how Article 8 CFR is related to the fundamental right to respect for private life in Article 7 CFR. Some authors consider Article 8 CFR as *lex specialis*.[28] The ECJ cites both fundamental rights together, provided that the data have a connection to the private life.[29] At the same time, the ECJ takes into account the content of Article 8 (1) ECHR, which is almost identical in wording to Article 7 CFR.[30]

---

[25] Brühann (2015), para. 26; Kingreen (2022a), para. 4; Sobotta (2023), para. 16.

[26] Schröder (2018), para. 6; Eibl (2020), p. 237.

[27] Opinions of the Court 1/15, ECLI:EU:C:2017:592, para. 120; Franzen (2022), para. 6; Kotzur (2023), para. 2.

[28] Schneider (2022), para. 24.1; Augsberg (2015), para. 1. See in more detail Michl (2017), pp. 349 ff.

[29] Joined cases C-92/09 and C-93/09 *Schecke* ECLI:EU:C:2010:662, para. 47 and 52; case C-70/18 *A and Others* ECLI:EU:C:2019:823, para. 54; case C-362/14 *Schrems* ECLI:EU:C:2015:650, para. 39; joined cases C-293/12 and C-594/12 *Digital Rights Ireland* ECLI:EU:C:2014:238, para. 37; case C-131/12 *Google Spain* ECLI:EU:C:2014:317, para. 69; Opinion of the Advocate General *Villalón*, C-293/12, ECLI:EU:C:2013:845, para. 63 ff. Critically on this Breuer (2020), para. 22.

[30] Joined cases C-293/12 and C-594/12 *Digital Rights Ireland* ECLI:EU:C:2014:238, para. 35; joined cases C-92/09 and C-93/09 *Schecke* ECLI:EU:C:2010:662, para. 52.

At the level of EU secondary law, the General Data Protection Regulation[31] (GDPR) and the Regulation (EU) 2018/1725[32] (EUDPR) are of particular relevance.[33] While the former lays down requirements for the data processing by private and public bodies of the Member States, the latter regulates the data processing by Union institutions.

In conclusion, the European data protection law protects against the unlawful processing of personal data by third parties.[34] In accordance with Article 3 No. 1 EUDPR and Article 4 No. 1 GDPR, personal data is any information that relates to identified or identifiable natural persons. Due to this limitation of EU secondary law and the similar interpretation of the EU primary law by the ECJ,[35] legal entities are excluded from the protection of (personal) data.[36] In this respect, legal entities are subject to data protection only indirect via the protection of trade secrets according to Directive (EU) 2016/943[37] and Article 16 CFR.[38] Data processing covers the collection, storage, use and deletion of the data, cf. Article 3 No. 3 EUDPR and Article 4 No. 2 GDPR.[39] Under these conditions, the collection of personal data during the onboarding process already affects the data protection guarantees. The same applies to the collection of the transaction data, as there is a sufficient personal reference with the recording of the parties to the transaction as well.[40]

To justify the processing of data, special requirements are always needed. In EU primary law, this requires (among others) a legitimate public interest, cf. Articles 8 (2), first sentence, 52 (1), second sentence, CFR. EU secondary law also requires

---

[31] Regulation (EU) 2016/679 of the European Parliament and of the Council of 27 April 2016 on the protection of natural persons with regard to the processing of personal data and on the free movement of such data, and repealing Directive 95/46/EC (4 May 2016) *OJ L 119/1.*

[32] Regulation (EU) 2018/1725 of the European Parliament and of the Council of 23 October 2018 on the protection of natural persons with regard to the processing of personal data by the Union institutions, bodies, offices and agencies and on the free movement of such data, and repealing Regulation (EC) No 45/2001 and Decision No 1247/2002/EC (21 November 2018) *OJ L 295/39.*

[33] See for more detail on the development of EU secondary data protection law Breuer (2020), para. 15 ff. and Kühling et al. (2021), para. 127 ff.

[34] Case C-291/12 *Schwarz* ECLI:EU:C:2013:670, para. 25; joined cases C-293/12 and C-594/12 *Digital Rights Ireland* ECLI:EU:C:2014:238, para. 36; case C-362/14 *Schrems* ECLI:EU:C:2015:650, para. 42.

[35] Cf. Case C-291/12 *Schwarz* ECLI:EU:C:2013:670, para. 26; joined cases C-92/09 and C-93/09 *Schecke* ECLI:EU:C:2010:662, para. 53, according to which legal persons can claim the protection of Articles 7 and 8 CFR '(. . .) only in so far as the official title of the legal person identifies one or more natural persons'.

[36] Legally debated for the EU primary law, cf. Kingreen (2022b), para. 12 with further references; Knecht (2019), para. 3.

[37] Directive (EU) 2016/943 of the European Parliament and of the Council of 8 June 2016 on the protection of undisclosed know-how and business information (trade secrets) against their unlawful acquisition, use and disclosure (15 June 2016) *OJ L 157/1.*

[38] Cf. Jarass (2021), para. 10; Augsberg (2015), para. 6; Kingreen (2022b), para. 10.

[39] Case C-291/12 *Schwarz* ECLI:EU:C:2013:670, para. 28; Kühling et al. (2021), para. 52.

[40] Cf. Eibl (2020), p. 366; Pfisterer (2016), pp. 557 ff.

the conduct of a task that is in public interest, cf. Article 5 (1) lit. a EUDPR and Article 6 (1) lit. e GDPR. For central bank digital currency, an often-cited legitimate public interest is the fight against illegal activities, such as money laundering and terrorism financing.[41] This addresses the central area of tension of central bank digital currency, in which fundamental rights of data protection and public interests meet. Due to the lack of personal contact in the digital space, it is considerably easier to conceal one's identity and thus facilitate illegal activities.[42] In addition, combating the laundering of money and the financing of terrorism are high-level public interests which require the monitoring of payment transactions and financial flows.[43]

6.2.2 *Principles of Data Protection*

Some selected data protection principles for the processing of data are also relevant for the analysis.

6.2.2.1 Purpose Limitation

The principle that crucially constitutes the data protection law is the principle of purpose limitation.[44] According to this principle, the collected data may only be processed for the legitimate purpose for which it was lawfully collected, cf. Article 8 (2), first sentence, CFR and Article 5 (1) lit. b GDPR.[45] Hence, the commercial exploitation of data collected for the purpose of combating money laundering and terrorism financing is not permissible, cf. Article 15 (2), second sentence, EU-Money-Transfer-Regulation.[46]

6.2.2.2 Data Minimisation

The principle of data minimisation is also important. According to this principle, the processing of personal data is only permitted if it is absolutely necessary to achieve

---

[41] Panetta (2022); ECB (2019), p. 1.

[42] Panetta (2022); ECB (2019), p. 1.

[43] For the particular relevance of the public interests: joined cases C-293/12 and C-594/12 *Digital Rights Ireland* ECLI:EU:C:2014:238, para. 42; Opinion of the Advocate General *Legér*, C-317/04, ECLI:EU:C:2005:710, para. 223; Frenz (2009), para. 1451. For the necessity of monitoring financial flows: Spoerr (2013), para. 85.

[44] Wolff (2013), para. 11; Kühling et al. (2021), para. 349.

[45] Breuer (2020), para. 35; Wolff (2013), para. 11; Kühling et al. (2021), para. 349.

[46] Heinson (2019), para. 101.

the purpose of the processing.[47] This means that as little personal data as possible shall be processed.[48] As a matter of priority, anonymised or pseudonymised data records are to be used instead.[49] Deleting identifying characteristics and replacing them with pseudonyms, combining data into data bundles (aggregation) or introducing random errors in a controlled manner are approved techniques of anonymisation.[50] However, it should be noted that even when using pseudonymisation, the obligation to comply with the data protection law still remains.[51] The principle of data minimisation should also be taken into account through the technical design of the data processing systems (so-called privacy by design), cf. Article 25 (1) GDPR.[52] Since the principle of data minimisation is similar to the principle of proportionality, it must also be examined whether alternatives exist which provide for a higher degree of data protection and which can achieve the purpose of the processing in the same way.[53]

6.2.2.3 Other Principles

Furthermore, there are other principles that shape the data protection law. The principle of storage limitation requires to provide for storage and deletion periods of the collected data, cf. recital 39, sentences 8 and 10, of the GDPR and Article 5(1) lit. e GDPR. This principle specifies the principle of data minimisation in terms of time.[54] In addition, in order to exclude unauthorised access to the collected data, certain security standards must be maintained when processing data, cf. Article 15 (4) EU-Money-Transfer-Regulation, recital 3, sentence 12, of the GDPR and Article 5 (1) lit. f, Article 32 GDPR. Last but not least, a public or private concern on the processing of personal data is required and that concerns needs to outweigh the data subject's concern on protection.[55] As a rule, such an outweighing concern results from the legislative instruction according to which the data processing is permissible for a specific purpose, cf. Article 94 (1) PSD2, Article 43 of the 5th AMLD.[56]

---

[47] Cf. joined cases C-203/15 and C-698/15 *Tele2 Sverige* ECLI:EU:C:2016:970, para. 103; Kühling et al. (2021), para. 354; Wolff (2013), para. 23.

[48] Joined cases C-203/15 and C-698/15 *Tele2 Sverige* ECLI:EU:C:2016:970, para. 96.

[49] Wolff (2013), para. 42; Kühling et al. (2021), para. 357.

[50] Kühling et al. (2021), para. 276 referring to Art.-29-Datenschutzgruppe, Stellungnahme 5/2014 zu Anonymisierungstechniken, WP 216, 10.04.2014.

[51] Kühling et al. (2021), para. 281.

[52] Kühling et al. (2021), para. 356.

[53] Wolff (2013), para. 26, 29.

[54] Pötters (2022), para. 26; Breuer (2020), para. 36.

[55] Wolff (2013), para. 45.

[56] Wolff (2013), para. 46.

6.3 Privacy-Friendly Design

Now that an overview of the legal framework of data protection has been gained, the following section will analyse the ECB's design of the digital euro with regard to the data protection.

For the design of the digital euro, the ECB assumes five possible levels of privacy.[57] Level 1 is the complete anonymity of the end-user; there is no KYC procedure. Diametrically opposed to this is level 5, where the financial intermediaries and the central banks have complete insight to KYC data and transaction data. However, these two design options are not considered by the ECB. The ECB does not favour complete anonymity. From a technical point of view, guaranteeing complete anonymity would not be possible for the account-based digital euro because every internet access could be traced individually.[58] But complete anonymity is also ruled out for offline payments with the digital euro as a bearer-instrument because the identification is necessary at least once for the registration and the compliance with the anti-money laundering and anti-terrorism regulations needs to be safeguarded as well.[59] Instead, the ECB prefers level 3, in which a KYC check is carried out and the transaction data can be viewed by the financial intermediaries (so-called standard design option). Levels 2 and 4 are not completely ruled out, but are not (yet) favoured. Level 2 involves a KYC check, but the balances and transactions are not visible to neither the financial intermediaries nor the central banks. In level 4, there is a KYC check as well, but small-value payments are supposed to be guaranteed a higher degree of privacy.

In particular, the latter aspect mentioned is worth a closer technical look. The ECB suggests to use partially private or anonymous transaction procedures, should the protection of data be given a higher weighting by the EU co-legislators.[60] These procedures depend on the manifestation of the digital euro. For example, for the digital euro as a bearer-instrument, offline payments should be made possible with physical devices (e.g. payment cards) which have biometric access requirements, so that the data stored on them are accessible to the holder only, but are subject to a cap.[61] For the account-based digital euro, the ECB could rely on its earlier experimental phase, which has already been presented in parts.[62] This was a two-tier model based on the Corda technology, in which the central banks issued the digital units and the financial intermediaries distributed the units to the end-users.[63] The end-users participated in the network by using pseudonyms.[64] The special feature

[57] On this see: ECB (2022), slides 12 and 13.

[58] ECB (2020), p. 27 fn. 47.

[59] ECB (2020), p. 27. Cf. also Panetta (2022).

[60] Panetta (2022); ECB (2020), p. 27.

[61] Panetta (2022).

[62] ECB (2019). See Chap. 2.

[63] ECB (2019), p. 4.

[64] ECB (2019), p. 5.

was that, in addition to a notary node to solve the double-spending problem, there was also an AML Authority. This authority periodically issued time-limited so-called 'anonymity vouchers' to the end-users.[65] When using the vouchers at a ratio of 1:1 to the amount to be transferred, the end-user does not have to disclose any transaction data to the AML Authority. The vouchers were free of charge and not exchangeable between the end-users. Therefore, anonymous payments were limited to the amount of vouchers available per person and per issuing period and thus de facto solely possible for small-value payments. A transaction without using the vouchers was only effective if it was additionally confirmed by the AML authority.[66] In principle, the central banks merely knew the total amount of units of the digital euro in circulation, but they gained the knowledge of individual units with assigned user pseudonyms in the case that these units were returned back for the exchange into other forms of money (e.g. cash or scriptural money).[67] The experiment was mainly criticised for not enabling payments peer-to-peer and for depending on the technical stability and accessibility of financial intermediaries.[68] Moreover, even when the vouchers were used, the small-value payments were not completely anonymous, as at least the financial intermediaries were involved in the settlement of the transaction.[69] Furthermore, during the onboarding the KYC data were still processed.

However, since the European Commission is planning to create a central EU anti-money laundering authority,[70] the voucher solution for small-value payments does not seem unlikely for designing the digital euro. Here, it could be worth considering to additionally apply complex technical procedures, such as those already developed by the ECB and the Bank of Japan in project STELLA.[71] The STELLA project analysed technical possibilities that, when using distributed ledger technology, could restrict the access to the transaction data by any network participant and thus improve data protection (so-called privacy-enhancing technologies or PETs).[72] Implementing those technologies was one of the key lessons learned from the ECB experiment just presented.[73] PETs are needed because although pseudonymisation takes place by default when the DLT is used, this alone is not sufficient for the protection of data as the ledger is still visible to the network

[65] On this and the following see ECB (2019), p. 6.

[66] ECB (2019), p. 8.

[67] ECB (2019), p. 9.

[68] ECB (2019), pp. 9 and 10.

[69] Bitkom (2020), p. 17.

[70] Proposal for a Regulation of the European Parliament and of the Council establishing the Authority for Anti-Money Laundering and Countering the Financing of Terrorism and amending Regulations (EU) No 1093/2010, (EU) 1094/2010, (EU) 1095/2010, COM/2021/421 final.

[71] ECB and Bank of Japan (2020).

[72] ECB and Bank of Japan (2020), p. 1.

[73] ECB (2019), p. 9.

participants.[74] A total of three PETs were tested, which will be briefly presented below.

PET 1 leads to the segregation of information. According to this, there is no central ledger in the DLT network that is shared with all network participants with all recorded transactions, but rather each participant merely has access to a subset of transaction data previously determined according to fixed rules ('need-to-know-basis').[75] PET 2 is used if there is to be only one central ledger in the network.[76] In this case, the transaction data is cryptographically encrypted by using the zero-knowledge proof method. This is a cryptographic method for verifying information without having to disclose the information itself.[77] The transaction records encrypted in this way are stored in the ledger in a way which enables the network participants to see that a transaction took place without disclosing any information about the transaction itself (e.g. the parties, content, scope).[78] PET 3 tries to prevent information from being linked to each other (so-called unlinking).[79] The information about the transaction shall be separated from the information about the parties to the transaction. This can be done by separating the transaction relationships between transferor and recipient, so that third parties can see the scope and content of the transaction, but not between which persons the transaction took place. Furthermore, the parties can also be separated from the pseudonyms used in the transaction, for example by using one-time pseudonyms.[80] A combination of the PETs is possible as well.

6.4 Opinion

Now, these design options need to be assessed in the light of the legal framework outlined above. In doing so, one needs to bear in mind the fundamental area of tension: The guarantee of the highest possible level of data protection, which comes as close as possible to the anonymity and privacy of cash, in contrast to the public interests in the highest possible level of transparency. Central bank digital currency shall not create a lawless anonymous space that favours criminal activities, especially terrorism financing. However, it must be borne in mind that the use of money is supposed to involve an exchange of values amongst each other. Those who voluntarily use public money in the form of the digital euro and thus contribute to strengthening the competitiveness and political autonomy of the EU shall not have to

---

[74] ECB and Bank of Japan (2020), p. 5 fn. 11.

[75] ECB and Bank of Japan (2020), p. 6.

[76] ECB and Bank of Japan (2020), p. 8.

[77] For more details see ECB and Bank of Japan (2020), p. 10.

[78] ECB and Bank of Japan (2020), p. 10.

[79] On this and the following see ECB and Bank of Japan (2020), p. 11.

[80] ECB and Bank of Japan (2020), p. 12.

unintendedly pay for it with their data. This would contradict the current concept of central bank money, i.e. cash, which is available to everyone.

The main concern when assessing the protection of data is the question of who should gain knowledge of which data and to what extent. This applies both to the relationship of the transaction parties to each other and to other network participants, especially the state representatives (central banks of the Eurosystem) and private actors (financial intermediaries). When it comes to the transmission of data between the transaction parties, the legal analysis needs to distinguish and use current payment practices for orientation. For example, it is common practice to not settle large-value payments completely anonymously. Each transaction partner has a legitimate interest in knowing the other, for example to prevent fraudulent activities. In contrast, small-value payments are usually settled anonymously; here one might think of buying bread rolls or newspapers. This is based on the trust in the value-creating factors of the medium of exchange, i.e. money, usually in the form of cash.[81] However, this trust in the value of money is just as guaranteed for the digital euro as a digital form of central bank money. Therefore, regarding the extent of the data transmission between the transaction parties it seems comprehensible to distinguish according to the size of the transaction amount and to technically transmit less or more data about the party. In relation to the state and the financial intermediaries, a different decision will have to be made. It is true that the central banks have no interest in the commercial exploitation of user data.[82] But since the state itself does not always trust its probity,[83] it seems reasonable to limit the amount of data that can be viewed by the central banks to what is essential to fulfil their tasks. However, taking into account the 'functional limit'[84] of the judiciary, the central banks should be granted a margin of appreciation. In this context, the data could also be technically designed in a more privacy-friendly way with the help of PETs. In the case of financial intermediaries, it should be noted that they are subject to due diligence obligations under the anti-money laundering law. Therefore, they have to process a minimum amount of data.[85] Nonetheless, this appears to be less problematic insofar as, on the one hand, they are bound by the current law (EU-Money-Transfer-Regulation, GDPR, national laws) and, on the other hand, anonymous payments are technically possible, at least for smaller amounts (see above). Only the data collection in the context of the onboarding process will be inevitable. In this respect, there is a parallel to the use of cash. Cash is brought into the economic cycle exclusively through account-based procedures. It reaches the commercial banks

[81] Cf. Ohler (2021), pp. 30 ff.

[82] Brunnermeier and Landau (2022), p. 25; Nagel (2022).

[83] For the compulsory enforcement against public authorities see Sections 169 ff. of the German Code of Administrative Procedure and the legislative proposal of the German Federal Council, German parliamentary paper 20/2533, p. 1. Cf. also BVerfG, 24.03.2018 – 1 BvQ 18/18 and Administrative Court Gießen, 03.09.2019 – 8 K 2064/18.GI.

[84] Classen (2016), p. 540.

[85] Similar also joined cases C-465/00, C-138/01 and C-139/01 *Österreichischer Rundfunk* ECLI: EU:C:2003:294, para. 74 and Frenz (2009), para. 1405.

from the central banks.[86] The end-users receive new cash by withdrawing it from cash desks at bank branches, ATMs or within the framework of cash-back procedures at the retail checkout.[87] However, the same amount withdrawed must always be debited from a bank account.[88] But only identified users have access to this account.

Distinguishing in this way also corresponds to the users' expectations. According to the ECB's public opinion survey mentioned at the beginning, about 20% of the respondents would agree to the financial intermediaries or the central banks having knowledge of the transaction data in order to protect the public interest (i.e. combating money laundering).[89] 10% of the respondents favoured a selective privacy for small-value payments and again 10% would accept a one-off identification, provided that full privacy applies to all subsequent transactions.[90] From a technical perspective, all respondents regarded the use of the DLT and the PETs mentioned above as helpful tools to protect their data.[91]

Moreover, distinguishing between large-value and small-value payments is also reflected in the current legal AML/CFT-framework. Pursuant to Article 12 (1) AMLD the Member States may allow obliged entities not to apply certain customer due diligence measures with respect to electronic money if (amongst other) the payment instrument has a maximum monthly payment transactions limit of EUR 150 and the maximum amount stored electronically does not exceed EUR 150. Furthermore, Article 2 (5) EU-Money-Transfer-Regulation allows to not apply the regulation to transfers of funds to a payee's payment account permitting payment exclusively for the provision of goods or services if (amongst other) the amount of the transfer of funds does not exceed EUR 1 000. These provisions express a trade-off between the efficiency of payment systems and the terrorism risk potential of small transfers of funds.[92]

Hence, to protect the end-users' privacy with regard to small-value payments as best as possible, there are two options. First, the EU co-legislators could decide to exempt financial intermediaries from their anti-money laundering due diligence obligations and thus create an alternative in the digital space that is more comparable to cash.[93] However, a fully anonymous use of the digital euro with small-value payments is not likely. The Financial Action Task Force (FATF) considers retail-CBDC as likely to be highly attractive to criminals and terrorists for ML/TF purposes.[94] FATF opts for the same due diligence obligations as if the CBDC was

[86] Haug (2022), para. 50; Verbeck (2017), p. 156.

[87] Verbeck (2017), pp. 191, 196, 232.

[88] Cf. Verbeck (2017), pp. 134, 187, 197.

[89] ECB (2021), p. 18.

[90] ECB (2021), p. 18.

[91] ECB (2021), p. 19.

[92] Cf. recital 16 EU-Money-Transfer-Regulation.

[93] Advocating this is Nagel (2022).

[94] FATF (2020), p. 26 no. 91.

an electronic transaction using fiat currency.[95] Thus, not applying the due diligence obligations at all does not seem feasible. However, as a middle way, it appears expedient to allow for simplified due diligence obligations under Article 15 AMLD. This would require the EU co-legislators to amend the AMLD and add a provision that declares small-value payments with the digital euro as an area of lower risk. What seems questionable is the amount above which a transaction could not be considered as 'small-value'. To be considered as small-value, several provisions in the AMLD (e.g. Article 2 (5), Article 11 (b) (ii)) and in the EU-Money-Transfer-Regulation (Article 2 (5), Article 7 (3)) suggest that a transaction should in any case not exceed the amount of EUR 1000. Moreover, Article 12 (1) AMLD suggests that a small-value payment would have to be assumed in any case for an amount below EUR 150. Hence, a small-value payment will range somewhere between EUR 150 and EUR 1000. To decide on the particular threshold will be a task of the EU co-legislators. Furthermore, in addition to the simplified due diligence obligations of the financial intermediaries, the PETs should be used to enhance privacy as well.

Since the financial intermediaries are to be regarded as data controllers within the meaning of Article 4 No. 7 GDPR,[96] the data protection principles outlined above take effect, which means that the end-users are protected from commercial exploitation of their data without consent. It is true that data leaks on the part of the financial intermediaries cannot be ruled out from the outset. However, due to the technical due diligence requirements of Article 32 GDPR, the risk should at least be reduced and should also be within the usual range as it exists today.

Therefore, in order to balance the conflicting interests of anonymity or privacy and the fight against illegal activities, it seems to be reasonable to opt for a technical design of the digital euro that hides the data on small-value payments as far as possible from the financial intermediaries and anonymises the parties to the transaction. These small-value payments also have a rather lower risk potential according to the previous legislative conception. For the digital euro as a bearer-instrument, ensuring a higher degree of privacy can be done by using physical devices with a fixed technical ceiling. For the account-based digital euro, using the PET encryption procedures in addition to the simplified due diligence obligations of the financial intermediaries appears reasonable.

6.5 Conclusion

The protection of data is of great importance when designing the digital euro. At the same time, the legitimate public interest in combating illegal activities in the digital space must be respected. In this area of conflict and in accordance with general principles of data protection law, the parties involved should merely gain knowledge

[95] FATF (2020), p. 27 no. 94.

[96] Heinson (2019), para. 55.

of the data to the extent that is absolutely necessary to fulfil their respective tasks. Small-value payments also have a lower crime risk potential and should be subject to a higher degree of privacy or anonymity. Taking both requirements into account and implementing them in the technical design of the digital euro seems possible, given the current state of technology.

References

AfD parliamentary group (2022) Parliamentary motion. German parliamentary paper 20/2359

Albers M (2010) Grundrechtsschutz der Privatheit. DVBl 2010:1061–1069

Auer R, Böhme R (2020) The technology of retail central bank digital currency. BIS Q Rev:85–100. https://www.bis.org/publ/qtrpdf/r_qt2003j.pdf. Accessed 31 July 2023

Augsberg (2015) Art. 8 GRC. In: Groeben H, Schwarze J, Hatje A (eds) Europäisches Unionsrecht, 7th edn. Nomos, Baden-Baden

Bitkom (2020) Infopapier digitaler Euro auf der Blockchain. https://www.bitkom.org/sites/main/files/2020-04/200423_infopapier_digitaler-euro-auf-der-blockchain.pdf. Accessed 31 July 2023

Breuer (2020) § 25. In: Heselhaus S, Nowak C (eds) Handbuch der Europäischen Grundrechte, 2nd edn. Beck, München

Brühann (2015) Art. 16 AEUV. In: Groeben H, Schwarze J, Hatje A (eds) Europäisches Unionsrecht, 7th edn. Nomos, Baden-Baden

Brunnermeier M, Landau J-P (2022) The digital euro: policy implications and perspectives. https://www.europarl.europa.eu/RegData/etudes/STUD/2022/703337/IPOL_STU(2022)703337_EN.pdf. Accessed 31 July 2023

Classen C (2016) Europäische Rechtsgemeinschaft à l'allemande? Anmerkung zum Urteil des BVerfG vom 21.06.2016, 2 BvR 2728/13. EuR 2016:529–543. https://doi.org/10.5771/0531-2485-2016-5-529

ECB (2019) Exploring anonymity in central bank digital currencies. In Focus Series No. 4. https://www.ecb.europa.eu/paym/intro/publications/pdf/ecb.mipinfocus191217.en.pdf. Accessed 31 July 2023

ECB (2020) Report on a digital euro. https://www.ecb.europa.eu/pub/pdf/other/Report_on_a_digital_euro~4d7268b458.en.pdf. Accessed 31 July 2023

ECB (2021) Eurosystem report on the public consultation on a digital euro. https://www.ecb.europa.eu/pub/pdf/other/Eurosystem_report_on_the_public_consultation_on_a_digital_euro~539fa8cd8d.en.pdf. Accessed 31 July 2023

ECB (2022) Civil Society Seminar: shaping the digital euro. 13 June 2022. https://www.ecb.europa.eu/pub/conferences/html/ecb_civilsoc.en.html. (speech) and https://www.ecb.europa.eu/pub/conferences/shared/pdf/shaping_the_digital_euro.pdf. (slides) Accessed 31 July 2023

ECB, Bank of Japan (2020) STELLA – joint research project of the European Central Bank and the Bank of Japan, Balancing confidentiality and auditability in a distributed ledger environment. https://www.ecb.europa.eu/paym/intro/publications/pdf/ecb.miptopical200212.en.pdf. Accessed 31 July 2023

Eibl J (2020) Privatheit durch Bargeld? Mohr Siebeck, Tübingen

FATF (2020) Report to the G20 Finance Ministers and Central Bank Governors on so-called Stablecoins. https://www.fatf-gafi.org/publications/virtualassets/documents/report-g20-so-called-stablecoins-june-2020.html?hf=10&b=0&s=desc(fatf_releasedate). Accessed 31 July 2023

Franzen (2022) Art. 16 AEUV. In: Franzen M, Gallner I, Oetker H (eds) Kommentar zum europäischen Arbeitsrecht, 4th edn. Beck, München

Frenz W (2009) Handbuch Europarecht, vol 4. Springer, Berlin and Heidelberg. https://doi.org/10.1007/978-3-540-31117-1
Haug (2022) § 106. In: Ellenberger J, Bunte H (eds) Bankrechtshandbuch, 6th edn. Beck, München
Heinson (2019) § 14. In: Specht L, Mantz R (eds) Handbuch Europäisches und deutsches Datenschutzrecht. Beck, München
Jarass (2021) Art. 16 GRC. In: Jarass H (ed) Charta der Grundrechte der EU, 4th edn. Beck, München
Kingreen (2022a) Art. 16 AEUV. In: Calliess C, Ruffert M (eds) EUV/AEUV Kommentar, 6th edn. Beck, München
Kingreen (2022b) Art. 8 GRC. In: Calliess C, Ruffert M (eds) EUV/AEUV Kommentar, 6th edn. Beck, München
Knecht (2019) Art. 8 GRC. In: Becker U, Hatje A, Schoo J, Schwarze J (eds) Schwarze EU-Kommentar, 4th edn. Nomos, Baden-Baden
Kotzur (2023) Art. 16 AEUV. In: Geiger R, Khan D, Kotzur M, Kirchmair L (eds) EUV/AEUV, 7th edn. Beck, München
Kühling J et al (2021) Datenschutzrecht, 5th edn. C.F. Müller, Heidelberg
Michl W (2017) Das Verhältnis zwischen Art. 7 und Art. 8 GRCh – zur Bestimmung der Grundlage des Datenschutzgrundrechts im EU-Recht. DuD 2017(41):349–353. https://doi.org/10.1007/s11623-017-0789-9
Nagel J (2022) Digitaler Euro – Chancen und Risiken? https://www.imfs-frankfurt.de/news-medien/details/news/digitales-zentralbankgeld-zugaenglich-machen-vortrag-von-bundesbankpraesident-dr-joachim-nagel-im-video.html. Accessed 31 July 2023
Ohler C (2021) Unkonventionelle Geldpolitik. Mohr Siebeck, Tübingen
Panetta F (2018) 21st century cash: central banking, technological innovation and digital currencies. SUERF Policy Note No. 40. https://www.suerf.org/policynotes/3251/21st-century-cash-central-banking-technological-innovation-and-digital-currencies. Accessed 31 July 2023
Panetta F (2022) A digital euro that serves the needs of the public: striking the right balance. Introductory statement at the Committee on Economic and Monetary Affairs of the European Parliament, 30.03.2022. https://www.ecb.europa.eu/press/key/date/2022/html/ecb.sp220330_1~f9fa9a6137.en.html
Pfisterer V (2016) "Finanzprivatsphäre" in Europa. EuR 2016:553–569
Pötters (2022) Art. 5. In: Gola P, Heckmann D (eds) DS-GVO, 3rd edn. Beck, München
Schneider (2022) Syst. B. In: Wolff H, Brink S (eds) BeckOK Datenschutzrecht, 40th edn. Beck, München
Schröder (2018) Art. 16 AEUV. In: Streinz R (ed) Beck'scher Kurzkommentar EUV/AEUV, 3rd edn. Beck, München
Sobotta (2023) Art. 16 AEUV. In: Grabitz E, Hilf M, Nettesheim M (eds) Das Recht der Europäischen Union, 78th edn. Beck, München
Spoerr (2013) Syst. J. In: Wolff H, Brink S (eds) Datenschutzrecht in Bund und Ländern. Beck, München
Verbeck D (2017) Einführung in die Bargeldökonomie der Bundesrepublik Deutschland. Kohlhammer, Stuttgart
Wolff (2013) Syst. A. In: Wolff H, Brink S (eds) Datenschutzrecht in Bund und Ländern. Beck, München

Chapter 7
Private Law

Abstract This chapter aims at enquiring fundamental questions of civil law related to CBDC. What is central bank digital currency in civil law, i.e. what is its legal nature? How can central bank digital currency be used in legal relations? How is a digital currency to be treated in individual compulsory enforcement and under insolvency law? Can end-users lend CBDC to banks for them to work with? Since the European private law is only developed in a very fragmented way and does not cover the aforementioned aspects, this chapter analyses paradigmatically the legal situation under the national law of some Member States. It mainly focuses on German civil law but occasionally and briefly outlines the legal situation in Austria and Spain when appropriate. Methodologically, the assessment follows an inductive approach by considering previous findings on comparable crypto-assets and making them fruitful for the mostly very complex problem areas. The chapter concludes that the legal situation for the digital euro is not clear in every regard and that this is detrimental to its usability. Therefore, the chapter further enquires if and how these aspects can be uniformly regulated on the European level and proposes a possible regulatory approach.

7.1 Legal Nature of the Digital Euro in Private Law

First and foremost, to understand the digital euro or central bank digital currency in general, it is crucial to clarify its legal nature in the private law system.

7.1.1 Central Bank Digital Currency as a Bearer-Instrument

As mentioned, the classification of central bank digital currency as a bearer-instrument seems to be legally challenging.

L. Kriese, *Central Bank Digital Currency*,
https://doi.org/10.1007/978-3-031-44738-9_7

7.1.1.1 Legal Situation in Germany

The legal situation in Germany is governed by the German Civil Code (BGB). This contains various provisions spread throughout the Code which can be used to clarify the legal nature of an object.

Security

Since CBDC is regarded as a central bank's liability, one could think of the digital euro as a security in the sense of a bearer bond according to Section 793 BGB or a promissory note according to Section 952 BGB.[1] However, both provisions require two features that need to be considered more closely in the case of digital currencies. First, the medium must document a claim. Second, the medium must be a deed.

Claim

To begin with, it is necessary that the medium certifies a claim in the sense of a promise of performance, cf. Sections 793 (1), first sentence, 952 (2) BGB. This must be a claim under private law.[2] Therefore, it needs to be enquired whether the central bank money represented by the digital euro as a bearer-instrument is a claim in this sense. At first glance, this could be assumed because central bank money in the form of banknotes is usually recorded as a liability in central banks' balance sheets.[3] More revealing is the historical legal nature of banknotes. In the nineteenth and twentieth centuries, when banknotes were still covered by gold, the Sections 4, 14 and 18 of the Bank Act (BankG[4]) contained an obligation for the issuing institution to redeem the banknotes for gold coins.[5] Due to this obligation to redeem, banknotes were then legally regarded as bearer bonds within the meaning of Section 793 BGB for a long time.[6] However, in today's monetary system the currency is no longer backed by gold, so the holder of the media can no longer exchange them for their cover-value at the central banks.[7] Thus, the issuers of the banknotes do not promise any performance to the holder that goes beyond the issuance and fixing of the paper with the nominal value.[8]

---

[1]See for example Thießen (2021), p. 27; Diehl (2021), para. 42; Lehmann (2021), para. 109; Spindler (2020), para. 28.

[2]Henssler (2020), para. 510; Vogel (2023), para. 9.

[3]Athanassiou (2018), pp. 48, 57, 185; Bechtel et al. (2022), para. 30.

[4]Bankgesetz v. 14.03.1875, RGBl. 1875, p. 177 (Banking Act of 1875).

[5]Häde (1991), p. 151.

[6]RG, 28.11.1921 – VI 282/21, RGZ 103, 231 (234); Herrmann (2010), p. 19; Häde (1991), p. 158.

[7]Kirchhartz (2014), para. 13.

[8]Häde (1991), p. 158.

However, some legal provisions provide for a right of the holder to exchange the banknotes and coins either into other forms of central bank money or into other forms of legal tender, cf. Article 3 (2) of Decision ECB/2010/29,[9] Article 3 (1) of Decision ECB/2013/10[10] each in conjunction with Article 288 (4) TFEU and Section 3 (2) MünzG.[11] However, the right of the holder to exchange the medium into other forms of central bank money is not due to the medium itself, but results from other legal provisions.[12] Furthermore, the provisions mentioned concern the exchange of coins and banknotes in the case they were damaged. However, it can be derived from Section 798 (1) BGB that the right of the holder to exchange the medium in the case it is damaged needs to be strictly distinguished from the actual claim in the meaning of Section 793 (1) BGB that the medium certifies. Thus, the claims of the holder for exchanging the banknotes into other forms of central bank money under statutory law are not sufficient to regard banknotes as certifying a claim in the legal sense.

Even the (partial) accounting as a liability may not establish the legal nature of cash as a debt claim.[13] This is mainly due to the different accounting of cash. Coins are recognised as assets in the balance sheets of the national central banks.[14] Banknotes on the other hand are recorded as the liability item 'banknotes in circulation'. However, this is merely historically justified due to the former legal nature as bearer bonds.[15] Moreover, not all liabilities in a balance sheet are always payment debts; they can also serve as items to maintain the balance sheet equation.[16] Furthermore, the purpose of recording banknotes on the balance sheet is rather to inform the public about the volume of banknotes in circulation.[17]

Hence, if conventional cash is not a debt claim of its holder against its issuer within the meaning of private law, it is not conceivable why a digital form of currency should be treated differently. Any claims of the holders to exchange CBDC into other forms of central bank money would probably also result from legal provisions (yet to be created) and not be based in the central bank digital currency itself.

---

[9] Decision of the European Central Bank of 13 December 2010 on the issue of euro banknotes (ECB/2010/29) (9 February 2011) *OJ L 35/26*, lastly amended by Decision (EU) 2022/2546 (22 December 2022) OJ L 328/136.

[10] Decision of the European Central Bank of 19 April 2013 on the denominations, specifications, reproduction, exchange and withdrawal of euro banknotes (ECB/2013/10) (30 April 2013) OJ L 118/37, lastly amended by Decision (EU) 2020/2090 (15 December 2020) OJ L 423/62.

[11] Münzgesetz v. 16.12.1999 (BGBl. I p. 2402), zuletzt geändert am 22.12.2011 (BGBl. I p. 2959) (Coinage Act).

[12] Freimuth (2022), para. 23; Häde (1991), p. 157/158; Langner (2020), para. 15.17.

[13] Fögen (1969), p. 18; Häde (1991), p. 157.

[14] See the balance sheet of the Deutsche Bundesbank as per 31.12.2021.

[15] Huber (2018), p. 173.

[16] Fögen (1969), p. 18.

[17] Fögen (1969), p. 18.

This means that there is no claim that the token could certify, i.e. that the question of the legal nature of the claim under private law does not need to be pursued further.

Deed

Furthermore, the recognition of a bearer-instrument as a deed also seems questionable. A deed in the sense of the above-mentioned provisions is the written embodiment of a thought, cf. Section 793 (2), second sentence, BGB.[18] When using the Blockchain or Corda technology the digital euro as a bearer-instrument is only a digital data record.[19] It lacks any physicalness, so that it cannot constitute a deed (for more on the physicalness see below).[20]

Nonetheless, applying Section 952 BGB or Section 793 BGB by analogy could be worth considering. One may assume an unintended gap in the provisions.[21] However, currency tokens do not represent a right in the sense of a claim, so that the typical connection between the claim and the medium for securities is missing.[22] Thus, in any case the different interests are not comparable.

Interim Result

Therefore, in the absence of a claim against the issuer, a digital currency is not a security, neither in direct application of the above-cited provisions nor by analogy.

Res

Next, it is questionable whether central bank digital currency can be considered as '*res*' in the sense of Section 90 BGB. According to this provision, only physical objects are *res* within the meaning of the law.

The prerequisite for physicalness is that the object in question is sensually perceptible, spatially delimited and controllable.[23] When determining physicalness, it is the public conception of that object that is decisive; the scientific view tends to take a subordinate position.[24] However, the digital euro as a bearer-instrument is a digital record that represents a certain value and is technically assigned to a certain

---

[18] Füller (2023), para. 2.

[19] See above Sects. 2.2 and 2.3.2.

[20] Cf. Varmaz et al. (2021), para. 60; Lehmann (2021), para. 130; Omlor (2021b), para. 43. Other opinion are Kaulartz and Matzke (2018), pp. 3282 and 3283. See also District Court (Landgericht) Berlin, 27.05.2020 – 2 O 322/18, juris para. 124.

[21] Other opinion is Omlor (2021b), para. 45.

[22] Cf. Omlor (2021b), para. 44; Siedler (2021), para. 23.

[23] District Court (Landgericht) Konstanz, 10.05.1996 – 1 S 292/95, juris para. 3; Stieper (2021a), para. 9; Stresemann (2021), para. 8.

[24] Lahusen (2021), p. 8; Schmidt (2020), para. 1.

holder through a (central or distributed) ledger. As with all crypto-assets, it is data that is not sensually perceptible and spatially delimited.[25] Viewed in isolation, due to its lack of physicality central bank digital currency cannot be considered as *res* within the meaning of Section 90 BGB.

However, central bank digital currency can be embodied in some way. The Eurosystem's experiments to enable the access to and the transfer with units of the digital euro as a bearer-instrument via physical devices (HBIs) have already been presented.[26] The ledger will also probably be stored on the physical TIPS servers of the Eurosystem. Hence, one could consider applying the settled case-law of the German Federal Supreme Court of Justice (BGH). The so-called 'embodiment jurisprudence' states that data embodied on a data carrier are to be regarded as physical objects within the meaning of Section 90 BGB.[27] However, this case-law is predominantly declared to be inapplicable with regard to the *in rem*-assessment of crypto-assets, as it should only refer to the question of whether specific areas of the law of obligations (law of sales, tenancy and contracts for work and services) can be applied to the data embodied in this way.[28] If one were to assume the applicability of this case-law, the data would also need to be concretely linked to specific *res*.[29] With regard to the ledger, such a link must be denied. The ledger only records the transactions of the digital units and enables to subsequently and technically assign the units to certain owners.[30] They are not a register of the digital units per se. However, the physical devices (HBIs) need to be examined in more detail. For the legal assessment, the technical functionality is crucial. If the HBIs are intended to solely serve for the transfer of and the access to the digital units, then they are comparable to payment cards. Such cards do not cause the electronic fiat money accessible with them to be regarded as a physical object. However, the ECB seems to lean towards a different view. For example, the ECB clarified several times that it is aiming for the local storage of the digital euro on the HBI.[31] The Bundesbank stated in its report on the Eurosystems' experiments that 'the HBI entitles the holder of a hardware device the ownership and full custody of the currency stored in the device'.[32] However, this appears to be doubtful. From a technical point of view, it is questionable whether indeed the euro tokens or only the transactions are stored on

---

[25] Schmidt (2020), para. 3; Omlor (2021b), para. 30; Rückert (2016), p. 296; Langenbucher (2018), p. 405.

[26] ECB (2020), pp. 30 and 31 and above Sect. 2.4.4.

[27] BGH, 15.11.2006 – XII ZR 120/04, juris para. 15 (with further references). A fundamentally different understanding of this case-law has Stresemann (2021), para. 25. Cf. also Spiegel (2020), p. 55.

[28] Shmatenko and Möllenkamp (2018), p. 497; Maute (2020a), para. 14. Cf. also District Court Konstanz, 10.05.1996 – 1 S 292/95, juris para. 3. Generally rejecting the case-law of the BGH is Omlor (2021a), para. 41.

[29] Langenbucher et al. (2020), para. 35.

[30] Cf. Shmatenko and Möllenkamp (2018), p. 497.

[31] ECB (2022), slide 6; ECB Appendix (2021), p. 2.

[32] Deutsche Bundesbank (2021), p. 4.

the devices or whether in general the device is only used for enabling mobile access to the digital units. In favour of the latter interpretation is the fact that although in principle the offline-CBDC should be similar to cash and the HBI could be compared to a prepaid card, this can hardly be achieved with the current state-of-the-art technology.[33] This is also shown by the way the Sand Dollar already works in practice. This CBDC 'can be accessed flexibly with either a mobile phone application or using a physical payment card to access your digital wallet'.[34] For the Sand Dollar, the HBI is only used as means of access. Furthermore, the fact that, according to the ECB, the offline devices have to synchronise with the online ledger of the Eurosystem at a certain point in time in order to solve the double-spending problem,[35] also suggests that technically only the transactions and a corresponding balance are stored on the HBI. Hence, the HBI will probably just serve as means of access. Thus, it cannot be assumed that the digital euro is embodied on the HBI in the sense of the BGH's case-law. Ultimately, with regard to the ownership of rights the BGH in its more recent case-law also strictly distinguishes between the physical data carrier and the immaterial data itself.[36] This argues against the applicability of the embodiment jurisprudence to central bank digital currency. Thus, CBDC as a bearer-instrument cannot be considered as *res* within the meaning of Section 90 BGB.

Intangible Object

According to Section 90 BGB, *res* are physical objects. The German Civil Code understands objects as goods, i.e. physical and other objects, and rights.[37] Since central bank digital currency is neither *res* nor a right (see above), only the catch-all category of 'other objects' remains for legal recording. These are generally understood to be immaterial and individual goods or objects with a certain economic value.[38] Central bank digital currency as a bearer-instrument is a data set and lacks embodiment. The specific euro tokens can also be individualised via the transactions that are stored in the respective ledger.[39] In addition, due to their use as a medium of exchange they also have a certain economic value. Existing literature therefore

---

[33] See Sect. 2.4.4 (with further references).

[34] https://www.sanddollar.bs/individual (Accessed 31.07.2023).

[35] ECB (2021), p. 5; ECB (2020), pp. 31 and 32.

[36] BGH, 10.07.2015 – V ZR 206/14, para. 20 (*Kohl-Tonbänder*). See also Spindler (2011), pp. 271 and 272 and Stieper (2021b), para. 12.

[37] Peukert (2011), p. 96.

[38] Kuhlmann (2014), p. 694; Stresemann (2021), para. 1; Greier (2016), p. 252. Critical towards the criterion of economic value is Stieper (2021a), para. 7.

[39] Cf. Omlor (2021a), para. 45; Koch (2018), p. 362.

assumes that crypto-assets are legally unregulated, other intangible objects.[40] According to the above, this legal classification can also be applied to the legal nature of central bank digital currency as a bearer-instrument under private law. However, since CBDC is not legally recognised as rights, classifying it as intangible objects should not lead to confuse it with intellectual property rights, which are legally recognised intangible objects.

Interim Result

In summary, central bank digital currency as a bearer-instrument in German private law is neither a security nor *res*. Rather, it is an intangible object that is not regulated by law.

7.1.1.2 Legal Situation in Other Member States

The legal framework for classifying central bank digital currency as a bearer-instrument differs broadly across the Member States.

In Austria, the legal framework for the assessment is the Austrian General Civil Code (ABGB[41]). This distinguishes between rights in person (Article 15 ABGB) and rights *in rem* (Article 285 ABGB). According to Article 285 ABGB, everything in the legal sense is called *res* which is distinct from the person and serves for the use of people. Article 292 ABGB states much clearer than in the German legal system: 'Physical *res* are those which fall within the senses; otherwise they are called intangible; e.g. the right to hunt, to fish and all other rights'.[42] Interestingly, rights are equated with *res* (Article 298 ABGB), but are nevertheless transferred by means of cession (Articles 1392, 1393 ABGB). The legal situation for rights to intangible objects such as central bank digital currency as a bearer-instrument is simplified by Article 353 ABGB. This provision states: 'Everything that belongs to someone, all his physical and intangible things, are called his property'.[43] Hence, there is no difficulty in establishing a property right to the bearer-instrument under Austrian private law.

---

[40] Langenbucher (2018), p. 407; Baier (2019), p. 126 with further references; Kütük and Sorge (2014), p. 644; Omlor (2019b), p. 290; Beck and König (2015), p. 130; Engelhardt and Klein (2014), p. 357.

[41] Allgemeines bürgerliches Gesetzbuch für die gesammten deutschen Erbländer der Oesterreichischen Monarchie, StF: JGS Nr. 946/1811, zuletzt geändert durch Gesetz v. 20.04.2023, BGBl. I Nr. 38/2023.

[42] Translated from German.

[43] Translated from German.

In Spain, the legal situation under the Spanish Código Civil[44] (CC) is again different. Article 333 CC distinguishes between movable and immovable goods (*bienes muebles e inmuebles*). Here it appears doubtful whether central bank digital currency as a bearer-instrument can be seen as a movable good because according to Article 335 CC it must be possible to transport it from one place to another. This requires the physical change of the location of the good, which does not occur when the Eurosystem's ledger is transcribed. Hence, Spanish private law does not provide for rules applicable to central bank digital currency as a bearer-instrument.

7.1.2 Account-Based Central Bank Digital Currency

With regard to the legal nature of account-based central bank digital currency, it should be noted that although it is issued by the ECB and is regarded as its liability item, it is only accessible via an account held with the central bank or with financial intermediaries. It is therefore scriptural money. In terms of its legal nature, this is a claim of the account holder against the account-holding institution for payout.[45] The question of whether this claim arises from an abstract acknowledgement of indebtness (Sections 780, 781 BGB), which finds its *causa* in the legal relationship between the account holder and the account provider (payment service framework contract),[46] or from the national law that implements Article 87 (2), first sentence, PSD2 (for e.g. Section 675t (1), first sentence, BGB[47]) does not need to be pursued further at this point. Hence, an account-based digital euro is a claim against the respective account provider under private law.

7.1.3 Interim Result

The legal nature of the digital euro differs for its various functionalities. An account-based digital euro is a claim of the account holder against the respective account provider. The legal situation for the digital euro as a bearer-instrument is not uniform across the Member States. Commonly, it is regarded as an intangible object which may or may not be regulated under private law.

---

[44]Real Decreto de 24 de julio de 1889 por el que se publica el Código Civil, Gaceta de Madrid 25.07.1889, No. 206 (BOE-A-1889-4763), lastly amended by Ley 4/2023, 28.02.2023 (BOE-A-2023-5366).

[45]ECB (2020), p. 25; Herresthal (2020), para. 7b; Häuser (2019), para. 509; Omlor (2014), p. 131.

[46]Häuser (2019), para. 510 and 511.

[47]German parliamentary paper 16/11643, p. 112; Schwintowski (2018), para. 265; Schmieder (2022a), para. 10; Jungmann (2023), para. 36.

7.2 Usability in Legal Relations

To ensure widespread acceptance, it is also important that the end-users are able to use CBDC in legal relations, for example as means of payment. In this regard, the law and the public often refer to 'money'. Hence, CBDC in the law of monetary obligations will be examined. Furthermore, to use central bank digital currency, the technical change of ownership when transferring units also needs to be recognised as a legal change in ownership. This also needs to be enquired further.

7.2.1 Law of Monetary Obligations

Regarding the legal nature of banknotes in German private law, it is assumed that they are to be treated only as money, i.e. (physical) tokens of value intended for the use as means of payment in commercial transactions.[48] Although the BGB uses the term 'money' in numerous provisions (e.g. Sections 232 (1), 244/245, 250/251, 342, 488 (1), first sentence, 935 (2), 1113 (1) BGB), it does not define it. The question of whether a medium is to be regarded as 'money' can be answered from both an economic and a legal perspective.[49]

7.2.1.1 Concept of Money in Economics

The concept of money in economics is predominantly determined by a functional view based on the three functions of money.[50] For a medium to be considered money, it must be suitable to be exchanged against goods and services (medium-of-exchange function), as a reference unit for the value of various goods (unit-of-account function) and for the accumulation of values over a certain period of time without the loss of value (store-of-value function).[51] However, these functions of money are not significantly affected by a digital representation of the currency. If the technical requirements are met by the recipients, the digital currency can also be used as a medium of exchange for goods and services or as a reference unit for their value. The digital representation of the currency also does not affect the store-of-value

---

[48] Ohler (2008), p. 319; RG, 28.11.1921 – VI 282/21, RGZ 103, 231 (235); Häde (1991), p. 159.

[49] Langenbucher et al. (2020), para. 18; Omlor (2021c), A64; for an overview see Grundmann (2022), para. 10.

[50] Peto (2002), p. 14; Schaal (1998), p. 18; Borchert (2003), p. 22. Cf. the Opinion of the Advocate General *Pitruzella*, C-422/19, ECLI:EU:C:2020:756, para. 77.

[51] Borchert (2003), pp. 27 ff.; Lehmann (2016), para. 163.

function in any different way[52] than the previous cash does, i.e. it behaves neutrally.[53] The digital euro is therefore money within the economic sense.

7.2.1.2 Concept of Money in Law

The legal concept of money is divided into several varieties,[54] but in its predominant form it is fundamentally based on the state theory of money developed by *Knapp*, according to which money constitutively requires sovereign recognition and normative design.[55] With regard to the embodiment of the money medium, a distinction is usually made between the concrete and the abstract concept of money.[56] Money in the concrete sense is any embodied medium that is legally recognised as means of payment and perceived as a medium of exchange by the public.[57] So far, the only means of payments with legal tender are banknotes and coins denominated in euro, Article 128 (1), third sentence, TFEU, Articles 10 and 11 Regulation (EU) 974/98. It is possible *de lege ferenda* to grant the legal tender status to the digital euro (see above). However, both manifestations (bearer-instrument and account-based) lack embodiment in any case.[58] Thus, the digital euro is not money in the concrete sense.[59] However, for the lack of embodiment, this understanding also precludes scriptural money, although this is generally regarded as 'money' by the public.[60] For this reason, the abstract concept of money has been developed which dispenses with the embodiment and the legal obligation to accept, and solely requires a normative recognition and the use as a universal means of exchange.[61] A normative recognition requires the openness of the legal system for the considered form of money, i.e. central bank digital currency.[62] For the use as a universal medium of exchange, there must be ascertainable acceptance, especially through the sufficient dissemination and use in the exchange for goods and services.[63] Assuming an increasing affinity for digital payments, especially amongst the younger generation, and the

---

[52] For restrictions to the store-of-value-function for reasons of financial stability and monetary policy see Chap. 8 and Sect. 9.2.

[53] Strobel (2021), p. 561.

[54] For an overview see Herrmann (2010), pp. 62 ff. and Omlor (2014), pp. 64 ff.

[55] Knapp (1923), p. 6; Schaal (1998), pp. 19 and 20; Grundmann (2022), para. 10; Opinion of the Advocate General *Pitruzella*, C-422/19, ECLI:EU:C:2020:756, para. 78; Siekmann (2018), para. 6.

[56] Herrmann (2010), p. 71.

[57] Mann (1960), p. 5; Omlor (2014), pp. 100 ff.

[58] Advocating the abolishment of this criterion are Omlor and Birne (2020), p. 6; see also Proctor (2012), para. 1.47.

[59] Cf. also Omlor (2021c), A83b.

[60] Haug (2022), para. 47 and 53.

[61] Omlor (2014), p. 98.

[62] Omlor (2021c), A67.

[63] Omlor (2021c), A83c.

corresponding availability of technical requirements, the latter mentioned prerequisite will probably be fulfilled when the digital euro is introduced. With the recognition as legal tender and, if necessary, the amendment of the national payment services law,[64] the criterion of normative recognition should also be over-fulfilled, with the consequence that the digital euro, in the absence of embodiment, cannot be classified as money in the concrete sense, but certainly in the abstract sense.[65]

7.2.1.3 Interim Result

If certain conditions are met, central bank digital currency is also money in the economic and legal sense. Hence, it can be used in legal relations to discharge payment obligations that require the transfer of money.

7.2.2 Legal Change of Ownership

Transferring money leads to a change of ownership. From a technical perspective, this will be done by transcribing the ledger that technically assigns the particular digital euro unit to the public key of the recipient. However, to ensure widespread usability this technical transfer also needs to unfold a legal effect. The following section will enquire how the ownership of central bank digital currency in its manifestations can change.

7.2.2.1 General Mechanism in the German Civil Code

The German Civil Code strictly separates two levels which are in general independent of each other's effectiveness (so-called 'principle of separation and abstraction'). The first level often consists of a contract creating an obligation such as a contract of sale or tenancy. The second level is the disposition needed to fulfil the obligation. Hence, the first level is the *causa* for the result of the second level. Changing the ownership of goods or rights can only be done by a disposition (transaction *in rem*). A disposition is any legal act by which another right or legal relationship is directly repealed, transferred, encumbered or its content changed.[66] Thus, any disposition always refers to a subjective right that can be disposed.[67] A subjective right is the entitlement assigned to the individual by the legal system to

[64] Cf. for e.g. Article 675c (2) BGB for e-money.

[65] Omlor and Birne (2020), p. 6; cf. Omlor (2021c), A67.

[66] BGH, 24.10.1979 – VIII ZR 289/78, juris para. 20; Neuner (2020a), para. 31.

[67] Peukert (2011), p. 100.

satisfy his interests at will.[68] It means that a person is 'entitled to something'.[69] The entitled person must be able to exclude others from using the 'something' and this 'something' must be legally assigned to him (so-called 'exclusion-and-assignment function').[70] When considering whether the position to be disposed is subject to a subjective right, its marketability must also be taken into account as an indication.[71] However, the normative assignment of the position to an owner by the legal system is ultimately decisive.[72]

In legal and economic relations, the disposition is commonly executed by the act of a party. This form of disposition requires in principle three prerequisites. First, the parties need to agree on the change of ownership (consent). Second, an action is required that makes the change public (act of publicity). And third, the party wanting to confer the ownership on the other party needs to be authorised to do so, either because she is the actual owner or the owner empowered her to do so (power of disposition). The act of publicity varies according to the specific position that is to be transferred. For transferring movable *res*, the BGB in principle requires the parties to hand over the object (*manu traditio*, cf. Sections 929 ff. BGB).[73] For transferring a right related to immovable objects such as real estate, the change needs to be entered into the land register (cf. Section 873 BGB). For transferring other rights and claims, the consent of the parties is sufficient enough (cf. Sections 413, 398 BGB).

The German Civil Code also provides for the case that the transferor does not have the power of disposition. The Code enables the recipient to acquire with good faith. This has four requirements. First, a transaction with a third person is necessary, i.e. transferor and recipient must not be identical. Second, the appearance of a legal position, i.e. the *prima facie* entitlement of the transferor. This varies according to the position that shall be transferred. For movable *res*, it is the possession of the object (cf. Section 1006 (1) BGB). For rights related to immovable objects it is the fact that the transferor is registered in the land register (cf. Section 891 BGB). For transferring other rights and claims there is in principle[74] no *prima facie* entitlement because those are not embodied and cannot be assigned to the transferor clearly and for everyone to see. Hence, a *bona-fide* acquisition of claims is not possible. Third, the good faith of the recipient is necessary, i.e. the recipient shall not know that the transferor lacks the power of disposition (cf. Sections 932 (2), 892 BGB). Fourth and lastly, a *bona-fide* acquisition must not be excluded, for e.g. because the object to be transferred was stolen (cf. Section 935 BGB).

---

[68] Neuner (2020b), para. 6; Rüthers et al. (2020), para. 63; Enneccerus and Nipperdey (1959), § 72; Leipold (2019), para. 33; Bork (2016), para. 281; Habersack (1996), p. 21.

[69] Neuner (2020b), para. 9.

[70] Neuner (2020b), para. 10; Peukert (2011), p. 56.

[71] Peukert (2011), p. 100.

[72] Neuner (2020b), para. 2; Peukert (2011), p. 108; Bork (2016), para. 281.

[73] Baur and Stürner (2009a), para. 10; Wellenhofer (2022a), para. 6.

[74] An exception would be a case in that the claim which is ceded is embodied in a deed (cf. Article 405 BGB).

7.2.2.2 Central Bank Digital Currency as a Bearer-Instrument

As outlined above, central bank digital currency as a bearer-instrument is commonly regarded as an intangible object across Member States' private law. From a technical point of view, it is a digital token. Therefore, the previous findings on crypto-assets in the literature can be used for the legal qualification. Various positions are represented there in this regard.[75]

German Law

Following the structure of the mechanism underlining the German Civil Code, it first needs to be enquired whether there is a subjective right to central bank digital currency as a bearer-instrument which can be subject to a disposition. Secondly, it will be enquired how the literature legally classifies the act of transfer.

Subjective Right to CBDC as a Bearer-Instrument

As stated above, a subjective right is a position that has been legally assigned to someone and enables him to exclude others from using this position.

Regarding the question of whether the owner can exclude others from using the position, it is argued for crypto-assets, also across legal systems,[76] that due to the use of cryptographic methods to trigger a transaction, the holder of the tokens can exclude third parties from using the tokens.[77] However, as set out above, it is decisive whether there are specific provisions in the legal system that grant exclusivity.[78] In contrast, it is not sufficient that excluding others from using the position is solely based on technical and factual circumstances, without any legal recognition.[79] As postulated by *Skauradszun*,[80] such legal recognition for crypto-securities in general may perhaps be seen in Section 1 (11), fourth sentence, KWG.[81] This provision is based on Article 1 No. 2 lit. d of the 5th AMLD.[82] However, both

---

[75] For an overview to the legal debate see Maute (2020b), para. 4 ff.

[76] See for e.g. Völkel (2019a), para. 3.23 (for Austria); Dobrauz-Saldapenna and Schrackmann (2019), para. 16.15 (for Switzerland with further references); Rietzler et al. (2019), para. 17.19 (for Liechtenstein with further references).

[77] Foerster (2020), para. 18.

[78] Habersack (1996), pp. 26 and 27.

[79] BVerfG, 24.11.2004 – 1 BvR 1306/02, juris para. 9; BGH, 18.01.2012 – I ZR 187/10, juris para. 23 and 24, 27; BGH, 05.07.2005 – VII ZB 5/05, juris para. 11; BGH, 22.11.2001 – I ZR 138/99, juris para. 51; Maute (2020a), para. 41.

[80] Skauradszun (2020), p. 1233.

[81] Gesetz über das Kreditwesen in der Fassung der Bekanntmachung v. 09.09.1998 (BGBl. I p. 2776), zuletzt geändert am 22.02.2023 (BGBl. I p. 51) (German Banking Act).

[82] Directive (EU) 2018/843 of the European Parliament and of the Council of 30 May 2018 amending Directive (EU) 2015/849 on the prevention of the use of the financial system for the

provisions exclude crypto-securities issued by central banks from the scope of application. Hence, a legal recognition of the holder being able to technically and factually exclude others from using central bank digital currency as a bearer-instrument does not exist so far.

The question of whether digital (crypto) token are legally assigned to the holder also proves to be debatable. Mirroring the discussion on the legal nature of software, it is argued that the intended and authorised use of the technical infrastructure creates a good that is exclusively assigned to a legal entity and cannot be duplicated due to the technical characteristics of the DLT.[83] Yet it can be countered that the assignment of goods to owners is a task of the (private law) legal system and thus cannot be justified on purely technical grounds.[84] Likewise, for crypto-assets it has been argued so far that although they cannot be used technically without the knowledge of the private key and transactions are irreversible due to the use of the DLT, this factual assignment is not recognised by law.[85]

In addition to this assignment based on technology, economic considerations are often cited. Since tokens are tradable and have a certain asset value, according to this view a legal assignment must take place.[86] This consideration is based on the market value theory, according to which a factual asset value is the beginning of every debate on the legal assignment, so that the conclusion applies 'if economic value, then subjective right'.[87] Nonetheless, to conclude from the asset value of an object that it is also legally recognised is subject to circular reasoning:[88] the asset acquires its de facto economic value through the possibilities of its owner to use this asset. However, these possibilities only result from the legal system, which in turn is supposed to follow economic values. The market value theory thus establishes a right to a good of economic value, although the economic value depends precisely on the existence and the scope of that right.[89] Moreover, on the basis of the market value theory, an economic devaluation of the good would consequently always have to lead to the loss of the right to this good.[90] This does not appear reasonable because legally protectable interests can also exist in economically worthless goods.[91]

purposes of money laundering or terrorist financing, and amending Directives 2009/138/EC and 2013/36/EU (19 June 2018) *OJ L 156/43.*

[83] Foerster (2020), para. 5 and 6.

[84] Cf. Heinze (2018), para. 11.

[85] Greier (2016), p. 252; Kuhlmann (2014), p. 695; Walter (2019), p. 3611; Lerch (2015), p. 196.

[86] Linardatos (2020), p. 200 who speaks about the law seizing the common perception of trade. Cf. further Maute (2020a), para. 30.

[87] Peukert (2008), p. 733 (with further references); Ehmann (2000), pp. 665 and 666; Timmann (2008), pp. 65 and 66; Hubmann (1955), p. 57; Weimann (1995), p. 68.

[88] For this and the following see Peukert (2011), p. 118.

[89] Cohen (1935), p. 815. Cf. also Ehmann (1988), p. 239.

[90] Timmann (2008), p. 66.

[91] Cf. BVerfG, 05.08.2020 – 2 BvR 1985/19, juris para. 40 and 41 on the question whether extracting food from garbage containers is to be penalised under criminal law.

Furthermore, there is no general legal rule in the *lex lata* according to which every de facto asset is assigned to the person who created it, hereby excluding all others.[92]

Furthermore, it has been argued that a legal assignment can also result from the fact that a position needs to be or is subject to protection under the legal system. In other words, if a position is protected by legal means, then the position is also assigned to the beneficiary. The need to protect the holder of digital currency tokens should on the one hand result from their asset value.[93] On the other hand, crypto-assets are said to be covered by the fundamental right to property granted in Article 14 (1), first sentence, of the Basic Law for the Federal Republic of Germany.[94] Moreover, the digital unit should only exist once, should be freely transferable and used for payment purposes, so it should be comparable to the property ownership of cash which should result in equal protection.[95] Hence, some argue that crypto-assets as data are subject to defensive claims for protection (Sections 823 (1), (2) BGB in conjunction with Sections 202a, 303a, 303b of the German Criminal Code (StGB); Section 826 BGB) and must therefore be recognised as a right due to the requirement of unity of the legal order itself.[96] However, the normative assignment of a position to an owner requires more than mere defensive claims.[97] These claims only prevent or sanction violations of the subjective right.[98] Thus, these defensive rights do not arise from a subjective right, but are based directly on an statutory provision.[99] Hence, they are a necessary, but not sufficient condition for a subjective right.[100] The decisive factor is whether the position itself is legally recognised, not any claims that follow from this position.[101] Subjective rights must be determined independent of a violation by the positive legal assignment of powers of a legal or factual nature.[102] So far, such assignments and thus normative recognition do not exist for crypto-assets in the form of central bank digital currency as a bearer-instrument.

In conclusion, there are no subjective rights linked to central bank digital currency as a bearer-instrument.

---

[92] Peukert (2008), p. 2.

[93] Omlor (2021a), para. 45.

[94] Walter (2019), p. 3613.

[95] Athanassiou (2018), pp. 99 and 100; Koch (2018), p. 363; Walter (2019), p. 3613.

[96] Linardatos (2020), pp. 201 and 202; Greier (2016), p. 256; Effer-Uhe (2018), p. 519; Jacobs and Arndt (2019), p. 568.

[97] Paulus (2020), pp. 137 and 138.

[98] Habersack (1996), pp. 24 and 25.

[99] Peukert (2011), pp. 100 and 101.

[100] Heinze (2018), para. 7.

[101] Effer-Uhe (2018), p. 520.

[102] Peukert (2008), pp. 56, 58.

Transfer Mechanisms

If there is no subjective right, then there is no base for a disposition (see above). To cope with that fact, the literature developed several theories to still enable a change in ownership that is recognised by law.

Mechanism of Movable Things by Analogy

To begin with, one could consider to apply the mechanisms to change the ownership of movable *res*. This change in ownership is based on the Sections 929 ff. BGB. However, since these provisions require *res* in the sense of Section 90 BGB, CBDC is not embodied and there is no subjective right, a direct application of the provisions is ruled out. Therefore, some consider an application by analogy.[103]

However, even (and especially) when applying a provision by analogy, some principles of property law must be respected. For example, the principle of certainty/ speciality. This principle requires that the transfer of rights *in rem* relate to a closely specified object.[104] Thus, in principle the aggregate transfer of tangible assets is precluded.[105] However, due to the registration of each transaction in the ledger, each digital token can be individualised in a sufficient manner.[106] This will also apply in the case of central bank digital currency because it is hardly conceivable that the Eurosystem will allow the uncontrolled creation of euro tokens by anyone, but will rather register each created token in a separate ledger.[107] This should ensure to comply with the principle of speciality. Furthermore, there is the principle of publicity. This principle requires that the change of ownership becomes externally recognisable to third parties through the transfer.[108] Regarding crypto-assets it is argued that this publicity is achieved through entering the transaction in the ledger, which enables to assign the tokens to their holder without doubt.[109]

However, most frequently it is argued that an application by analogy is not consistent with the *numerus clausus* of property law.[110] Due to the nature of rights *in rem* as absolute rights[111] with *erga omnes*-effect, there may only exist the

[103] See for e.g. Omlor (2021a), para. 45 ff.; Walter (2019), p. 3613; Spindler and Bille (2014), pp. 1362 and 1363; Koch (2018), p. 362. Similar also Athanassiou (2018), p. 98. For the prerequisites of an application by analogy see Wank (2020), para. 110; see also BGH, 17.03.2022 – III ZR 79/21, juris para. 3 and Möllers (2021a), para. 117.

[104] Baur and Stürner (2009a), para. 17; Wilhelm (2021), para. 21.

[105] Wilhelm (2021), para. 20.

[106] Koch (2018), p. 362; Omlor (2021a), para. 45.

[107] Cf. Sect. 2.4.3 Cf. similarly also Spiegel (2020), p. 106.

[108] Wellenhofer (2022a), para. 5; Wilhelm (2021), para. 35.

[109] Koch (2018), p. 362. Similar also Spindler and Bille (2014), pp. 1362 and 1363.

[110] Engelhardt and Klein (2014), p. 357; Langenbucher et al. (2020), para. 39; Skauradszun (2021a), p. 373.

[111] For a definition see Neuner (2020b), para. 53 ff.

manifestations that are regulated and created by the statutory law.[112] Furthermore, this principle of *numerus clausus* is supplemented by restricting the parties' freedom to structure the private law (so-called type-constraint).[113] According to that principle, the parties to a transaction shall not contractually create new types of rights relating to the ownership of objects.[114] However, the alleged inconsistency with the two principles mentioned is countered by the fact that applying the Sections 929 ff. BGB is not aiming at creating new types of rights, but rather at applying the existing property law provisions and using the advantages of this transfer technique for new manifestations of objects.[115] Methodologically, this view extents the existing concept of *res* to intangible objects but does not create new rights for these objects.[116]

Then, the requirements for a transfer according to Section 929 (1), first sentence, BGB would need to be met. As set out above, the parties need to agree on the change of ownership. When examining crypto-assets based on the distributed ledger technology, some argue that a consent between the parties is not required because from a technical point of view it is sufficient if the transferor unilaterally authorises the transaction.[117] To still ensure the consistency with the mechanism of transfer underlying the Civil Code, one could construct an anticipated consent through the participation in the DLT network. However, those advocating this construction of anticipated consent make an exception for classical DLT networks such as the Bitcoin blockchain. These networks are to be characterised by decentralisation and the distance from the sovereign which should result in a lack of legal commitment on part of the participants.[118] For central bank digital currency, the assessment is likely to be different. The participants in such a network of CBDC want to use the digital currency units precisely as means of payment. It is hardly conceivable that this should not be based on the parties' intention to be legally bound. Furthermore, depending on the technical infrastructure, cryptographic methods are used to trigger a transaction.[119] This requires at least an exchange of the public keys, which serve as the address the digital units are assigned to. This exchange could also be seen as the necessary consent.

Secondly, an act of publicity is required. For movable *res* this is typically the handover of the object, i.e. the transferor enabling the recipient to exercise the effective control over the object.[120] Some authors see this 'handover' in the transfer of the position of the single unit in in the ledger, which results of the fact that the ledger is rewritten because the payer has triggered the transaction by means of his

---

[112] Wellenhofer (2022a), para. 2; Ellenberger (2023), para. 16.

[113] Wilhelm (2021), para. 14.

[114] Wellenhofer (2022a), para. 3; Neuner (2020b), para. 56.

[115] Koch (2018), pp. 363 and 364.

[116] Like here Arndt (2022), p. 79. Cf. also Walter (2019), p. 3612.

[117] Cf. Omlor (2019a), p. 327.

[118] Omlor (2019a), p. 328; Omlor (2021a), para. 47.

[119] See Sect. 2.2.

[120] Baur and Stürner (2009b), para. 12, 16; Wellenhofer (2022b), para. 7.

private key.[121] However, others argue that normally the change of ownership is settled with handing over the object, whereas in the case of crypto-assets, depending on the technology used, the network as a whole or individual nodes must still verify the transaction before the ledger can be rewritten.[122]

Thirdly, the transferor needs to have the power of disposition. This proof of authorisation should be seen in the knowledge of the private key because only this knowledge allows to trigger the transaction.[123]

Mechanism of Other Rights and Claims by Analogy

Another approach could be to use the mechanism to transfer claims and other rights. In the Civil Code, this is regulated in the Sections 398, 413 BGB. According to Section 398, first sentence, BGB a claim may be transferred by the obligee to another person by contract with that person (assignment). Section 413 BGB extends the assignment provisions to the transfer of 'other rights'. Sections 398, 413 BGB therefore contain general rules on the transfer of rights, which may be applied in case no other specific rules intervene.[124] It is undisputed that a token is not a claim (see above).

Hence, it needs to be enquired whether a digital currency token constitutes an 'other right' within the meaning of Section 413 BGB. This term is generally understood to mean only subjective rights.[125] The provision of Section 413 BGB does not create subjective rights, but only describes the type of legal succession to already existing subjective rights.[126] As set out above, there is no subjective right to digital currency tokens yet. Hence, a direct application of Sections 398, 413 BGB is predominantly[127] rejected.[128] This will also have to apply to central bank digital currency.

As a result, some authors consider to apply the Sections 398, 413 BGB by analogy because these provisions are most reasonable for classifying the transfer of other objects.[129] However, due to the very structure of the aforementioned

---

[121] Koch (2018), p. 362; Kuhlmann (2014), p. 696; Omlor (2021a), para. 47.

[122] Skauradszun (2021a), p. 373.

[123] Omlor (2021a), para. 47; Koch (2018), p. 364.

[124] Cf. Wilhelm (2021), para. 7.

[125] Cf. Langenbucher et al. (2020), para. 38; Omlor (2019a), p. 327.

[126] Peukert (2011), p. 106.

[127] Nonetheless advocating a direct application Köndgen (2018), para. 131. Frequently cited for a direct application is also Mössner (2022), para. 104.4. In my opinion this is incorrect because Mössner refers in the paragraph cited to para. 102 and thus only states that not the token itself but solely the claims under the law of obligations to which the transferor is entitled against third parties are transferred according to Sections 398, 413 BGB.

[128] Instead of many see Omlor (2019b), p. 290 and Maute (2020b), para. 5.

[129] Paulus and Matzke (2018), pp. 452 and 453; Omlor (2021a), para. 47a. Not clear in this regard are Spindler and Bille (2014), pp. 1362 and 1363. With modifications Skauradszun (2021a), p. 376: Sections 413, 398, 399, second alternative, BGB by analogy.

provisions, it is often argued against their application by analogy. According to these provisions, the legal succession already settles with the agreement between the parties, whereas crypto-assets need a multi-act acquisition procedure, i.e. triggering and verifying the transaction and transcribing the ledger.[130] In addition, since a *bona-fide* acquisition is not possible (see above), the marketability and the tradeability of the tokens would be restricted.[131] In view of the qualification of the digital euro as money in the legal sense (see above), the latter fact appears to be of particular interest because Section 935 (2) BGB explicitly provides for *bona-fide* acquisitions of money.

Approach of Combined Mechanisms

Another approach is conducted by *Ammann* who considers to use the mechanisms for transferring real estate property pursuant to Sections 873, 925 (1) BGB by analogy.[132] According to him, the functioning of the DLT shows a clear parallel to the land register because in both cases a validation procedure takes place before a change is registered, the registration is irreversible and the ledger being accessible by everyone leads to public faith that is comparable with Section 892 BGB.[133] However, Section 925 (1), first sentence, BGB requires that the consent of the parties is certificated by a notary. *Koch* criticised that this would be impractical.[134] Building on this foundation, *Arndt* proposes an overall analogy of Sections 873, 929 BGB.[135] According to this application by analogy, the transfer of tokens should take place by consent and registration, using Sections 929, first sentence, 873 (1) BGB by analogy without the notarial certification.[136] The registration is fulfilled if the entire (factual) transaction is settled and the ledger is transcribed, even if the transferor only transfers his private key to the recipient (i.e. an offline-transaction in the purely factual meaning), so that the latter can in fact dispose of the transferor's currency units.[137] A *bona-fide*, unencumbered acquisition should then also be possible using Sections 892, 932 ff. BGB by analogy.[138]

---

[130] Langenbucher et al. (2020), para. 38; Skauradszun (2021a), p. 374; Omlor (2019a), p. 327; Arndt (2022), p. 129; Spiegel (2020), p. 105.

[131] Koch (2018), p. 363; of different opinion is Linardatos (2020), pp. 211 and 212, who generally objects the need for a *bona-fide* acquisition, but nonetheless grants it in the individual case using Sections 413, 398 BGB in conjunction with Section 172 BGB by analogy.

[132] Ammann (2018), p. 382.

[133] Ammann (2018), pp. 382 and 383.

[134] Koch (2018), p. 364.

[135] Arndt (2022), p. 113.

[136] Arndt (2022), p. 114.

[137] Arndt (2022), p. 114.

[138] Arndt (2022), p. 115.

Recognition Under the Law of Obligations and Factual Transaction

However, the predominant view in the literature on crypto-assets rejects any application of the aforementioned provisions by analogy at all. As already set out, the mechanisms of the Civil Code are based on a disposition which in turn needs a subjective right. Since this is missing for crypto-assets, their transfer cannot be a disposition.[139] Therefore, the transfer can only be recorded under the law of obligations by means of the claims that arise from the contract concerning the crypto-assets (cf. Section 453 (1), first sentence, second alternative, BGB).[140] On the second level, i.e. the level of the disposition, there was only a 'material act'.[141] However, a material act as *terminus technicus* is a factual act which, by virtue of the statutory law, provokes a legal consequence independent of what was intended by the actor, such as the combination/intermixture/processing (Sections 946 ff. BGB) or the finding (Section 965 BGB).[142] Due to the lack of a subjective right, the transfer of a token does not result in a legal consequence by virtue of the statutory law, so the term 'material act' is perhaps to be understood in the sense of a purely factual transaction.[143]

Opinion

Above all, it should be noted that the legal situation for recording the transfer of central bank digital currency is unsatisfactory. All the solutions presented above for the legal recording of the transfer face good legal arguments both for and against.

Starting point for the legal debate is the fact that any change of ownership requires a disposition and that this requires the existence of a subjective right. All presented theories that consider the application of statutory mechanisms by way of analogy, go beyond of what is methodologically lawful. These solutions ignore the lack of a subjective right and have to modify their transfer prerequisites, in some cases considerably and to a previously unknown[144] extent. They lead to at least a double, if not multiple application of the mentioned norms by way of analogy. Thus, the legal recognition of the transfer would move so far away from the original statutory provisions and, moreover, acquire significance for an unforeseeable number of cases and areas of law that this appears to be a task of the legislature rather than of the

[139] Maute (2020b), para. 3.

[140] Peukert (2011), pp. 108 ff.

[141] Paulus and Matzke (2018), pp. 451 and 453; Kaulartz and Matzke (2018), p. 3280; Lerch (2015), p. 196; Beck and König (2015), p. 131; Engelhardt and Klein (2014), p. 357; Kütük and Sorge (2014), pp. 644 and 645; Kuhlmann (2014), p. 696; Heckelmann (2018), p. 508; Omlor (2019b), pp. 290 and 291; Langenbucher et al. (2020), para. 39.

[142] Neuner (2020c), para. 13 and 14; Ellenberger (2023), para. 9.

[143] Like here Maute (2020b), para. 8; Linardatos (2020), p. 185.

[144] For the modifications when transferring the right conferring prospective entitlement pursuant to Section 929 BGB by analogy see Wellenhofer (2022c), para. 27 ff.; Baur and Stürner (2009c), para. 34 ff.

judicial application of the law, which is in principle limited to individual cases.[145] Admittedly, using a combination of the transfer mechanisms seems tempting because in this way existing liens on the token could be made visible if one were to use a legal register comparable to the land register.[146] However, also including the transaction of solely the private key appears problematic. In these cases, there is no visible transfer in the register in the technical sense and the transaction is also more similar to the handover principle that is characteristic for movable *res*.

Nonetheless, the solution which advocates a change of ownership purely by law of obligations with an act of transfer as a legal nullum at the level of disposition does not seem convincing either. This construction is alien to the Civil Code and cannot be reconciled with the principle of separation and abstraction, which, especially in the case of a change of ownership, strictly distinguishes between the contractual obligation and the disposition which is required for the change.[147] Moreover, with the assumption of a purely factual transaction act, there is no legal protection[148] of the acquirer's good faith.[149] In factual transactions, this is generally harmless because the *bona-fide* protection is intended to help to overcome a lack of authorisation which is not a prerequisite in purely factual transactions.[150] However, since CBDC is classified as money in the legal sense, it must be respected that money circulates in the economy and the *bona-fide* acquisition is necessary to safeguard the smooth functioning of the financial and economic system.[151] Furthermore, coping with the acquisition solely under the law of obligation could lead to gaps in the legal protection in cases where those transactions are null and void, for e.g. because the transferor was not legally capable of contracting (cf. Sections 104 ff., 134, 138, 142 (1) BGB).[152] In such cases, there is often only a claim for restitution under the law of enrichment (Section 812 (1), first sentence, first alternative, BGB) and in the case of insolvency only a pro rata satisfaction under Section 38 of the German Insolvency Act (InsO).[153]

In conclusion, it must be noted that the German Civil Code cannot cover the change of the 'ownership' of central bank digital currency as a bearer-instrument.[154]

---

[145] Cf. Wank (2020), para. 37 and 128; Jachmann-Michel (2022), Art. 95 para. 15.

[146] Arndt (2022), p. 103.

[147] Skauradszun (2021a), p. 372. Cf. also Linardatos (2020), p. 187.

[148] Not meant is a possible good faith that grounds on the fact that the ledger based on the DLT is technically irreversible. However, in this direction arguing is Spiegel (2020), p. 107, according to whom a lack of power of disposition is not imaginable due to the technical characteristics of DLT. This, however, solely focuses on a factual but not a legal empowerment of the transferor.

[149] Cf. Koch (2018), p. 363.

[150] Arndt (2022), p. 24; Maute (2020c), p. 225.

[151] Cf. BGH, 14.06.2013 – V ZR 108/12, juris para. 9; Klinck (2023), para. 37; Linardatos (2020), p. 210.

[152] Maute (2020c), p. 225; Linardatos (2020), p. 189.

[153] Linardatos (2020), p. 190.

[154] Like here but for crypto-assets Langenbucher (2018), p. 410. For a solution *de lege ferenda* see Sect. 7.4.4.

Indeed *Arndt* rightly points out that '(. . .) one [must] simply observe all transactions (. . .), but cannot evaluate them'.[155]

Law in Other Member States

As outlined above, in Austrian law central bank digital currency as a bearer-instrument is a legally recognised intangible object which can be subject to property rights under Article 353 ABGB. Although classifying the legal nature appears to be simple, the exact opposite applies to the act of transfer. When interpreting the Sections 353 ff. ABGB, the Austrian jurisprudence and literature predominantly applies the mentioned provisions solely to physical objects due to the statutory structure of these provisions.[156] Hence, the change of ownership of intangible objects cannot be covered by Austrian private law. Other parts of the literature advocate to abolish this teleological reduction or at least consider an application of the transfer provisions under property law by analogy.[157] However, since this requires considerable legal doctrinal justification for a *bona-fide* acquisition of intangible objects,[158] some advocates of these positions also argue for a legislative action taken by the legislator.[159]

In Spain, the ownership of property legally changes when the recipient takes possession of the object based on a contract under the law of obligations without the need of any further consent or power of disposition, cf. Article 609 (1) CC. In this respect, in contrast to German law, Spanish law knows a principle of separation, but no principle of abstraction.[160] However, the requirement of taking possession does not cover intangible goods. Moreover, Spanish private law does not provide for the *bona-fide* protection of movable property, cf. Article 464 (1) CC.[161] Furthermore, the official title of chapter 7 of title 4 of book 4 (Article 1526 ff. CC) speaks of provisions on the transfer of claims and other incorporeal rights (*De la transmisión de créditos y demás derechos incorporales*). However, as can be seen in Article 1526 (2) CC, these provisions only relate to the rights that are linked to the movable and immovable objects, but not to the objects themselves. Spanish law therefore does not contain an answer to the question of the transfer of central bank digital currency as a bearer-instrument any more than German law does.

---

[155] Arndt (2022), p. 40 (comments added).

[156] Eccher (2010a), para. 1; Fleißner (2018), p. 438; Pachinger et al. (2021), para. 19 and 20 (each with further references).

[157] Fleißner (2018), pp. 440 ff.; Völkel (2019a), para. 3.23.

[158] It is legally debated whether intangible objects are movable things within in the meaning of Section 293 ABGB because only those are covered by Section 367 ABGB, on this cf. Völkel (2019a), para. 3.14 (with further references) and Völkel (2019b), para. 4.58.

[159] Fleißner (2018), p. 442.

[160] Adomeit et al. (2018), p. 47.

[161] Adomeit et al. (2018), p. 49.

7.2.2.3 Account-Based Central Bank Digital Currency

Since account-based central bank digital currency is by its legal nature a claim, at first glance the transfer could be made by assignment (for e.g. according to Section 398 BGB). However, it is also scriptural money. The transfer of scriptural money is governed by the special provisions on payment services laid down in the PSD2.[162] The transfer is then made by transmitting a sum of money on the payer's instructions, cf. Article 4 (5), (25) PSD2.[163] This is done by the payer's PSP reducing its liabilities related to the payer through a debit entry and the payee's PSP increasing its liabilities related to the payee to the same extent through a credit entry.[164] Thus, in contrast to the assignment, not the claim of the payer against his PSP is transferred to the payee, but as a consequence of the transfer a separate claim of the payee against his PSP for payout is established.[165]

7.2.2.4 Interim Result

In conclusion, changing the ownership of account-based central bank digital currency takes place through debit entries and credit entries. In contrast, the change of ownership of central bank digital currency as a bearer-instrument cannot be covered under the private law of the Member States.

7.3 Special Areas of Civil Law

For central bank digital currency to be widely useable in legal and economic relations, it is not only important to classify the legal nature and the way of changing the ownership. It is also necessary to examine what happens when the creditor wants to enforce a claim for payment which is due in central bank digital currency (see Sect. 7.3.1). Or if the debtor is insolvent but owns a significant amount of CBDC units (see Sect. 7.3.2). And for the broader economic use, it needs to be enquired whether the end-users can lend CBDC to banks for them to work with (see Sect. 7.3.3).

---

[162] Omlor (2019a), p. 327; Schmieder (2022b), para. 4.

[163] Foerster (2023), para. 68; Casper (2023), para. 50.

[164] ECB (2020), p. 25; Omlor (2014), p. 133.

[165] Cf. Häuser (2019), para. 480. For the legal debate on when the claim for payout emerges see Häuser (2019), para. 510. For the legal nature of the claim see also Sect. 7.1.2.

7.3.1 *Central Bank Digital Currency in Individual Compulsory Enforcement*

Before examining how to enforce claims against or because of central bank digital currency, the following section will first provide a brief overview of the law regulating the compulsory enforcement procedure in Germany, the German Code of Civil Procedure (ZPO).[166]

7.3.1.1 Compulsory Enforcement Procedure in the German Code of Civil Procedure

In the system of compulsory enforcement, one needs to distinguish the reason for the compulsory enforcement and the object the creditor enforces against. The creditor can enforce for monetary claims (Sections 802a–882i ZPO) or for other claims (Sections 883–898 ZPO).[167] If he enforces for a monetary claim, it must be clarified whether the compulsory enforcement is against movable (Sections 803–863 ZPO) or immovable (Sections 864–871 ZPO) property. Enforcing against movable property contains physical objects (Sections 808–827 ZPO) or claims and other property rights (Sections 828–863 ZPO). Enforcing for a monetary claim against physical objects is effected by the attachment (Sections 808 ff. ZPO) and the realisation, the latter usually taking place in the form of a public auction (Section 814 (1) ZPO).[168] Enforcing for a monetary claim against claims and other property rights is effected by the court's attachment order (Section 829 ZPO) and transfer order (Section 835 ZPO).[169] If the creditor wants to enforce for a monetary claim against immovable property, this is done by the registration of a security mortgage, a compulsory auction or a judicial sequestration, Section 866 (1) ZPO.

Compulsory enforcement can also serve to obtain the surrender of objects (Sections 883 ff. ZPO), to ensure that actions are taken (Sections 887 ff. ZPO) or refrained from (Section 890 ZPO) and to ensure that the debtor makes a declaration of intent (Sections 894 ff. ZPO).

Hence, one needs to distinguish between the reason and the object of the compulsory enforcement. On the one hand, it seems conceivable that the creditor of a monetary claim wants to enforce against central bank digital currency. On the other hand, it is possible that a creditor wants to enforce a claim for 'restitution' of central bank digital currency, for example as a result of an erroneous transaction. In

---

[166] For more detail see Lackmann and Racz (2021), §§ 15 ff. and Schilken (2010a). For the basic requirements of the enforcement procedure see Werner (2021), para. 86 ff.

[167] For this and the following see Brox and Walker (2018), para. 7 and 8 and Gaul (2010a), para. 6 ff.

[168] Brox and Walker (2018), para. 206a.

[169] Lackmann and Racz (2021), para. 268; Brox and Walker (2018), para. 501.

both cases, a distinction must be made between a bearer-instrument and the account-based central bank digital currency.

7.3.1.2 Compulsory Enforcement for Monetary Claims Against Central Bank Digital Currency

The first constellation this section analyses is a situation where there is a creditor who aims at enforcing a monetary claim and a debtor who owns central bank digital currency.

Central Bank Digital Currency as a Bearer-Instrument

Since central bank digital currency is not immovable property, cf. Section 864 (1) ZPO, the compulsory enforcement can only be carried out against movable property. Since a bearer-based CBDC is not embodied, it cannot be seized as physical objects. Thus, one might consider to apply Sections 829, 835 ZPO because according to their headings, both provisions refer to monetary claims.[170] Although central bank digital currency as a bearer-instrument is money in the legal sense, it does not constitute a monetary claim within the meaning of Sections 829, 835 ZPO. A monetary claim within that meaning is to be understood as any claim directed to a sum of money.[171] Furthermore, according to the wording of Section 829 (1), first sentence, ZPO there must be a three-person relationship between the enforcement creditor, the enforcement debtor and the third-party debtor. However, central bank digital currency as a bearer-instrument is not a claim against a third party (see above). Therefore, the provisions on seizing money cannot be applied directly. It therefore needs to be enquired more closely whether the compulsory enforcement can be based on Section 857 (1) ZPO. According to this provision, the above provisions shall apply mutatis mutandis to compulsory enforcement against other property rights that are not subject to compulsory enforcement against the immovable property. Hence, central bank digital currency as a bearer-instrument must therefore be regarded as an 'other property right'.

Property Right

A property right is any right that embodies a value in such a way that the realisation of the attached right satisfies the creditor's monetary claim.[172] Moreover, this right

---

[170] Cf. Badstuber (2019), p. 250; Ammann (2018), p. 385; Koch (2020), p. 87; Bausch and Heetkamp (2018).

[171] Flockenhaus (2022a), para. 5.

[172] BGH, 09.02.2012 – VII ZB 117/09, juris para. 23; Ahrens (2021), para. 4; Schilken (2010b), para. 41; Koch (2021), para. 2; Flockenhaus (2022b), para. 2; Würdinger (2017), para. 7.

must be seizable according to general principles and may neither concern a monetary claim (Section 829 ZPO) nor a claim for surrender (Section 846 ZPO) nor be subject to compulsory enforcement against immovable property.[173] Furthermore, the provision of Section 857 ZPO does not cover purely factual relationships through which the debtor occupies a position of economic value nor possibilities of action that are not marketable rights.[174] A right can only be liable to attachment if it can also be transferred, cf. Section 851 (1) ZPO.[175] It is true that central bank digital currency can be transferred de facto. Moreover, it also embodies a value that can satisfy the creditor when being liable to attachment. However, it does not constitute a right (see above). Thus, directly applying Section 857 ZPO is rejected for crypto-assets,[176] which must also apply accordingly to central bank digital currency.

Deviating from the conventional understanding described above, *Jacobs and Arndt* prefer a different interpretation of the term 'property right' within the meaning of Section 857 (1) ZPO for crypto-assets.[177] According to them, Section 857 (1) ZPO mentions the term 'right' only because the debtor's entire assets are subject to the compulsory enforcement and an item is assigned to the debtor's assets through rights. Further, they agree to the fact that crypto-assets are assigned on a purely factual basis through the technical power of control over the assets. However, they advocate to assign the crypto-assets to their owner also by law, as only the owners were entitled to use the assets and to exclude others from using them. Furthermore, they resort to a teleological interpretation. The principle of effective compulsory enforcement mirroring the prohibition of self-help requires the comprehensive access to the debtor's assets. This should also result from the requirement of the unity of the legal order because the holders of the crypto-assets could at least assert claims for protection (Section 823 (2) BGB in conjunction with Sections 303a and 303b StGB). Moreover, they argue that the factual relationship of the holders to their crypto-assets is reified freedom, which is protected by Article 14 (1) of the German Basic Law (GG) and which converts the factual relationship into a legal relationship.

On closer examination, this view does not apply a different interpretation of the term 'property right', but rather attempts to extend the existing understanding of the term 'subjective right' to crypto-assets by advocating a legal assignment of crypto-assets to their holders. Moreover, this opinion attempts to extend the compulsory enforcement to purely factual positions by interpreting Section 857 (1) ZPO contrary to its wording.[178] This way of interpreting contradicts the general doctrine of legal

[173] Riedel (2023), § 857; Smid (2020), para. 12 and 13; Kemper (2021), para. 2; Lackmann and Racz (2021), para. 294.

[174] Smid (2020), para. 9; Kemper (2021), para. 4; Lackmann and Racz (2021), para. 294.

[175] Flockenhaus (2022b), para. 1; Smid (2020), para. 13; Schilken (2010b), para. 46.

[176] Koch (2020), p. 87; Badstuber (2019), pp. 251 and 252; Koch (2021), para. 35; Jacobs and Arndt (2019), p. 564.

[177] See for the following Jacobs and Arndt (2019), pp. 565 ff.

[178] Cf. meanwhile namely Arndt (2022), p. 38: 'Insofar it follows clearly from the wording 'other property *right*' that the Code of Civil Procedure only allows for the compulsory enforcement against

methodology according to which the wording of a provision forms the limit of lawful interpretation.[179] Furthermore, positions that are solely recognised by means of defensive claims are not sufficient for a legal assignment and cannot establish a (subjective) right. Irrespective of the question whether crypto-assets as well as central bank digital currency are to be regarded as property in the meaning of the constitutional understanding,[180] this does not lead to a direct application of Section 857 ZPO. Even for property per constitution, there are areas such as the legal nature, transfer, protection, pledging and attachment and insolvency, that require a regulation by the legislator due to their effects on a multitude of aspects relevant to fundamental rights.[181] It is up to the legislator to decide whether new legal provisions have to be created or whether existing provisions only have to be amended. Even if Article 14 (1), first sentence, GG creates an obligation for the legislator to enact particular provisions, the legislator would still be granted a certain margin of appreciation for implementing that obligation, cf. Article 14 (1), second sentence, GG. Hence, the teleological aspects mentioned are not to be considered when interpreting Section 857 ZPO, but rather when applying this provision by analogy as a judicial development of the law.

Application by Analogy

Thus, the following section enquires whether Section 857 ZPO can be applied by analogy.[182] This requires a gap in the specific part of the statutory system which appears to be unseen by the legislator. Moreover, the interests of the case directly covered by the provision and of the case not covered must be comparable. A statutory gap can be affirmed. It also appears to be unseen by the legislator. This can be derived from the purpose of § 857 ZPO as a catch-all provision for all assets that are not explicitly listed in the ZPO.[183] The provision intends to provide comprehensive access to the debtor's assets for the creditor.[184] In particular, one needs to bear in mind that the compulsory enforcement intends to satisfy the creditor, so that the aspects of accomplishing that aim in practice need to be considered as well.[185] It should not be possible for the debtor to evade the compulsory enforcement

---

legal but not *factual* positions of economic value.' (Translated from German; italic accentuation also in the original).

[179] Möllers (2021b), para. 36.

[180] On this see Ipsen (2021), para. 722 with further references.

[181] Papier and Shirvani (2022), para. 152. Other opinion is Arndt (2022), p. 181 who sees the judge obliged to create a subjective right for crypto-assets by means of interpreting the *lex lata* in accordance with the constitution.

[182] For the prerequisites of an application by analogy see Wank (2020), para. 110; see also BGH, 17.03.2022 – III ZR 79/21, juris para. 3 and Möllers (2021a), para. 117.

[183] Effer-Uhe (2018), p. 524; Ahrens (2021), para. 1; Lüke (2015a), para. 1; Lackmann and Racz (2021), para. 293; Paulus (2020), p. 140.

[184] Nober (2022), para. 2; Paulus (2020), p. 134; Gaul (2010b), para. 5; Koch (2020), pp. 87 and 88.

[185] Paulus (2020), p. 140.

by converting his assets into digital units that were still unknown at the time the ZPO came into force, i.e. by 'fleeing into the virtual currency'.[186]

However, the interest situation of the cases covered and not covered by the provision in question also have to be comparable. When comparing the attachment of central bank digital currency with the attachment of property rights covered by Section 857 ZPO, it can be argued that in both cases an asset is obtained which can be used to satisfy the creditor and which does not have to be similar to a claim because of Section 857 (2) ZPO.[187] Nonetheless, the comparability can also be doubted, namely when examining the legal consequences and the manner of the compulsory enforcement under Section 857 ZPO. For example, the compulsory enforcement is effected by the court's attachment order, Sections 857 (1), 829 (1) ZPO. In the absence of a third-party debtor, the court's prohibition to make a payment to the debtor (so-called *arrestatorium*) laid down in Section 829 (1), first sentence, ZPO is dispensable in the case of central bank digital currency as a bearer-instrument. However, in this case, the court's order to the debtor that he is to refrain from any disposition over the right (so-called *inhibitorium*) is a prerequisite for the attachment to be effective, Sections 857 (2), 829 (1), second sentence, ZPO. The legal effect of the attachment is that the creditor is entitled to a lien by attachment on the object of the compulsory enforcement, Section 804 (1) ZPO.[188] Due to crypto-assets lacking legal quality, critics of an application by analogy hint at the doctrinal fact that for encumbering something with a lien, a full right is required, which does not exist in the case of crypto-assets.[189] Thus, applying Section 857 (1) ZPO would lead to a legal consequence (a lien) that would not be possible under the material law of the German Civil Code.[190] Furthermore, it appears to be problematic whether the attachment of CBDC is feasible in practice. With the attachment, the debtor is no longer able to legally dispose of the attached object to the detriment of the creditor, Sections 857 (1), (2), 829 (1), second sentence, ZPO. From a factual point of view, it is then also not possible to dispose of an incorporeal object in a way that would be detrimental to the compulsory enforcement. This situation is likely to be different with central bank currency based on the distributed ledger technology. The legal *inhibitorium* exists.[191] However, the debtor can still factually trigger a transaction of the attached units with his private key, which is detrimental to the compulsory enforcement because of its irreversibility.[192] According to the current technical conception, the existence of a court-ordered *inhibitorium* would not be examined within the framework of the double-spending

[186] Koch (2020), p. 87; Effer-Uhe (2018), p. 516; Greier (2016), p. 256; Koch (2021), para. 35.

[187] Cf. Effer-Uhe (2018), p. 524; Koch (2020), p. 88.

[188] Brox and Walker (2018), para. 616.

[189] Jacobs and Arndt (2019), p. 567; Arndt (2022), p. 38.

[190] Arndt (2022), p. 38.

[191] As well as the protection under criminal law through the offence requiring an application for prosecution of Section 288 StGB, cf. Effer-Uhe (2018), p. 525.

[192] Cf. Paulus (2020), p. 140; Effer-Uhe (2018), p. 516.

control.[193] In order to safeguard the effectiveness of the compulsory enforcement, it is necessary to prevent the debtor from factually disposing of the CBDC. This can be done by obtaining the private key of the debtor.[194] For this purpose, the creditor has a claim for information against the debtor pursuant to Sections 857 (1), 836 (3), first sentence, ZPO.[195] If the latter refuses to cooperate, a search by the bailiff (Section 758 ZPO) or an affidavit in conjunction with coercive detention (Sections 857 (1), 836 (3), second and fourth sentences, 802g ff. ZPO) can take place.[196] Alternatively, it is proposed to restrict the debtor's possibility of disposing by transferring the attached units to the public key of an authority's account using Sections 808 ff. ZPO by analogy.[197] If the debtor is unwilling to cooperate, the bailiff can obtain knowledge of the private key by way of coercive detention at the request of the creditor as well, Sections 802a (2), first sentence, No. 2, 802c, 802f, 802g ZPO. However, since the coercive detention is limited to a duration of six months maximum, Section 802j (1) ZPO, a particularly persistent[198] debtor can still evade compulsory enforcement and continue to dispose of the central bank digital currency, impairing the purpose of compulsory enforcement. These technical characteristics of central bank currency based on the DLT tend to argue against the interest situations being comparable.[199]

In addition to these aforementioned aspects, another one seems to speak against an application of Section 857 ZPO by analogy. The attachment creates a lien, Section 804 (1) ZPO. If (im)movable property is subject to the attachment, this lien can be 'acquired away' in good faith based on the mixed private-public law theory,[200] Sections 136, 135 (2), 932, 936, 892 BGB.[201] That means that due to the good faith of the acquirer, the lien will expire. Such a possibility does not exist for central bank digital currency as a bearer-instrument because the Sections 929 ff. BGB are not applicable (see above). Hence, this is comparable to the attachment of claims, where, although the debtor disposes of the claim, a *bona-fide* acquisition free of encumbrances at the expense of the creditor is not possible.[202] However, the

[193] Cf. Sects. 2.2 and 2.4.

[194] Effer-Uhe (2018), pp. 516 and 517.

[195] Effer-Uhe (2018), p. 525.

[196] Badstuber (2019), p. 251; Jacobs and Arndt (2019), p. 569; Effer-Uhe (2018), p. 525.

[197] Jacobs and Arndt (2019), p. 570; Paulus (2020), p. 140; Effer-Uhe (2018), p. 525; Strauch and Handke (2020), para. 16 and 17.

[198] See for an example of particular persistent debtors the press release of the Administrative Court of Münster, 13.05.2022 – 7 K 1552/21, http://www.justiz.nrw.de/JM/Presse/presse_weitere/PresseOVG/archiv/2022_01_Archiv/17_06_2022_1/index.php. (Accessed 31.07.2018).

[199] Like here Strauch and Handke (2020), para. 21 who nonetheless recommend to file a request for applying Sections 808 ff. ZPO by analogy and Section 857 ZPO by analogy in parallel to avoid the liability of attorneys.

[200] For the legal debate on the legal nature of the lien by attachment see Brox and Walker (2018), para. 380 ff.

[201] BGH, 11.07.1962 – VIII ZR 125/61, WM 1962, 1177 (1177); Lüke (2015b), para. 54.

[202] Brox and Walker (2018), para. 618.

debtor can still effectively dispose of the central bank digital currency as a bearer-instrument despite the attachment. In a form in which the CBDC enjoys a higher degree of privacy or anonymity,[203] executing the existing lien by attachment against the new (de facto) owner of the digital units will face serious challenges.[204] This factually provokes what is legally not possible: the expiration of the lien as a result of a change of ownership. In addition, a lien that could be held against any acquirer of the central bank digital currency without regard to their good faith would enormously restrict the marketability of digital money and deter law-abiding citizens from making transactions.[205] *Effer-Uhe* therefore considers to abandon the *inhibitorium* directed at the debtor and hereby enables the acquirers of digital assets to acquire without encumbrances.[206] However, this practice would invalidate the requirement of Section 857 (2) ZPO, which is mandatory for the attachment of CBDC to be effective. Such a modified application of the provision by analogy would, like the transfer provisions (see above), be so dislodged from the wording of the statutory law that it seems to be upon the legislator to enact such a legal provision.[207]

As a result, the interests concerned are not comparable. Hence, Section 857 ZPO cannot be applied by analogy.

Interim Result

Thus, it must be noted that the compulsory enforcement for a monetary claim against central bank digital currency as a bearer-instrument is not admissible neither by directly applying Section 857 ZPO nor by analogy. As with the recording of the change of ownership, legally covering the compulsory enforcement under the ZPO is not possible.

Account-Based Central Bank Digital Currency

Since account-based CBDC is by its legal nature a claim for payout, the provisions for the attachment of monetary claims under Sections 829, 835 ZPO can be used for the compulsory enforcement. This is carried out by a court's attachment order and the realisation by a court's transfer order, whereby both orders are usually issued in the same document (so-called 'PfÜB').[208] The local court (Amtsgericht) is the court responsible for execution, Section 828 (1), (2) ZPO, while the senior judicial officer

[203] See Sect. 6.4.

[204] Effer-Uhe (2018), p. 523.

[205] Cf. Effer-Uhe (2018), pp. 517 and 523.

[206] Effer-Uhe (2018), p. 524.

[207] Like here in the result also Effer-Uhe (2018), p. 524.

[208] Brox and Walker (2018), para. 501.

is functionally responsible for executing, Section 20 (1) No. 16 RPflG.[209] Although the accounts held with banks are usually a current account,[210] the debtor's claim against the account provider for payout of the balance is not subject to the prohibition of attachment under Section 357 of the Commercial Code (HGB) and can therefore be seized independently as a monetary claim.[211] Due to the *arrestatorium* contained in the attachment order pursuant to Section 829 (1), first sentence, ZPO, the account provider may not execute any cash payments to the debtor or execute any transfer orders from the debtor when the claim for payout is seized.[212] For that to become effective, the court's attachment and transfer order has to be delivered to the account provider as third-party debtor, Sections 829 (3), 835 (3), first sentence, ZPO. The realisation then takes place either by transferring the claim for payout for collection, § 835 (1), first alternative, ZPO, which means that the debtor remains the legal owner of the claim, but the creditor acquires a right to confiscation, which he can then assert with a confiscation lawsuit against the account provider, Section 836 (1) ZPO.[213] Or the realisation takes place as a transfer in lieu of payment, Section 835 (1), second alternative, ZPO, which means that the creditor becomes the owner of the claim for payout, but also bears the insolvency risk of the account provider, Section 835 (2) ZPO.[214] However, in both cases of transfer the one-month moratorium on payment must be observed, Section 835 (3), second sentence, first half, ZPO.

Interim Conclusion

The compulsory enforcement for monetary claims against central bank digital currency as a bearer-instrument is not possible under the current legal situation. In contrast, the compulsory enforcement against account-based central bank digital currency is carried out as an attachment of claims pursuant to Sections 829, 835 ZPO.

[209] Rechtspflegergesetz in der Fassung der Bekanntmachung v. 14.04.2013 (BGBl. I p. 778, ber. 2014 I p. 46), zuletzt geändert am 22.02.2023 (BGBl. I p. 51) (Act on Senior Judicial Officers).

[210] Schmieder (2022a), para. 37.

[211] BGH, 30.06.1982 – VIII ZR 129/81, juris para. 24; BGH, 08.07.1982 – I ZR 148/80, juris para. 13.

[212] Brox and Walker (2018), para. 527.

[213] Cf. Brox and Walker (2018), para. 634 and 638 ff.

[214] Cf. Brox and Walker (2018), para. 635.

7.3.1.3 Compulsory Enforcement for Claims on Transfer of Central Bank Digital Currency

Finally, some cases have to be considered, in which the creditor demands the transfer of units of central bank digital currency. This may be the case after an erroneous transfer of the units. Legally disputed is solely the compulsory enforcement for a claim on the transfer of central bank digital currency as a bearer-instrument. Sections 883 ff. ZPO provide for the compulsory enforcement that serves to obtain the surrender of objects or to ensure that actions are taken or refrained from. Since the tokens are intangible, the only possibility for the compulsory enforcement is the enforcement that serves to ensure that actions are taken, pursuant to Sections 887, 888 ZPO. In this regard, it is disputed how to exactly legally classify crypto-assets. Their classification largely depends on whether the transfer of the crypto-assets can be classified as a fungible (Section 887 ZPO) or non-fungible (Section 888 ZPO) action. An action is fungible if it does not depend exclusively on the will of the debtor but can also be taken by a third party, cf. Sections 887 (1), 888 (1), first sentence, ZPO. To distinguish both forms of actions, the perspective of the creditor is decisive. In particular, one needs to enquire whether it is economically indifferent to the creditor who the person is that takes the action owed (then Section 887 ZPO) or whether it is important to the creditor that only the respective debtor takes the action (then Section 888 ZPO).[215]

Building on these foundations, some authors in the literature apply Section 887 ZPO because the creditor had no specific interest in particular units of the digital currency that is to be protected under law.[216] Rather, what mattered to him economically, was only a certain sum of units and this sum could also be transferred by third parties in place of and at the expense of the actual debtor.[217]

In contrast, the majority of the authors consider to apply Section 888 ZPO because for triggering the transaction it is necessary to know the private key and only the debtor has this knowledge.[218] However, a small number of authors considers to apply Section 887 ZPO in the case that the private key is stored on a physical device (for e.g. an offline wallet) because the creditor or the bailiff could then obtain the knowledge of the key by seizing the device according to Section 808 ZPO by analogy[219] or Section 883 ZPO by analogy[220] and thus trigger the transaction even without the debtor cooperating.

---

[215] BGH, 27.11.2008 – I ZB 46/08, juris para. 8; Regional Court of Appeal (OLG) Koblenz, 02.01.2014 – 3 W 648/13, juris para. 27; Lackmann (2022), para. 8; Gruber (2020), para. 9.

[216] Koch (2021), para. 36; Koch (2020), p. 88.

[217] Effer-Uhe (2018), p. 529.

[218] Kütük and Sorge (2014), p. 645; Paulus and Matzke (2018), p. 464; Bausch and Heetkamp (2018); Lackmann (2022), para. 10; Kaulartz (2016), p. 479; Badstuber (2019), p. 252.

[219] Paulus and Matzke (2018), p. 464.

[220] Jacobs and Arndt (2019), p. 572.

Eventually, applying the correct provision depends on the specific circumstances of the individual case.[221] Usually the creditor is only interested in the sum owed in total being satisfied, especially in the case of central bank digital currency. However, this can in principle be done by anyone at the expense of the actual debtor. Hence, in the majority of cases, the compulsory enforcement for a claim on the transfer of central bank digital currency as a bearer-instrument should be carried out in accordance with Section 887 ZPO.

7.3.2 Central Bank Digital Currency Under Insolvency Law

In addition to the compulsory enforcement for individual claims, the important aspect of the parties being insolvent also needs to be examined. On the one hand, it seems possible that the end-user becomes insolvent and his creditors demand access to the digital assets. On the other hand, it must also be taken into account that the financial intermediaries (credit institutions, wallet providers etc.) may fall victim to insolvency or over-indebtedness. In both cases, it is questionable whether central bank digital currency forms part of the insolvency estate and what rights third parties, for example the end-users, bear in the insolvency of the financial intermediaries. In the digital world cross-border legal cases are much more common. However, the European insolvency law only partly provides for applicable provisions. Rather, according to Article 7 (1) of the Insolvency Regulation,[222] the law applicable to insolvency proceedings and their effects shall be that of the Member State within the territory of which such proceedings are opened. For the following section, the centre of the debtor's main interests is assumed to be in German territory, so that the provisions of the German Insolvency Code (InsO) are applicable, cf. Article 3 (1) Insolvency Regulation.

7.3.2.1 Insolvency Estate

This first raises the question of whether central bank digital currency forms part of the insolvency estate and can thus be used to satisfy the insolvency creditors, cf. Article 7 (2) lit. b Insolvency Regulation.

---

[221] Like here also Strauch and Handke (2020), para. 25.

[222] Regulation (EU) 2015/848 of the European Parliament and of the Council of 20 May 2015 on insolvency proceedings (5 June 2015) OJ L 141/19, lastly amended by Regulation (EU) 2021/2260 (20 December 2021) OJ L 455/4.

Abstract Scale

Pursuant to Section 35 (1) InsO, the insolvency estate is defined as all assets owned by the debtor on the date the proceedings were opened and those acquired during the proceedings. In addition to Section 35 InsO, Sections 36 and 47 InsO must also be consulted when determining the insolvency estate.[223] The former provision forms the principle and both latter provisions specify exceptions to it, so that in terms of legal methodology there is a rule-exception relationship between these three provisions.[224] Pursuant to Section 36 (1), first sentence, InsO, objects not subject to execution do not form part of the insolvency estate. Pursuant to Section 47, first sentence, InsO, anyone entitled to claim the separation of an object from the insolvency estate under a right *in rem* or *in personam* is not an insolvency creditor. This definition of the insolvency estate raises two issues. It is questionable how the terms 'assets' and 'owned' in Section 35 (1) InsO are to be interpreted.

For defining the concept of assets, there are essentially two opposing views: The view based on considerations connected to the compulsory enforcement and the view based on economic considerations. The first view defines the term 'assets' within the meaning of Section 35 (1) InsO as the entire assets of the debtor that can be seized in the (individual) compulsory enforcement proceedings.[225] This covers all rights and objects of pecuniary value which are owned by the debtor and which the compulsory enforcement can be directed against.[226] In contrast, according to the economic view, 'assets' are all monetary goods of a person, i.e. all assets in the economic sense of the debtor are included.[227]

When defining the concept of assets, it must be borne in mind that insolvency law is a special part of civil law. In this context, the term 'assets' is frequently used without having a uniform definition. Therefore, the term must be interpreted and applied depending on the context and the specific meaning and purpose of its field of application. Insolvency law aims at satisfying the interests of creditors by giving them joint access to the debtor's assets.[228] Thus, the creditors are to be provided with an object that is liable for the debtor's obligations.[229] This requires an economic value. This value must also be seizable (liable) in the specific case. Hence, in principle any economic value of the debtor is covered. Only in a second step it is then to be examined whether this value is seizable and in the case it is not, the value

---

[223] Graf-Schlicker and Kexel (2010), para. 1; Schumacher (2011), para. 1; Imberger (2011), para. 2.

[224] Hirte and Praß (2019), para. 11; Wimmer (2020), para. 1.

[225] Häsemeyer (2007), para. 9.06; Weis (2001), para. 62; Arndt (2022), pp. 41 and 42; Hess (2013), para. 76; Ries (2020), para. 1; Büteröwe (2016), para. 5.

[226] Hirte and Praß (2019), para. 7.

[227] OLG Düsseldorf, 10.07.2013 – I-15 U 28/12, juris para. 65; Graf-Schlicker and Kexel (2010), para. 7; Kirchner (2023), para. 5; Paulus and Berg (2019), p. 2135; Peukert (2011), p. 107.

[228] Cf. German parliamentary paper 12/2443, p. 83.

[229] Hirte and Praß (2019), para. 6; Kirchner (2023), para. 4a.

needs to be sorted out of the insolvency estate.[230] This corresponds best to the systematic structure of Sections 35 (1), 36 (1), first sentence, InsO.[231] The fact that the assignment of an object to the insolvency estate is incidental to its seizability also allows for exceptions that ground on its meaning and purpose. As can be seen from the provisions listed in Section 36 (1), second sentence, InsO that protect the debtor in certain cases of compulsory enforcement, the 'primacy of enforceability'[232] serves welfare state considerations.[233] Therefore, if the insolvency debtor lacks social protection in the individual case, the principle that any economic value forms part of the insolvency estate remains despite a possible lack of seizability.

The term 'owned' in Section 35 (1) InsO expresses that the liable economic value must be assigned to the insolvency debtor.[234] For that assignment it is questionable whether a factual assignment is sufficient. The predominant view rejects this and requires a legal assignment of the value to the debtor.[235] This reasoning is also consistent in view of Section 47, first sentence, InsO because it removes objects from the insolvency estate whose legal owner is not the debtor.[236]

Application to Central Bank Digital Currency

In view of this scale, it must be enquired whether central bank digital currency in its two alternative manifestations has an economic value that can be seized and that is legally assigned to the insolvency debtor.

There is no doubt about the economic value of both account-based central bank digital currency and the one as a bearer-instrument as a form of money. Account-based CBDC is also seizable as a monetary claim and assigned to the account holder (see above). Therefore, it forms part of the insolvency estate.

For CBDC as a bearer-instrument, the classification is more complex. Regarding comparable crypto-assets, it is predominantly assumed that those are part of the insolvency estate while at the same time attributing legal quality to them.[237] However, this cannot be applied in the same way to central bank digital currency as a bearer-instrument.

First, it must be considered that, according to the opinion represented here, this manifestation of CBDC is not fully seizable (see above). However, in principle, one

[230] Hirte and Praß (2019), para. 13.

[231] Cf. Arndt (2022), pp. 42 and 43.

[232] Skauradszun (2021b), p. 2611.

[233] Weis (2001), para. 63; Schumacher (2011), para. 1; Arndt (2022), p. 44.

[234] Paulus and Berg (2019), p. 2134.

[235] German parliamentary paper 12/2443, p. 124; Hirte and Praß (2019), para. 25.

[236] Neuner (2020d), para. 19.

[237] Kütük and Sorge (2014), p. 645; Effer-Uhe (2018), p. 530; Peters (2019), para. 407; Strauch and Handke (2020), para. 39; Skauradszun (2021b), p. 2614; Kirchner (2023), para. 37a; d'Avoine and Hamacher (2022), p. 9.

can circumvent the lack of seizability in two ways. On the one hand, the central bank digital currency is object of the compulsory enforcement at least partially (Sections 887, 888. ZPO). *Arndt* counters that this is not sufficient to assign CBDC to the insolvency estate because including actions into the insolvency proceedings would lead to a repayment of debts through forced labour.[238] However, his view cannot be followed in this sweeping manner because with the provision of Section 888 ZPO the legislator has precisely provided for the 'forced labour for debt redemption' postulated by *Arndt* in the individual compulsory enforcement. Why this legislator's decision should apply to an individual creditor, but not to a majority of creditors, is not quite convincing. Moreover, as explained, surrendering units of CBDC is often a fungible act that does not require any personal 'forced labour' on the part of the debtor. Thus, CBDC being seizable under Sections 887, 888 ZPO perhaps seems to be sufficient.[239] On the other hand, the problem of CBDC being seizable in individual cases only partially could possibly also be solved by using the above-mentioned exception to the assumption that assets need to be seizable in order to form part of the insolvency estate. If, for example, the debtor converts his residual assets into digital assets shortly before insolvency in order to avoid the compulsory enforcement, he appears to be less in need of protection. Hence, one could consider to not apply the rule that the assignment of an object to the insolvency estate is incidental to its seizability, if needed with the application of the provisions mentioned in Section 36 (1), second sentence, InsO by analogy.

Secondly, there is no subjective right that is correlated to central bank digital currency as a bearer-instrument. As a consequence, the debtor cannot acquire the legal ownership necessary for an assignment. However, it seems worth to consider that a purely factual or technical based assignment is preferable to a legal assignment, bearing in mind the purpose of the insolvency law.[240] In this way, one could achieve the most comprehensive and equal satisfaction of creditors possible.[241] For this, it is mainly a question whether an economic value exists.[242] If one were to insist on the assets being assigned by law, the debtor could 'digitise' or 'tokenise' his assets and, in view of the existing legal uncertainties, evade the compulsory enforcement even though he possesses a considerable economic value. This appears to be unjustified in terms of equity. The debtor would then be granted the opportunity to 'escape into the digital world'. However, it must be considered that due to the lack of legal quality of the central bank digital currency, there could be third parties 'whose' tokens are in the factual possession of the debtor, for example as a result of an erroneous transfer. Those third parties could not invoke a right to separation and would therefore have to tolerate a realisation of 'their' economic values with the help

[238] Arndt (2022), p. 42 fn. 95.

[239] Like here Kütük and Sorge (2014), p. 645; Effer-Uhe (2018), p. 530.

[240] Cf. Arndt (2022), p. 44.

[241] Henckel (2004), para. 2.

[242] Regional Court of Appeal (OLG) Düsseldorf, 10.07.2013 – I-15 U 28/12, juris para. 66; Amey (2019), p. 17.

of the state, de facto without rights. However, this in turn appears to be contradictory as well. Economic transactions precisely stay alive via the exchange of monetary goods, also in digital form, and the legislator balances this with the provisions of Sections 47 ff. InsO. Therefore, in order to avoid perceived 'injustices' it would be necessary to weigh the interests of the creditors against the need for protection of the third parties. If one were to prefer a purely factual assignment to an assignment by law and if central bank digital currency as a bearer-instrument were thus to form part of the insolvency estate, one would have to proceed generously at the level of granting rights to separation as well. However, when interpreting strictly based on the applicable law and respecting the will of the legislator,[243] central bank digital currency as a bearer-instrument in principle does not form part of the insolvency estate because it is not assigned to its holder by law. Nonetheless, this result can also be acceptable in terms of legal policy in order to increase the pressure on the legislator to act.

Interim Result

According to an interpretation based on the applicable law, the account-based central bank digital currency but not the bearer-instrument forms part of the insolvency estate. This could only be addressed by an interpretation that is more strongly oriented towards the intention of satisfying the creditors. In addition, it should be pointed out that perhaps the severest problem to overcome in practice is that the trustee in insolvency must in any case be aware of the fact whether the debtor possesses such digital assets.[244] This asymmetrical distribution of information can only be overcome by the debtor's duty to provide information, which can be enforced by imprisonment, Sections 97 (1), (2), 98 (2) No. 1 InsO.[245] Furthermore, it is likely that the debtor is more willing to disclose if he is pointed at further disadvantageous consequences, such as the refusal of the residual debt discharge under Sections 300 (3), 290 (1) No. 5 InsO and a possible criminal liability under Section 283 (1) No. 1, 8 StGB.[246]

7.3.2.2 Third Party's Rights to Separation

In insolvency proceedings it always needs to be considered that the assets found and taken possession of by the trustee in insolvency at the debtor's premises (Section 148

[243] Cf. German parliamentary paper 12/2443, p. 124. See for critical opinions on interpreting law according to the will of the historical legislator Larenz and Canaris (1995), pp. 149 ff.; Wank (2017), pp. 31 ff.; Herzberg (2005), p. 4.

[244] Chesley and Fernando (2019), 4.1; d'Avoine and Hamacher (2022), p. 9.

[245] Kütük and Sorge (2014), p. 646.

[246] d'Avoine and Hamacher (2022), p. 11.

(1) InsO) actually belong to a third party, cf. Article 8 (1), (2) lit. c Insolvency Regulation. These must then be separated (Sections 47, 48 InsO) or the third party must be satisfied separately (Sections 49 ff. InsO).

Account-Based Central Bank Digital Currency

For example, in the case of the account-based central bank digital currency, the rights of third parties could be affected in the event of the insolvency of a financial intermediary, such as the account provider. However, since account-based central bank digital currency is by its legal nature not a legal position *in rem*, its holder is not entitled to a right to separation or separate satisfaction.[247] Rather, the holder is an ordinary creditor in insolvency and thus is referred to a proportional satisfaction, Section 38 InsO. This result would only differ if the account is intended to solely receive funds which are subject to a fiduciary[248] commitment.[249]

Central Bank Digital Currency as a Bearer-Instrument

If the law is interpreted in a way that central bank digital currency as a bearer-instrument forms part of the insolvency estate, it is also conceivable that the CBDC is 'owned' by a third party. Admittedly, since the bearer-based CBDC lacks legal quality, the third party neither bears a right to separation nor a right to separate satisfaction. Nevertheless, for crypto-assets there are some authors who want to grant a right to separation derived from Section 47, first sentence, InsO.[250] The reason given is that the third party is in need of protection[251] and that the token is similar to *res* due to its individuality by technical design.[252]

Pursuant to Section 47, first sentence, InsO, anyone entitled to claim the separation of an object from the insolvency estate under a right *in rem* or *in personam* is not an insolvency creditor. This provision is worded more openly, as it does not explicitly presuppose an absolute right.[253] Admittedly, if one were to broadly interpret the objects covered by the insolvency estate, then the need for protection speaks in favour of granting a right to separation or separate satisfaction. However, the aforementioned provision itself does not establish a claim or right on its own, but

[247] Cf. Regional Court of Appeal (OLG) Köln, 05.11.2008 – 2 U 16/08, juris para. 31.

[248] For a definition of the term see Bäuerle (2022), para. 67.

[249] BGH, 24.06.2003 – IX ZR 120/02, juris para. 10; Haneke (2023), para. 95. For the requirements of a fiduciary commitment see BGH, 24.06.2003 – IX ZR 75/01, juris para. 17.

[250] Effer-Uhe (2018), p. 530; Linardatos (2020), p. 207. Other opinion are Kütük and Sorge (2014), p. 645.

[251] Strauch and Handke (2020), para. 45.

[252] Linardatos (2020), p. 192.

[253] Cf. German parliamentary paper 12/2443, p. 124.

requires an existing right of the third party and only allows the third party to assert this right contrary to the usual blocking effect of the insolvency proceedings.[254] Therefore, it must be distinguished according to the reason for which the central bank digital currency as a bearer-instrument 'owned' by the third party has reached the debtor. If this is due to an erroneous transaction, the third party is only entitled to a claim for restitution under the law of enrichment, which does not entitle to separation.[255] Although it might be similar to *res*, there is no right *in rem*, so that no right to separation can be established. However, if the debtor possesses the digital units because of a contract of agency (Section 662, 675 BGB), the claim for restitution under Section 667, first alternative, BGB (in conjunction with Section 675 (1) BGB) grants a right to separation to the third party irrespective of the legal nature.[256]

7.3.2.3 Conclusion

To conclude, the account-based central bank digital currency is subject to the insolvency estate. In the event of the insolvency of the account provider the holder is not entitled to any rights to separation or separate satisfaction, but is rather to be treated as a normal creditor in insolvency. In contrast, central bank digital currency as a bearer-instrument is generally not part of the insolvency estate. In the case of an assignment to the insolvency estate on the basis of an extensive interpretation of the statutory law and in the event of the insolvency of a third party, the holder only bears a right to separation if the third party received the CBDC as part of a contract of agency.

7.3.3 Central Bank Digital Currency in the Deposit Business

Last but not least, as a special question, the following section will enquire the effects of central bank digital currency on the 'backbone of the financial economy',[257] the very important deposit business of the commercial banks.

---

[254] Brinkmann (2019), para. 3.

[255] Cf. BGH, 09.01.2018 – XI ZR 17/15, juris para. 22.

[256] Haneke (2023), para. 57; Brinkmann (2019), para. 62a; Strauch and Handke (2020), para. 46.

[257] Servatius (2020), para. 2.

7.3.3.1 Terminology

In the absence of a uniform definition of the term across all legal areas, it was long disputed what is meant by the term 'deposit-taking business'.[258] Today there is agreement that deposits are liabilities of credit institutions resulting from the acceptance of customer funds.[259] Due to their balance sheet nature as liabilities, deposits are part of the banks' liability business for refinancing their lending business (e.g. granting loans).[260] Depending on the maturity of the customer's repayment claim, there are three different types of deposits. The demand deposits (giro deposit), which are due immediately at the customer's request, and the time and savings deposits, which have a term or notice periods.[261]

7.3.3.2 Central Bank Digital Currency as Deposits

Next, it is questionable whether central bank digital currency can also be accepted as a deposit by the commercial banks. This largely depends on the legal nature of the deposits.[262] For this classification, the predominant view also differentiates according to the maturity of the claim for restitution:[263] giro deposits due immediately are to be seen as an irregular safekeeping contract ('*depositum irregulare*') according to Section 700 BGB, cf. Sections 700 (1), third sentence, 695, first sentence, BGB. Time and savings deposits qualify as loans, cf. Sections 488 (3), 608 (1) BGB. Since both the account-based central bank digital currency and the bearer-instrument are money in the legal sense, the end-user can make them available to the commercial banks in the longer term in the form of time and savings deposits, subject to the technical possibilities of acceptance by the commercial bank, cf. Section 488 (1) BGB.

In contrast, the mere short-term acceptance of central bank digital currency is legally more complex. Due to the short-term nature, this form of acceptance is a *depositum irregulare* according to Section 700 BGB. Pursuant to Section 700 (1), first sentence, BGB, if fungible things are deposited in such a way that ownership is to pass to the depositary and the depositary is to be obliged to return things of the same type, quality and quantity, then in the case of money the provisions on loan

---

[258] For an overview to the legal debate see Langner (2022a), para. 7 ff.

[259] Cf. Article 3 (1) No. i) of the Council Regulation (EC) No 2531/98 of 23 November 1998 concerning the application of minimum reserves by the European Central Bank (27 November 1998) *OJ L 318/1*; Section 1 (1), second sentence, No. 1 KWG; Cf. case C-366/97 *Romanelli* ECLI: EU:C:1999:71, para. 13; Fischer and Boegl (2022), para. 22; Servatius (2020), para. 1.

[260] Servatius (2020), para. 1; Langner (2022a), para. 1.

[261] Fischer and Boegl (2022), para. 22; Langner (2022b), para. 5, 7; Keßler (2020), para. 10, 16.

[262] Cf. Bossu et al. (2020), p. 38 no. 83.

[263] For this and the following see BGH, 24.03.2009 – XI ZR 191/08, juris para. 11; BGH, 23.06.1965 – III ZR 251/63, juris para. 31; Canaris (1981), para. 1164 and 1165; Henssler (2023), para. 16.

contracts apply, and in the case of other things the provisions on contracts for the loan of things apply. Both, the object of the contract, i.e. a fungible object, as well as the obligation to pass the ownership to the depositary raise legal concerns.

The object of the contract proves to be problematic because both forms of central bank digital currency are no physical objects within the meaning of Section 90 BGB. It could also be derived from a ruling of the Federal Supreme Court of Justice (BGH) that an irregular safekeeping contract does not cover scriptural money and central bank digital currency as a bearer-instrument. In this ruling, the BGH states that the payout of cash in a bank branch is only the fulfilment of the redemption obligation according to Sections 700 (1), third sentence, 695 BGB.[264] Although the BGH does not comment on this explicitly, it could be concluded from the ruling that as an *actus contrarius* only depositing cash, but not depositing scriptural money is covered by Section 700 BGB. However, this seems inconsistent insofar as the BGH also classifies the giro deposit itself as an irregular safekeeping contract. In modern times this giro deposit is rarely increased by depositing cash. In the majority of cases, due to wage and salary payments, scriptural money is transferred.[265] However, if the legal practice also covers the transfer of scriptural money as a deposit intake, then Section 700 BGB needs to be applied to intangible forms of money at least by analogy.[266] Therefore, the lack of embodiment of the two forms of central bank digital currency does not prevent them from being accepted as deposits.

At most, the obligation to pass the ownership to the depositary could be problematic. This specific obligation serves to distinguish the contract from the regular safekeeping contract pursuant to Section 688 BGB, where only the possession needs to be transferred.[267] This duty to pass ownership to the depositary proves impossible to fulfil, especially with regard to central bank digital currency as a bearer-instrument as intangible good. However, the irregular safekeeping contract does not require the pass on of ownership to be effective because the pass on being effective is already the fulfilment of the contractual obligation.[268] As a contractual obligation, it is subject to the parties' private autonomous freedom of contract. As a consequence, they could waive the obligation to pass on ownership and instead, similar to Section 688 BGB, allow the transfer of the factual power of disposal over the token to the depositary. However, applying Section 688 BGB by analogy does not seem necessary in view of the interests at stake because CBDC is still money that is to be returned to the end-user only in terms of its amount, but not in its specific composition.

---

[264] BGH, 30.11.1993 – XI ZR 80/93, juris para. 16.

[265] Cf. Servatius (2020), para. 2.

[266] Gehrlein (2023), para. 2; Schur (2012), para. 7, 10; Fehrenbacher (2021), para. 3; Servatius (2020), para. 132.

[267] Zetzsche (2020), para. 1; Schur (2012), para. 1.

[268] Cf. Schur (2012), para. 11; Bieder (2020), para. 15 and 16 with further references to the outdated contrary opinion.

Thus, it can be stated that central bank digital currency in both forms can be a suitable object of the deposit business by credit institutions.

7.3.3.3 Aspects of Minimum Reserves Policy

In addition to these civil law aspects, monetary policy aspects also play a role in the deposit business. As an instrument of monetary policy, this refers to the ECB's minimum reserve policy based on Article 127 (2), first indent, TFEU in conjunction with Article 19.1 ESCB Statute. This policy requires credit institutions to hold a certain minimum amount denominated in euro on their accounts with the central banks as deposits, Article 3 (1) lit. b MRR-Regulation.[269] This so-called minimum reserve requirement is the product of the minimum reserve base and the minimum reserve ratio. The minimum reserve base is calculated, among other things, from the amount of deposits of a credit institution minus an allowance of EUR 100.000, Article 5 (1) lit. a, Article 6 (2) MRR-Regulation. The minimum reserve ratio is 0% for deposits with a term of more than 2 years, otherwise the ratio is 1%, Article 6 (1) MRR-Regulation. The minimum reserves calculated in this way are remunerated by the central banks over the minimum reserve period, Article 9 MRR-Regulation. The interest rate for this is 3.25% in June 2023, whereas both the shortfall and the excess of the target are sanctioned with a penalty interest rate (6.50% of the shortfall for the shortfall and 0.00% for the excess).[270] The minimum reserve policy ensures a steady demand for the money supplied by central banks and thus ultimately controls the supply with central bank money.[271] In doing so, the ECB should be sufficiently flexible to appropriately carry out the control of the money supply even under newly developed payment methods. This postulate of flexibility for new payment methods is derived from recital 5 of the MRR-Regulation 1998.[272] Admittedly, only electronic money is mentioned there as an example. However, the underlying idea can also be applied to digital money and could still be considered today for the interpretation and the application of the minimum reserve policy. It is true that the MRR-Regulation 1998 has been replaced by numerous MRR-Regulations so far.[273] Nonetheless, the replacements have always been

---

[269] Regulation (EU) 2021/378 of the European Central Bank of 22 January 2021 on the application of minimum reserve requirements (ECB/2021/1) (3 March 2021) *OJ L 73/1*.

[270] Charts provided by the Bundesbank on interest rates for minimum reserves for the year 2023, https://www.bundesbank.de/de/aufgaben/geldpolitik/mindestreserven/zinssaetze-und-reservesaetze/zinssaetze-und-reservesaetze-602548#tar-1.

[271] See for more details Ohler (2021), pp. 90 ff.

[272] Council Regulation (EC) No 2531/98 of 23 November 1998 concerning the application of minimum reserves by the European Central Bank (27 November 1998) *OJ L 318/1*.

[273] Regulation (EC) No 2818/98 of the European Central Bank of 1 December 1998 on the application of minimum reserve requirements (ECB/1998/15) (30 December 1998) OJ L 356/1; Regulation (EC) No 1745/2003 of the European Central Bank of 12 September 2003 on the application of minimum reserves (ECB/2003/9) (2 October 2003) *OJ L 250/10*; Regulation

made for the reasons of clarity and transparency.[274] If the minimum reserve policy should be used as an effective instrument for the management of the money supply in the future, central bank digital currency must be permitted as eligible deposits at credit institutions in both forms. Furthermore, the fulfilment of the minimum reserve requirement by the credit institutions vis-à-vis the central bank can also take place through the use of central bank digital currency. The wording of Article 3 (1) lit. b MRR-Regulation is more open in this respect, as it only requires that the minimum reserves be held on reserve accounts denominated in euro. Therefore, it appears permissible for credit institutions to accept central bank digital currency as a deposit and to use this in turn as a deposit on the minimum reserve accounts held with the central banks.

7.4 European Harmonisation

The previous sections have shown that classifying central bank digital currency as a bearer-instrument under private law systems in the Member States is arduous and controversial. It often needs an interpretation of the statutory law which exceeds the boundaries set by the legal doctrine for the judicial interpretation and development of the law. Central bank digital currency cannot be redeemed for gold because the gold coverage of the currency was abolished. Just like for fiat currency, this means that CBDC lacks any intrinsic value and could thus be not considered as a value itself beside the aspect that it is money. However, since the volume of CBDC in circulation will be regulated strongly,[275] this fundamental scarcity will lead to a certain economic value that does not allow for a lawless situation and requires a concrete (sovereign) assignment of goods.[276] This has not yet been provided for in the private law systems of the Member States. This circumstance will lead to legal uncertainties when using the central bank digital currency and can be detrimental to the objectives for which it shall be established.[277] Hence, the following section will enquire a regulatory approach on the European level which could solve the legal uncertainties connected to CBDC as a bearer-instrument in a unifying and harmonising manner.[278]

(EU) 2021/378 of the European Central Bank of 22 January 2021 on the application of minimum reserve requirements (ECB/2021/1) (3 March 2021) *OJ L 73/1*.

[274] Recital 1 of the Regulation (EC) No 1745/2003 and recital 1 of the Regulation (EU) 2021/378.

[275] For e.g. for reasons of financial stability, see Chap. 8.

[276] Cf. similarly Eccher (2010b), para. 3.

[277] Similar also Muscheler and Hunt (2021), p. 2 fn. 3; Grünewald (2022), p. 136.

[278] Other opinion is Skauradszun (2021a), pp. 379 ff. who prefers the national legislator to act.

7.4.1 Legal Basis of Competence

To do so, it must be clarified whether the EU co-legislators can act on the basis of Article 133 TFEU to harmonize the civil law status of CBDC. If this provision is understood to provide for a comprehensive legislative power under monetary law,[279] the question arises as to what extent provisions on civil law can also be set by the Union. In this respect, there are different views in the literature.

With reference to the wording of the predecessor provisions (Article 109 l (4), third sentence, TEC-Maastricht and Article 123 (4), third sentence, TEC-Nice), some authors argue that civil law provisions are not covered by the legislative competence under Article 133 TFEU.[280] Other authors refer to the wording of Article 133 TFEU, which is broader than that of the predecessor provisions, and argue that civil law areas are covered also.[281] As a mediating view, the predominant voices in the literature allow civil law regulations on the basis of Article 133 TFEU in the case that these are linked to monetary law.[282]

The latter view is to be agreed with because the wording 'measures necessary for the use (. . .)' does not imply a restriction to or an exclusion of a certain area of law. This is also consistent with the ECJ case-law.[283] In addition, as shown above, questions of civil law are closely linked to the usability of the currency in economic and legal transactions.[284] This is crucial for settling pecuniary obligations. Considering what has been stated so far, Union law provisions on the general treatment of intangible goods under civil law are likely to be inadmissible. In contrast, there is a sufficient connection to monetary law in the case of provisions specifically related to central bank digital currency as a bearer-instrument. In view of the far-reaching exclusion of the bearer-instrument form from legal and economic transactions in the Member States set out above, harmonising civil law provisions also appears necessary for the use of the euro as a single currency.

Hence, Article 133 TFEU represents a suitable basis of competence for harmonising the civil law with regard to central bank digital currency as a bearer-instrument.

---

[279] Khan and Richter (2023), para. 1; Selmayr (2015), para. 1.

[280] Sandrock (1997), p. 11; Sixt (1997), p. 435; Hahn and Häde (2010), para. 24; Becker (2022), para. 1.

[281] Selmayr (2015), para. 7 and fn. 31; Wutscher (2019), para. 2.

[282] Manger-Nestler (2017), para. 3; Kempen (2018), para. 2; Schefold (1996), p. 5; Schefold (1999), p. 277; Häde (2022), para. 2.

[283] See joined cases 422/19 and 423/19 *Hessischer Rundfunk* ECLI:EU:C:2021:63, para. 56.

[284] Cf. Schefold (1999), p. 272.

7.4.2 *Legal Limits of Exercising European Union's Competence*

If the Union bears the regulatory competence as aforementioned, it must respect the limits and rules imposed by the Treaties. One such rule on the exercise of competence to be respected by the Union is Article 345 TFEU.[285] According to this provision, the Treaties shall in no way prejudice the rules in Member States governing the system of property ownership. If Union provisions are to be made on the legal nature, the transfer and the treatment in the compulsory enforcement, the sphere of the Member States' property regimes could be affected. This depends on the interpretation of the term 'system of property ownership'. Numerous positions are advocated in this regard.[286]

On the one hand, it is assumed that Article 345 TFEU is a solution to the conflict of competences in favour of the Member States in the case of assigning property to the private or public sector as part of the general economic policy.[287] Therefore, the system of property ownership was a central means of shaping the economic policy of the Member States.[288] This narrow interpretation of the term could be justified by the genesis of the provision, which was based on the concern that the European Community could prevent national expropriation or privatisation efforts.[289] According to this view, there would be no conflict of competence when regulating fundamental civil law issues of the digital euro as a bearer-instrument.

On the other hand, positions in the literature neglect the reasons of origin and rather favour a broader interpretation of the term. Thus, the term 'system of property ownership' is to be understood as the entire provisions of Member States whose object is the institution of property.[290] This includes its exercise and use, the restrictions within the framework of its social responsibility, the expropriation and related rights as well as questions of allocation in the sense of private or public property.[291] According to this view, the main focus should be on the provisions on property that are found in the respective national constitutions.[292] Pursuant to the constitutional understanding of property in Germany, all assets assigned to the individual by the legal system with exclusive rights are protected as property.[293] Thus, the understanding of constitutional law is not restricted to the rules on property ownership under parliamentary law; rather, other subjective rights of value form part

[285] Manger-Nestler (2021), p. 8; Krajewski (2017), para. 11 with further references.

[286] For an overview to the legal debate see Kingreen (2022), para. 9 and Kühling (2018), para. 10 and 11 each with further references.

[287] Kingreen (2022), para. 10.

[288] Kühling (2018), para. 2.

[289] Bär-Bouyssière (2015), para. 1; Kühling (2018), para. 13.

[290] Bär-Bouyssière (2015), para. 6; Vedder (2018), para. 2; Wernicke (2023), para. 12.

[291] Vedder (2018), para. 2; Bär-Bouyssière (2015), para. 6; Khan (2023), para. 1.

[292] Wernicke (2023), para. 12 and 13; Krajewski (2017), para. 8.

[293] BVerfG, 31.03.1998 – 2 BvR 1877/97, juris para. 88.

of the competences of the Member States as well.[294] This view uses mainly the wording of Article 345 TFEU to justify its opinion.[295]

It is not necessary here to comment on whether Article 345 TFEU should be interpreted restrictively or rather broadly. The provisions to be made shall establish a subjective right to central bank digital currency as a bearer-instrument and regulate its usability in legal relations. This could indeed collide with the broad interpretation of the term in Article 345 TFEU with regard to the assignment of property. The respective literature on that cites ECJ case-law to justify the Member States' competences to generally assign property to owners. However, the cited case-law did not concern the assignment of factual assets to a holder in order to establish a legal position, but rather concerned state-organised expropriations in the course of economic policy measures.[296] Furthermore, according to the broad interpretation of the term, the Member States' competence for the system of property ownerships requires first of all the existence of property.[297] Since a subjective right to central bank digital currency as a bearer-instrument does not yet exists in the legal systems of the Member States (see above), the decisive question is whether the competence of the Member States also includes the power to decide independently on whether a certain object should be endowed with subjective exclusive rights or not. Under ECJ case-law on industrial property rights, this has led advocates of the broad conception to distinguish between the existence and the exercise of property. The former should be reserved exclusively for the Member States, while the latter should be subject to EU law.[298] However, the ECJ has clarified its position on this. It states: 'Thus, far from endorsing the argument that rules concerning the very existence of industrial property rights fall within the sole jurisdiction of the national legislature, the Court was anticipating the unification of patent provisions or harmonization of the relevant national legislation'.[299] It continues and states that '(...) neither Article 222 [= Article 345 TFEU] nor Article 36 of the Treaty reserves a power to regulate substantive patent law to the national legislature, to the exclusion of any Community action in the matter'.[300] With reference to later ECJ case-law, some argue that the cited case-law does not necessarily argues against a view that grants exclusive competence to the Member States linked to the existence of property.[301] In the cited decision, the ECJ states that 'that provision [Article 345 TFEU] merely

[294] Hatje (2009), p. 814 with reference to case C-10/89 *CNL-SUCAL/HAG* ECLI:EU:C:1990:359, para. 12; Bär-Bouyssière (2015), para. 7.

[295] Pießkalla (2008), p. 201; Krajewski (2017), para. 8; Kühling (2018), para. 13.

[296] Case C-309/96 *Annibaldi* ECLI:EU:C:1997: 631, para. 23.

[297] Schmidt-Preuß (2006), p. 475.

[298] Kühling (2018), para. 6 with reference to case C-24/67 *Parke-Davis* ECLI:EU:C:1968:11, p. 111; Wernicke (2023), para. 15 with reference to joined cases C-56/64 and C-58/64 *Grundig/ Consten* ECLI:EU:C:1966:41, para. 394 and joined cases C-92/92 and C-326/92 *Phil Collins* ECLI: EU:C:1993:847, para. 19, 22.

[299] Case C-350/92 *Spain/Council* ECLI:EU:C:1995:237, para. 19.

[300] Case C-350/92 *Spain/Council* ECLI:EU:C:1995:237, para. 22 (comments added).

[301] Schmidt-Preuß (2006), p. 475.

recognises the power of Member States to define the rules governing the system of property ownership and does not exclude any influence whatever of Community law on the exercise of national property rights'.[302] Thus, in this ruling the ECJ takes up the previous distinction between the existence and exercise of property rights. However, it does not explicitly state, abandoning its previously cited judgments, that the former is the exclusive prerogative of the Member States. Rather, it solely expresses that the exercise of property rights must in any case respect Union law requirements.

In view of these case-law, Article 345 TFEU does not preclude provisions enacted by the Union that establish subjective exclusive rights to property that does not yet exist under Member State law, at least if the Union has a competence to do so under the EU Treaties. As explained above, such a competence exists in the form of Article 133 TFEU.

7.4.3 Form of Legal Act

Last but not least, it must be considered which of the available legal acts the Union could use. According to Article 133, first sentence, TFEU, the European Parliament and the Council, acting in accordance with the ordinary legislative procedure, shall lay down the measures necessary for the use of the euro as the single currency. Pursuant to Article 289 (1), first sentence, TFEU, the ordinary legislative procedure shall consist in the joint adoption by the European Parliament and the Council of a regulation, directive or decision on a proposal from the Commission. Thus, in principle, the EU co-legislators are free to choose the form of action. Therefore, it is questionable whether the civil law aspects mentioned should be regulated by means of a regulation or a directive. Directives are only addressed to the Member States and need to be implemented into national law, Article 288 (3) TFEU. They are intended to harmonise Member States' law while assimilating as well as possible into the existing national legal framework.[303] Member States are free to choose the way they implement the directive into their national law, Article 288 (3) TFEU. If, as in this case, the directive is intended to confer subjective rights, there is a 'reservation of statutory provisions',[304] i.e. only legal statutes that directly affect the public are suitable for national implementation.[305] Thus, with regard to Austria, a mere change in the case-law on Sections 353 ff. ABGB would not be sufficient to implement a directive.[306] Regulations are abstract-general legal statutes regulating

[302] Case C-491/01 *British American Tobacco* ECLI:EU:C:2002:741, para. 147 (comments added).

[303] Nettesheim (2021), para. 84.

[304] König and Kleinlein (2020), para. 52.

[305] Nettesheim (2021), para. 92.

[306] Cf. König and Kleinlein (2020), para. 53.

fundamental aspects of longer-term significance.[307] They demand general and direct applicability and therefore serve as the most important instrument for unifying law in practice.[308]

It should be noted that according to Article 133, first sentence, TFEU, the measures must be necessary for the use of the euro as the single currency. Considering the aforementioned, the uniformity of the currency could be jeopardised if a directive is chosen as the form of action.[309] In addition, each directive must provide for an appropriate implementation period. Thus, due to the different status of intangible objects in the private law systems of the Member States, there is a risk that the cross-border use of central bank digital currency as a bearer-instrument will already be considerably impeded during the implementation period. Hence, despite the higher intensity of intervention it seems appropriate to use a regulation as the suitable form of action. The regulatory content could then be combined with the regulation establishing the digital euro in order to reduce the administrative burden.

7.4.4 Design and Content

The following section will now concentrate on the content of a possible harmonisation measure by the EU co-legislators. The result can be seen in the draft proposal for a regulation establishing the digital euro in the appendix to this book.

The regulation is intended to solve the main civil law problems of the digital euro as a bearer-instrument raised above. As set out, this manifestation of the digital euro is an intangible object. Hence, the following section will use the laws concerning intellectual property that confer rights on other intangible goods as a blueprint.

With regard to the legal nature, the holder of such a digital euro is to be granted a subjective right which entitles him or her to prevent all third parties not having his or her consent from using it. This is comparable to Article 9 (1), (2) Union trade mark Regulation[310] (UTMR), Article 19 (1) Community designs Regulation[311] (CDR) and Articles 5 (1), 8 (1) of the Regulation (EU) 1257/2012.[312]

This method can also be applied to the change of ownership of the digital euro as a bearer-instrument. Several provisions clarify that the right to the specific intangible

---

[307] Nettesheim (2021), para. 72 and 73.

[308] Cf. Article 288 (2) TFEU and König and Kleinlein (2020), para. 40.

[309] Selmayr (2015), para. 11, 23; Wutscher (2019), para. 1.

[310] Regulation (EU) 2017/1001 of the European Parliament and of the Council of 14 June 2017 on the European Union trade mark (16 June 2017) *OJ L 154/1*.

[311] Council Regulation (EC) No 6/2002 of 12 December 2001 on Community designs (5 January 2002) *OJ L 3/1*.

[312] Regulation (EU) No 1257/2012 of the European Parliament and of the Council of 17 December 2012 implementing enhanced cooperation in the area of the creation of unitary patent protection (31 December 2012) *OJ L 361/1*.

object can be transferred, see for e.g. Article 20 (1) UTMR, Article 28 CDR and Article 71 European Patent Convention[313] (EPC). These provisions are structured just like the national provisions when it comes to the change of ownership. They require an agreement of the parties and that the transfer is entered into a register to create publicity, cf. Articles 20 (4) UTMR, 28 lit. a CDR. For the digital euro, it must be borne in mind that the transfer can take place in several ways. For example, by transferring the digital units themselves, similar to today's online bank transfer. But it also seems conceivable to transfer the digital units 'offline' in the meaning that the HBI will be exchanged permanently between the parties, provided that the HBI is not intertwined with the identity of one party for reasons of anti-money laundering.[314] In contrast, the fact that the transferor merely enables the recipient to factually dispose of his (the transferor's) digital units, for example by disclosing the passwords that trigger the transaction, is not to be recorded as a transfer. This is because there is no longer an allocation recognisable for the public. When the digital euro is transferred, the technical position in the Eurosystem's ledger is changed. When the HBI is transferred, the possession of the HBI provides a legal *prima facie* evidence for the public to verify if the transferor is empowered to dispose of the money. However, when the passwords are revealed, the digital units are technically still assigned to the public key of the transferor, although the acquirer can dispose of them. This is not recognisable to the public and therefore cannot be regarded as a transfer. Next, it must be considered how these possibilities of changing the ownership can be recognised under law. The transfer of the HBI appears to be comparable to the transfer of movable tangible goods, so that it is sufficient if the regulation refers to the particular law of the Member States. Due to the special technical features of the DLT, the transfer of the digital units themselves cannot simply be integrated into existing schemes of dispositions. Here it seems appropriate to develop a separate act of transfer that uses the actual technical processes for orientation.

Since CBDC as a bearer-instrument is regarded as (digital) money, which has some parallels to cash, enabling end-users to acquire in good faith seems compelling. This should also apply if the digital euro went astray. This appears conceivable in the case when the passwords are lost or fell victim to hacking or the end-user loses the HBI. Since the digital units will be assigned to a pseudonym in the ledger, identification requires the means that enable the access, i.e. the passwords. Hence, if the passwords are lost, so are the digital units. Since CBDC is still money, this should not impair the possibility to acquire the digital units (for e.g. from the hacker), so that Section 935 (2) of the German Civil Code can be used for orientation. However, some cases must be respected as well in which the units are assigned to a legal entity other than the desired one due to a technical error. Since these cases can conceptually be regarded as 'lost' as well and a full-fledged right can in principle be acquired in good faith, a compensation should be provided for this. As not all Member States are

[313]Convention on the Grant of European Patents of 5 October 1973 as revised by the Act revising Article 63 EPC of 17 December 1991 and the Act revising the EPC of 29 November 2000.

[314]See Sect. 6.3.

familiar with the principle of separation and abstraction and the regulation provides for a valid acquisition of rights even in the case of loss, it should be possible for the Member States to provide for their own claims for restitution in their national law for these special cases.

Furthermore, it should be possible to establish rights *in rem*, such as a lien. For orientation, Articles 22 (1) UTMR, 29 (1) CDR and Article 71 EPC can be used accordingly. This can also enable to establish a lien by attachment on the digital euro. However, due to the technical design, any third-party rights *in rem* are not apparent to the acquirer. To preserve the fitness for economic circulation, it seems conceivable to adopt the provision of Section 936 of the German Civil Code accordingly, which allows a lapse of these rights due to a *bona-fide* acquisition.

With regard to the compulsory enforcement, it will be clarified that the compulsory enforcement may be carried out against the right to a digital euro as a bearer-instrument. Articles 23 (1) UTMR, 30 (1) CDR can serve as orientation here. The compulsory enforcement for monetary claims can be carried out against the digital euro or against the HBI. In the first case, due to the lack of embodiment, the application of the Member States' provisions on the seizure of claims is appropriate. However, it must be considered that the debtor can factually dispose of the digital euro despite the attachment in a manner that is detrimental to the compulsory enforcement. Therefore, the official organ for enforcement by execution shall be enabled to obtain the factual power of disposal over the seized digital units. This can be done, for example, by transferring the units to a wallet of the official organ.[315] In doing so, the debtor shall be obliged to cooperate and this obligation to cooperate shall be enforceable in accordance with the general provisions of the national compulsory enforcement law. For the compulsory enforcement against the HBI, it is appropriate to apply the national law provisions on the attachment of movable tangible goods.

There is no need for a special provision on the insolvency proceedings. Due to the granting of a subjective right to the digital euro as a bearer-instrument, the digital euro can be regarded as an 'object of property' in the meaning that it is an asset, cf. Article 7 (1) Regulation (EU) 1257/2012, Article 19 (1) UTMR, Article 27 (1) CDR. Hence, the bearer-based digital euro will form part of the insolvency estate. Furthermore, granting a subjective right will also lead to a right to separation in the event of the insolvency of a third party.[316]

As it is the case for intellectual property rights,[317] the owner of the digital euro should be granted protection as well. For this purpose, it appears to be sufficient to apply the national provisions the owner of property is entitled to, in particular claims

---

[315] Cf. Effer-Uhe (2018), p. 525; Greier (2016), pp. 254 and 255; Koch (2020), p. 89.

[316] Cf. for the right of use under the German Act on the Legal Protection of Designs see Bäuerle (2022), para. 52.

[317] See for e.g. Article 90 UTMR, for national law see Section 42 German Act on the Legal Protection of Designs and Section 14 (5), (6) German Act on the Protection of Trade Marks and other Signs.

for restitution, removal and omission of impairments of use and damages. However, since money is involved, the claim for restitution is usually limited to a restitution based on the sum in total.

7.5 Conclusion

As it has been shown, the civil law consideration of central bank digital currency is sometimes very complex. While the account-based form is a claim, transferable by means of credit and debit entries, subject to the compulsory enforcement and the insolvency proceedings, the bearer-instrument form as an intangible object is not recognised in the *lex lata* and thus cannot be transferred, pledged or seized and cannot form part of the insolvency estate. However, both manifestations are money in the legal sense and can be part of the banks' deposit business.

References

Adomeit K et al (2018) Einführung in das spanische Recht, 4th edn. Beck, München

Ahrens (2021) § 857. In: Prütting H, Gehrlein M (eds) ZPO, 13th edn. Wolters Kluwer, Hürth

Amey R (2019) Cryptocurrency: a guide for the rest of us, SouthSquare Digest (July 2019):14–17. https://southsquare.com/articles/cryptocurrency-a-guide-for-the-rest-of-us/. Accessed 31 July 2023

Ammann T (2018) Bitcoin als Zahlungsmittel im Internet. CR 2018:379–386

Arndt J (2022) Bitcoin-Eigentum. Mohr Siebeck, Tübingen

Athanassiou P (2018) Digital innovation in financial services – legal challenges and regulatory policy issues. International Banking and Finance Law Series, vol 34

Badstuber T (2019) Bitcoin und andere Kryptowährungen in der Zwangsvollstreckung. DGVZ 2019:246–255

Baier J (2019) Kriminalpolitische Herausforderungen durch Bitcoin und andere Kryptowährungen. CCZ 2019:123–129

Bär-Bouyssière (2015) Art. 345 AEUV. In: Groeben H, Schwarze J, Hatje A (eds) Europäisches Unionsrecht, 7th edn. Nomos, Baden-Baden

Bäuerle (2022) § 47. In: Braun E (ed) InsO, 9th edn. Beck, München

Baur J, Stürner R (2009a) Sachenrecht - § 4, 18th edn. Beck, München

Baur J, Stürner R (2009b) Sachenrecht - § 51, 18th edn. Beck, München

Baur J, Stürner R (2009c) Sachenrecht - § 59, 18th edn. Beck, München

Bausch S, Heetkamp S (2018) Wie kommt der "Kuckuck" auf den Bitcoin? Dispute Resolution-Magazin. https://www.deutscheranwaltspiegel.de/disputeresolution/archiv/wie-kommt-der-kuckuck-auf-den-bitcoin/. Accessed 31 July 2023

Bechtel et al (2022) Die Zukunft des Zahlungsverkehrs in einer DLTbasierten europäischen Wirtschaft. In: Kunschke D, Spitz M, Pohle J (eds) FinTech, 2nd edn. ESV, Berlin. https://doi.org/10.37307/b.978-3-503-20689-6.09

Beck B, König D (2015) Bitcoin: Der Versuch einer vertragstypologischen Einordnung von kryptographischem Geld. JZ 2015:130–138

Becker (2022) Art. 133 TFEU. In: Siekmann H (ed) The European Monetary Union – a commentary on the legal foundations. Bloomsbury Publishing, London

Bieder (2020) § 700. In: Staudinger Kommentar zum BGB, recast 2020, online-version via juris

Borchert M (2003) Geld und Kredit, 8th edn. Oldenbourg, München
Bork R (2016) Allgemeiner Teil des Bürgerlichen Gesetzbuchs, 4th edn. Mohr Siebeck, Tübingen
Bossu W et al (2020) Legal aspects of central bank digital currency: central bank and monetary law considerations. IMF Working Paper WP/20/254. https://www.imf.org/en/Publications/WP/Issues/2020/11/20/Legal-Aspects-of-Central-Bank-Digital-Currency-Central-Bank-and-Monetary-Law-Considerations-49827. Accessed 31 July 2023
Brinkmann (2019) § 47. In: Hirte H, Vallender H (eds) Uhlenbruck Insolvenzordnung, vol 1, 15th edn. Franz Vahlen, München
Brox H, Walker W (2018) Zwangsvollstreckungsrecht, 11th edn. Franz Vahlen, München
Büteröwe (2016) § 35. In: Schmidt K (ed) Insolvenzordnung, 19th edn. Beck, München
Canaris C (1981) Bankvertragsrecht, 2nd edn. De Gruyter, Berlin and New York
Casper (2023) § 675f. In: Säcker F et al (eds) Münchener Kommentar zum BGB, vol 6, 9th edn. Beck, München
Chesley R, Fernando M (2019) Cryptocurrency and its impact on insolvency and restructuring. INSOL International Special Report. https://de.scribd.com/document/526628323/Cryptocurrency-and-its-Impact-on-Insolvency-and-Restructuring-2019. Accessed 31 July 2023
Cohen F (1935) Transcendental nonsense and the functional approach. Columbia Law Rev 35:809–849
d'Avoine M, Hamacher P (2022) Kryptowährungen im Insolvenzverfahren. ZIP 2022:6–12
Deutsche Bundesbank (2021) Eurosystem experimentation regarding a digital euro – research workstream on hardware bearer instrument. https://www.ecb.europa.eu/paym/digital_euro/investigation/profuse/shared/files/deexp/ecb.deexp211011_2.en.pdf?33e4ca807a0c37e6fbfac8c447748501. Accessed 31 July 2023
Diehl (2021) Chapter 2. In: Omlor S, Link M (eds) Kryptowährungen und Token. R&W, Frankfurt a.M.
Dobrauz-Saldapenna, Schrackmann (2019) Distributed-Ledger-Regulierung in der Schweiz. In: Piska C, Völkel O (eds) Blockchain rules. Manz Verlag, Wien
ECB (2020) Report on a digital euro. https://www.ecb.europa.eu/pub/pdf/other/Report_on_a_digital_euro~4d7268b458.en.pdf. Accessed 31 July 2023
ECB (2021) Digital euro experimentation scope and key learnings. https://www.ecb.europa.eu/pub/pdf/other/ecb.digitaleuroscopekeylearnings202107~564d89045e.en.pdf. Accessed 31 July 2023
ECB (2022) Eurogroup meeting – roles of the Eurosystem and intermediaries in the digital euro ecosystem. 3 October 2022. https://www.ecb.europa.eu/paym/digital_euro/investigation/governance/shared/files/ecb.degov221003_businessmodels.en.pdf?fb8a6368c3206393ab66fd63e75bb3a6. Accessed 31 July 2023
ECB Appendix (2021) The Eurosystem's analysis of privacy-enhancing techniques in central bank digital currencies. https://www.ecb.europa.eu/pub/pdf/annex/ecb.sp210414_1_annex~43eee6196e.en.pdf?ed992ba1ebc6915fe12bf5d57013ae549. Accessed 31 July 2023
Eccher (2010a) § 307. In: Koziol H, Bydlinski P, Bollenberger R (eds) Kurzkommentar zum ABGB, 3rd edn. Verlag Österreich, Wien and New York
Eccher (2010b) § 285. In: Koziol H, Bydlinski P, Bollenberger R (eds) Kurzkommentar zum ABGB, 3rd edn. Verlag Österreich, Wien and New York
Effer-Uhe D (2018) Kryptowährungen in Zwangsvollstreckung und Insolvenz am Beispiel des Bitcoin. ZZP 2018:513–531
Ehmann H (1988) Informationsschutz und Informationsverkehr im Zivilrecht. AcP 188:230–380
Ehmann (2000) Das Allgemeine Persönlichkeitsrecht. In: Canaris C et al (eds) 50 Jahre Bundesgerichtshof – Festgabe aus der Wissenschaft, vol 1. München
Ellenberger (2023) Vor § 104. In: Grüneberg C (ed) Bürgerliches Gesetzbuch, 82nd edn. Beck, München
Engelhardt C, Klein S (2014) Bitcoins – Geschäfte mit Geld, das keines ist – Technische Grundlagen und zivilrechtliche Betrachtung. MMR 2014:355–360

Enneccerus L, Nipperdey H (1959) Allgemeiner Teil des Bürgerlichen Rechts, vol 1, 1st half-volume, 15th edn
Fehrenbacher (2021) § 700. In: Prütting H, Wegen G, Weinreich G (eds) BGB, 16th edn. Wolters Kluwer, Hürth
Fischer, Boegl (2022) § 112. In: Ellenberger J, Bunte H (eds) Bankrechtshandbuch, 6th edn. Beck, München
Fleißner L (2018) Eigentum an unkörperlichen Sachen am Beispiel von Bitcoins. ÖJZ 2018:437–443
Flockenhaus (2022a) § 829. In: Musielak H, Voit W (eds) ZPO, 19th edn. Franz Vahlen, München
Flockenhaus (2022b) § 857. In: Musielak H, Voit W (eds) ZPO, 19th edn. Franz Vahlen, München
Foerster (2020) § 9. In: Maume P, Maute L (eds) Rechtshandbuch Kryptowerte. Beck, München
Foerster (2023) § 675f BGB. In: Gsell B et al (eds) beck-online.Grosskommentar BGB, version 15.02.2023. Beck, München
Fögen H (1969) Geld- und Währungsrecht. Beck, München
Freimuth (2022) Art. 128 TFEU. In: Siekmann H (ed) The European Monetary Union – a commentary on the legal foundations. Bloomsbury Publishing, London
Füller (2023) § 952. In: Säcker F et al (eds) Münchener Kommentar zum BGB, vol 8, 9th edn. Beck, München
Gaul (2010a) § 9. In: Gaul H, Schilken E, Becker-Eberhard E (eds) Zwangsvollstreckungsrecht, 12th edn. Beck, München
Gaul (2010b) § 34. In: Gaul H, Schilken E, Becker-Eberhard E (eds) Zwangsvollstreckungsrecht, 12th edn. Beck, München
Gehrlein (2023) § 700. In: Hau W, Poseck R (eds) BeckOK BGB, version 01.05.2023, 66th edn. Beck, München
Graf-Schlicker, Kexel (2010) § 35. In: Graf-Schlicker M (ed) InsO, 2nd edn. RWS, Köln
Greier G (2016) Möglichkeiten strafprozessualer Sicherung von Bitcoins gemäß §§ 111b ff. StPO, Wistra 2016:251–257
Gruber (2020) § 887. In: Rauscher T, Krüger W (eds) Münchener Kommentar zur ZPO, vol 2, 6th edn. Beck, München
Grundmann (2022) § 245. In: Säcker F et al (eds) Münchener Kommentar zum BGB, vol 2, 9th edn. Beck, München
Grünewald S (2022) Legal interoperability of the digital euro: prospects and challenges. In: ESCB Legal Conference 2022. https://www.ecb.europa.eu/pub/pdf/other/ecb.escblegalconferenceproceedings2022~1646d63f3e.en.pdf?08c4311f6b5f39ecf6e6a188cc55c06d. Accessed 31 July 2023
Habersack M (1996) Die Mitgliedschaft – subjektives und "sonstiges" Recht. Mohr Siebeck, Tübingen
Häde U (1991) Geldzeichen im Recht der Bundesrepublik Deutschland. Nomos, Baden-Baden
Häde (2022) Art. 133 AEUV. In: Calliess C, Ruffert M (eds) EUV/AEUV Kommentar, 6th edn. Beck, München
Hahn H, Häde U (2010) Währungsrecht - § 14, 2nd edn. Beck, München
Haneke (2023) § 47. In: Fridgen A, Geiwitz A, Göpfert B (eds) BeckOK Insolvenzrecht, version 15.04.2023, 31st edn. Beck, München
Häsemeyer L (2007) Insolvenzrecht, 4th edn. Carl Heymanns Verlag, Köln
Hatje (2009) Wirtschaftsverfassung im Binnenmarkt. In: Bogdandy A, Bast J (eds) Europäisches Verfassungsrecht, 2nd edn. Springer, Berlin Heidelberg
Haug (2022) § 106. In: Ellenberger J, Bunte H (eds) Bankrechtshandbuch, 6th edn. Beck, München
Häuser (2019) B. In: Drescher I, Fleischer H, Schmidt K (eds) Münchener Kommentar zum Handelsgesetzbuch, vol 6, 4th edn. Beck, München
Heckelmann M (2018) Zulässigkeit und Handhabung von Smart Contracts. NJW 2018:504–510
Heinze (2018) Einleitung Sachenrecht. In: Staudinger Kommentar zum BGB, recast 2018, online-version via juris

Henckel (2004) § 35. In: Henckel W, Gerhardt W (eds) Jaeger Insolvenzordnung, vol 1, 1st edn. De Gruyter, Berlin
Henssler (2020) Funktionen, Begriff und wirtschaftliche Bedeutung der Wertpapiere. In: Brox H, Henssler M (eds) Handelsrecht, 23rd edn. Beck, München
Henssler (2023) § 700. In: Säcker F et al (eds) Münchener Kommentar zum BGB, vol 6, 9th edn. Beck, München
Herresthal (2020) Chapter 3 § 675t. In: Langenbucher K, Bliesener D, Spindler G (eds) Bankrechts-Kommentar, 3rd edn. Beck, München
Herrmann C (2010) Währungshoheit, Währungsverfassung und subjektive Rechte. Mohr Siebeck, Tübingen
Herzberg R (2005) Die ratio legis als Schlüssel zum Gesetzesverständnis? – Eine Skizze und Kritik der überkommenen Auslegungsmethodik. JuS 2005:1–8
Hess (2013) §§ 35, 36 InsO. In: Hess H (ed) Insolvenzrecht – Großkommentar, vol 1, 2nd edn. C.F. Müller, Heidelberg
Hirte, Praß (2019) § 35. In: Hirte H, Vallender H (eds) Uhlenbruck Insolvenzordnung, vol 1, 15th edn. Franz Vahlen, München
Huber J (2018) Monetäre Souveränität. Metropolis-Verlag, Marburg
Hubmann H (1955) Das Recht am Unternehmen. ZHR 117:41–60
Imberger (2011) § 47. In: Wimmer K (ed) Frankfurter Kommentar zur Insolvenzordnung, 6th edn. Luchterhand, Köln
Ipsen J (2021) Staatsrecht II – Grundrechte, 24th edn. Franz Vahlen, München
Jachmann-Michel (2022) Art. 95. In: Dürig G, Herzog R, Scholz R (eds) Grundgesetz Kommentar, 99th edn. Beck, München
Jacobs, Arndt (2019) Bitcoins in der Zwangsvollstreckung. In: Boele-Woelki K et al (eds) Festschrift für Karsten Schmidt zum 80. Geburtstag, vol I. München
Jungmann (2023) § 675t. In: Säcker F et al (eds) Münchener Kommentar zum BGB, vol 6, 9th edn. Beck, München
Kaulartz M (2016) Die Blockchain-Technologie. CR 2016:474–480
Kaulartz M, Matzke R (2018) Die Tokenisierung des Rechts. NJW 2018:3278–3283
Kempen (2018) Art. 133 AEUV. In: Streinz R (ed) Beck'scher Kurzkommentar EUV/AEUV, 3rd edn. Beck, München
Kemper (2021) § 857. In: Saenger I (ed) ZPO, 9th edn. Nomos, Baden-Baden
Keßler (2020) Bank- und Börsenrecht III. In: Joost D, Strohn L (eds) Handelsgesetzbuch, vol 2, 4th edn. Beck, München
Khan (2023) Art. 345 AEUV. In: Geiger R, Khan D, Kotzur M, Kirchmair L (eds) EUV/AEUV, 7th edn. Beck, München
Khan, Richter (2023) Art. 133 AEUV. In: Geiger R, Khan D, Kotzur M, Kirchmair L (eds) EUV/AEUV, 7th edn. Beck, München
Kingreen (2022) Art. 345 AEUV. In: Calliess C, Ruffert M (eds) EUV/AEUV Kommentar, 6th edn. Beck, München
Kirchhartz (2014) § 1. In: Erne R (ed) Claussen, Bank- und Börsenrecht, 5th edn. Beck, München
Kirchner (2023) § 35. In: Fridgen A, Geiwitz A, Göpfert B (eds) BeckOK Insolvenzrecht, version 15.04.2023, 31st edn. Beck, München
Klinck (2023) § 935 BGB. In: Gsell B et al (eds) beck-online.Grosskommentar BGB, version 01.06.2023. Beck, München
Knapp G (1923) Staatliche Theorie des Geldes, 4th edn. München and Leipzig
Koch P (2018) Die "Tokenisierung" von Rechtspositionen als digitale Verbriefung. ZBB 2018: 359–368
Koch R (2020) Die Zwangsvollstreckung in virtuelle Währungen. DGVZ 2020:85–90
Koch (2021) § 857. In: Kindl J, Meller-Hannich C (eds) Gesamtes Recht der Zwangsvollstreckung, 4th edn. Nomos, Baden-Baden
Köndgen (2018) § 675c BGB. In: Gsell B et al (eds) beck-online.Grosskommentar BGB, version 15.11.2018. Beck, München

König, Kleinlein (2020) § 2. In: Schulze R, Janssen A, Kadelbach S (eds) Europarecht, 4th edn. Nomos, Baden-Baden

Krajewski (2017) Art. 345 AEUV. In: Pechstein M, Nowak C, Häde U (eds) Frankfurter Kommentar EUV/GRC/AEUV. Mohr Siebeck, Tübingen

Kühling (2018) Art. 345 AEUV. In: Streinz R (ed) Beck'scher Kurzkommentar EUV/AEUV, 3rd edn. Beck, München

Kuhlmann N (2014) Bitcoins – Funktionsweise und rechtliche Einordnung der digitalen Währung. CR 2014:691–696

Kütük M, Sorge C (2014) Bitcoin im deutschen Vollstreckungsrecht - Von der "Tulpenmanie" zur "Bitcoinmanie". MMR 2014:643–646

Lackmann (2022) § 887. In: Musielak H, Voit W (eds) ZPO, 19th edn. Franz Vahlen, München

Lackmann R, Racz C (2021) Zwangsvollstreckungsrecht, 12th edn. Franz Vahlen, München

Lahusen B (2021) Verdinglichung durch Datenschutz. AcP 221:1–31

Langenbucher K (2018) Digitales Finanzwesen. AcP 218:385–429

Langenbucher et al (2020) Chapter 11. In: Langenbucher K, Bliesener D, Spindler G (eds) Bankrechts-Kommentar, 3rd edn. Beck, München

Langner (2020) ESCB/Eurosystem/National Central Banks. In: Amtenbrink F, Herrmann C (eds) The EU law of economic and monetary union. Oxford

Langner (2022a) § 44. In: Ellenberger J, Bunte H (eds) Bankrechtshandbuch, 6th edn. Beck, München

Langner (2022b) § 45. In: Ellenberger J, Bunte H (eds) Bankrechtshandbuch, 6th edn. Beck, München

Larenz K, Canaris C (1995) Methodenlehre der Rechtswissenschaft, 3rd edn. Springer, Berlin and Heidelberg

Lehmann M (2016) Grundriss des Bank- und Kapitalmarktrechts. C.F. Müller, Heidelberg

Lehmann (2021) Chapter 5. In: Omlor S, Link M (eds) Kryptowährungen und Token. R&W, Frankfurt a.M.

Leipold D (2019) BGB I – Einführung und Allgemeiner Teil, 10th edn. Mohr Siebeck, Tübingen

Lerch M (2015) Bitcoin als Evolution des Geldes: Herausforderungen, Risiken und Regulierungsfragen. ZBB 2015:190–204

Linardatos (2020) Der Mythos vom "Realakt" bei der Umbuchung von Bitcoins. In: Beyer E et al (eds) Privatrecht 2050 – Blick in die digitale Zukunft, 1st edn. Nomos, Baden-Baden

Lüke (2015a) § 857. In: Wieczorek B, Schütze R (eds) ZPO, 4th edn. De Gruyter, Berlin and Boston

Lüke (2015b) § 804. In: Wieczorek B, Schütze R (eds) ZPO, 4th edn. De Gruyter, Berlin and Boston

Manger-Nestler (2017) Art. 133 AEUV. In: Pechstein M, Nowak C, Häde U (eds) Frankfurter Kommentar EUV/GRC/AEUV. Mohr Siebeck, Tübingen

Manger-Nestler C (2021) Digitales Zentralbankgeld aus währungsrechtlicher Sicht. RdZ 2021:4–11

Mann F (1960) Das Recht des Geldes, Frankfurt am Main and Berlin

Maute (2020a) § 4. In: Maume P, Maute L (eds) Rechtshandbuch Kryptowerte. Beck, München

Maute (2020b) § 5. In: Maume P, Maute L (eds) Rechtshandbuch Kryptowerte. Beck, München

Maute (2020c) Responsio – Warum die Übertragung von Bitcoins kein dingliches Rechtsgeschäft erfordert. In: Beyer E et al (eds) Privatrecht 2050 – Blick in die digitale Zukunft, 1st edn. Nomos, Baden-Baden

Möllers T (2021a) Juristische Methodenlehre - § 6, 4th edn. Beck, München

Möllers T (2021b) Juristische Methodenlehre - § 4, 4th edn. Beck, München

Mössner (2022) § 90 BGB. In: Gsell B et al (eds) beck-online.Grosskommentar BGB, version 01.03.2022. Beck, München

Muscheler K, Hunt C (2021) Recent legal developments in the area of crypto-assets and a digital euro. Institute for Law and Finance Working Paper Series No. 164. https://www.ilf-frankfurt.de/fileadmin/user_upload/ILF_WP164.pdf. Accessed 31 July 2023

Nettesheim (2021) § 9. In: Oppermann T, Classen C, Nettesheim M (eds) Europarecht, 9th edn. Beck, München

Neuner J (2020a) Allgemeiner Teil des Bürgerlichen Rechts - § 29, 12th edn. Beck, München
Neuner J (2020b) Allgemeiner Teil des Bürgerlichen Rechts - § 20, 12th edn. Beck, München
Neuner J (2020c) Allgemeiner Teil des Bürgerlichen Rechts - § 28, 12th edn. Beck, München
Neuner J (2020d) Allgemeiner Teil des Bürgerlichen Rechts - § 26, 12th edn. Beck, München
Nober (2022) § 857. In: Anders M, Gehle B (eds) ZPO, 80th edn. Franz Vahlen, München
Ohler C (2008) Die hoheitlichen Grundlagen der Geldordnung. JZ 2008:317–324
Ohler C (2021) Unkonventionelle Geldpolitik. Mohr Siebeck, Tübingen
Omlor S (2014) Geldprivatrecht. Mohr Siebeck, Tübingen
Omlor S (2019a) Kryptowährungen im Geldrecht. ZHR 183:294–345
Omlor S (2019b) Digitaler Zahlungsverkehr. JuS 2019:289–294
Omlor (2021a) § 33. In: Omlor S, Möslein F (eds) FinTech-Handbuch, 2nd edn. Beck, München
Omlor (2021b) Chapter 6. In: Omlor S, Link M (eds) Kryptowährungen und Token. R&W, Frankfurt a.M.
Omlor (2021c) Vorb. zu §§ 244 ff. In: Staudinger Kommentar zum BGB, recast 2021, online-version via juris
Omlor S, Birne A (2020) Digitales Zentralbankgeld im Euroraum. RDi 2020:1–10
Pachinger et al (2021) Chapter 20. In: Omlor S, Link M (eds) Kryptowährungen und Token. R&W, Frankfurt a.M.
Papier, Shirvani (2022) Art. 14. In: Dürig G, Herzog R, Scholz R (eds) Grundgesetz Kommentar, 99th edn. Beck, München
Paulus C (2020) Daten in der Zwangsvollstreckung. DGVZ 2020:133–140
Paulus C, Berg J (2019) Daten als insolvenzrechtlicher Vermögenswert des Schuldners. ZIP 2019: 2133–2142
Paulus D, Matzke R (2018) Smart Contracts und das BGB – Viel Lärm um nichts? ZfPW 2018: 431–465
Peters (2019) § 35. In: Stürner R, Eidenmüller H, Schoppmeyer H (eds) Münchener Kommentar zur Insolvenzordnung, 4th edn. Beck, München
Peto R (2002) Geldtheorie und Geldpolitik, 2nd edn. Oldenbourg, München
Peukert A (2008) Güterzuordnung als Rechtsprinzip. Mohr Siebeck, Tübingen
Peukert (2011) Sonstige Gegenstände im Rechtsverkehr. In: Leible S, Lehmann M, Zech H (eds) Unkörperliche Güter im Zivilrecht. Mohr Siebeck, Tübingen
Pießkalla M (2008) Die Kommissionsvorschläge zum "full ownership unbundling" des Strom- und Gasversorgungssektors im Lichte der Eigentumsneutralität des EG-Vertrags (Art. 295 EG). EuZW 2008:199–203
Proctor C (2012) Mann on the legal aspect of money, 7th edn. Oxford
Riedel (2023) § 857. In: Vorwerk V, Wolf C (eds) BeckOK ZPO, version: 01.03.2023, 48th edn. Beck, München
Ries (2020) § 35. In: Kayser G, Thole C (eds) Heidelberger Kommentar zur Insolvenzordnung, 10th edn. C.F. Müller, Heidelberg
Rietzler et al (2019) Liechtensteinisches Blockchain-Gesetz. In: Piska C, Völkel O (eds) Blockchain rules. Manz Verlag, Wien
Rückert C (2016) Vermögensabschöpfung und Sicherstellung bei Bitcoins – Neue juristische Herausforderungen durch die ungeklärte Rechtsnatur von virtuellen Währungseinheiten. MMR 2016:295–300
Rüthers B et al (2020) Rechtstheorie und Juristische Methodenlehre, 11th edn. Beck, München
Sandrock O (1997) Der Euro und sein Einfluß auf nationale und internationale privatrechtliche Verträge, RIW Beilage 1 zu Heft 8/1997
Schaal P (1998) Geldtheorie und Geldpolitik, 4th edn. Oldenbourg, München
Schefold D (1996) Die Europäische Verordnung über die Einführung des Euro. WM 1996 (47) Sonderbeilage Nr. 4:2–20
Schefold D (1999) Der Einfluß von EG-Währungsrecht auf nationale Zivilrechte. ZEuP 1999:271–293

Schilken (2010a) §§ 47 ff. In: Gaul H, Schilken E, Becker-Eberhard E (eds) Zwangsvollstreckungsrecht, 12th edn. Beck, München
Schilken (2010b) § 54. In: Gaul H, Schilken E, Becker-Eberhard E (eds) Zwangsvollstreckungsrecht, 12th edn. Beck, München
Schmidt (2020) § 90. In: Westermann H, Grunewald B, Meier-Reimer G (eds) Erman BGB, 16th edn. ottoschmidt, Köln
Schmidt-Preuß M (2006) Der Wandel der Energiewirtschaft vor dem Hintergrund der europäischen Eigentumsordnung. EuR 2006:463–488
Schmieder (2022a) § 26. In: Ellenberger J, Bunte H (eds) Bankrechtshandbuch, 6th edn. Beck, München
Schmieder (2022b) § 25. In: Ellenberger J, Bunte H (eds) Bankrechtshandbuch, 6th edn. Beck, München
Schumacher (2011) § 36. In: Wimmer K (ed) Frankfurter Kommentar zur Insolvenzordnung, 6th edn. Luchterhand, Köln
Schur (2012) § 700. In: Siebert W (ed) Soergel BGB, 13th edn. Kohlhammer, Stuttgart 2012
Schwintowski (2018) Chapter 9. In: Schwintowski H (ed) Bankrecht, 5th edn. Wolters Kluwer, Köln
Selmayr (2015) Art. 133 AEUV. In: Groeben H, Schwarze J, Hatje A (eds) Europäisches Unionsrecht, 7th edn. Nomos, Baden-Baden
Servatius (2020) Chapter 35. In: Langenbucher K, Bliesener D, Spindler G (eds) Bankrechts-Kommentar, 3rd edn. Beck, München
Shmatenko L, Möllenkamp S (2018) Digitale Zahlungsmittel in einer analog geprägten Rechtsordnung. MMR 2018:495–501
Siedler (2021) § 7. In: Omlor S, Möslein F (eds) FinTech-Handbuch, 2nd edn. Beck, München
Siekmann H (2018) Legal Tender in the Euro Area. IMFS Working Paper Series No. 122. https://www.imfs-frankfurt.de/fileadmin/user_upload/IMFS_WP_122.pdf. Accessed 31 July 2023
Sixt J (1997) Euro – Notwendigkeit oder Bedrohung? DZWir 1997:428–480
Skauradszun D (2020) Durchbruch bei der Pfändung und Verwertung von Kryptowerten nach § 857 Abs. 1 und 5 ZPO, § 1 Abs. 11 Satz 4 KWG n.F. WM 2020:1229–1236
Skauradszun D (2021a) Kryptowerte im Bürgerlichen Recht. AcP 221:353–398
Skauradszun D (2021b) Kryptowerte im Insolvenzverfahren des Anlegers oder Emittenten. ZIP 2021:2610–2617
Smid (2020) § 857. In: Rauscher T, Krüger W (eds) Münchener Kommentar zur ZPO, vol 2, 6th edn. Beck, München
Spiegel A (2020) Blockchain-basiertes virtuelles Geld. Mohr Siebeck, Tübingen
Spindler (2011) Der Schutz virtueller Gegenstände. In: Leible S, Lehmann M, Zech H (eds) Unkörperliche Güter im Zivilrecht. Mohr Siebeck, Tübingen
Spindler (2020) Chapter 33. In: Langenbucher K, Bliesener D, Spindler G (eds) Bankrechts-Kommentar, 3rd edn. Beck, München
Spindler G, Bille M (2014) Rechtsprobleme von Bitcoins als virtuelle Währung. WM 2014:1357–1369
Stieper (2021a) Vorb. §§ 90 ff. In: Staudinger Kommentar zum BGB, recast 2021, online-version via juris
Stieper (2021b) § 90. In: Staudinger Kommentar zum BGB, recast 2021, online-version via juris
Strauch, Handke (2020) § 10. In: Maume P, Maute L (eds) Rechtshandbuch Kryptowerte. Beck, München
Stresemann (2021) § 90. In: Säcker F et al (eds) Münchener Kommentar zum BGB, vol 1, 9th edn. Beck, München
Strobel B (2021) Digitaler Euro? – Ein Überblick über die rechtlichen und wirtschaftlichen Fragen. BKR 2021:556–561
Thießen F (2021) Der Digitale Euro – Stand der Entwicklung und Lücken in den Zielen. Kreditwesen 74(24):27–31
Timmann T (2008) Das Patentrecht im Lichte von Art. 14 GG. Mohr Siebeck, Tübingen

Varmaz et al (2021) Chapter 1. In: Omlor S, Link M (eds) Kryptowährungen und Token. R&W, Frankfurt a.M.
Vedder (2018) Art. 345 AEUV. In: Vedder C, Heintschel von Heinegg W (eds) Europäisches Unionsrecht, 2nd edn. Nomos, Baden-Baden
Vogel (2023) § 793 BGB. In: Gsell B et al (eds) beck-online.Grosskommentar BGB, version 01.04.2023. Beck, München
Völkel (2019a) Grundlagen der privatrechtlichen Einordnung. In: Piska C, Völkel O (eds) Blockchain rules. Manz Verlag, Wien
Völkel (2019b) Derivativer und originärer gutgläubiger Eigentumserwerb. In: Piska C, Völkel O (eds) Blockchain rules. Manz Verlag, Wien
Walter A (2019) Bitcoin, Libra und sonstige Kryptowährungen aus zivilrechtlicher Sicht. NJW 2019:3609–3614
Wank R (2017) Die Auslegung von Gesetzen, 6th edn. Franz Vahlen, München
Wank R (2020) Juristische Methodenlehre - § 15. Franz Vahlen, München
Weimann M (1995) Software in der Zwangsvollstreckung. Bochum
Weis (2001) §§ 35, 36 InsO. In: Hess H, Weis M, Wienberg R (eds) Kommentar zur Insolvenzordnung mit EGInsO, vol 1, 2nd edn. C.F. Müller, Heidelberg
Wellenhofer M (2022a) Sachenrecht - § 3, 37th edn. Beck, München
Wellenhofer M (2022b) Sachenrecht - § 7, 37th edn. Beck, München
Wellenhofer M (2022c) Sachenrecht - § 14, 37th edn. Beck, München
Werner (2021) Chapter 7. In: Omlor S, Link M (eds) Kryptowährungen und Token. R&W, Frankfurt a.M.
Wernicke (2023) Art. 345 AEUV. In: Grabitz E, Hilf M, Nettesheim M (eds) Das Recht der Europäischen Union, 78th edn. Beck, München
Wilhelm J (2021) Sachenrecht, 7th edn. De Gruyter, Berlin and Boston
Wimmer (2020) § 24. In: Gottwald P, Haas U (eds) Insolvenzrechts-Handbuch, 6th edn. Beck, München
Würdinger (2017) § 857. In: Bork R, Roth H (eds) Stein/Jonas ZPO, 23rd edn. Mohr Siebeck, Tübingen
Wutscher (2019) Art. 133 AEUV. In: Becker U, Hatje A, Schoo J, Schwarze J (eds) Schwarze EU-Kommentar, 4th edn. Nomos, Baden-Baden
Zetzsche (2020) § 700. In: Westermann H, Grunewald B, Meier-Reimer G (eds) Erman BGB, 16th edn. ottoschmidt, Köln

Part III
Analysing the Economic Aspects of Central Bank Digital Currency

Chapter 8
Economic Implications of Central Bank Digital Currency

Abstract This chapter is dedicated to the general economic implications of central bank digital currency such as the impacts on financial stability. The chapter evaluates the risks of a CBDC for bank disintermediation, either structural or cyclical. It sets out the legal context of the economic discussion on restricting the CBDC's store-of-value-function. In addition, it illustrates and assesses possible design options to prevent risks to financial stability such as remuneration and limits.

8.1 Bank Disintermediation Risks

In general, the economic discussion revolves around risks of bank disintermediation and, closely connected to this, financial stability.[1] Inspired by *Bindseil*, the risks for bank disintermediation connected to central bank digital currency can be divided into 'structural' disintermediation and 'cyclical' disintermediation.[2]

8.1.1 Structural Disintermediation

The discussion on structural disintermediation in the economic literature can be summarised under the keyword of sovereign money ('Vollgeld') or narrow banking system.

8.1.1.1 Current Banking System and Creation of Private Money

To understand this economic discussion newly aroused by central bank digital currency, one first needs to have a look at the current banking system and the role

[1] For a brief overview cf. Manger-Nestler (2021), pp. 5 and 6.

[2] Bindseil (2020), p. 8.

L. Kriese, *Central Bank Digital Currency*,
https://doi.org/10.1007/978-3-031-44738-9_8

of money. When it comes to money, private money in the form of scriptural money is the one with the highest portion in national economy's circulation.[3] This private money is created by banks through their lending business in which they create a claim against the borrower on their asset side of their balance sheet and a liability in form of a deposit on their liability side which lengthens the balance sheet and increases the private money in circulation.[4] If the debtor uses the loan by transferring a certain amount to another bank, the lending bank has to refinance itself either by deposits or borrowing from other banks or the central bank.[5] This influences the lending bank's seigniorage as it consists of the spread between the refinance interest rate it has to pay and the loan interest rate it receives.[6] In today's banking system, commercial banks have to refinance the private money only fractionally with the highly liquid public central bank money.[7] This system is called 'fractional banking' or 'fractional reserve system'. In this system, commercial banks' liquid assets are smaller in quantity than their deposit liabilities.[8] Most commercial banks' assets consist of loans which are illiquid because there is no secondary market where they can be sold very easily in a short period of time.[9] Hence, banks as intermediaries have to perform the difficult task of maturity transformation between on-demand liabilities (giro deposits) and illiquid assets.[10]

8.1.1.2 Sovereign Money and Narrow Banking

This difficulty of having enough liquid assets to satisfy the withdrawal of on-demand liabilities can lead to severe complications in times of financial crisis. If commercial banks' customers sense difficulties in withdrawing their savings and converting them into safe public money (cash), this will cause a bank run. Having in mind the world financial crisis starting in 1929, the first discussion to change the fractional banking system came up in 1933 with the so-called Chicago-Plan.[11] According to this, commercial banks' deposit liabilities should be covered to one hundred per cent with central bank reserves, creating a liquidity equilibrium of assets and liabilities.[12] In this system of 'narrow banking', banks would invest customers' deposits only in

---

[3] Broadbent (2016), p. 2.

[4] Felber (2014), p. 60; Gischer et al. (2020), pp. 60 and 64.

[5] Felber (2014), p. 60.

[6] Felber (2014), p. 62.

[7] Huber (2018), p. 22; Gischer et al. (2020), p. 65.

[8] Broadbent (2016), p. 5.

[9] Broadbent (2016), p. 5.

[10] Broadbent (2016), p. 5.

[11] Mayer (2015), p. 53; Broadbent (2016), p. 6 (with additional references).

[12] Mayer (2015), p. 55; Broadbent (2016), p. 5; Adrian and Mancini-Griffoli (2019), p. 12; Bindseil (2020), p. 30.

low-risk and highly liquid assets such as central bank reserves.[13] Closely connected to this is the system of sovereign money. This is a system in which the economy's money can only be created by central banks.[14] As in legal terms this would lead to a system in which central banks and the non-bank public (households and corporates) would be connected by a direct legal relationship and banks could only act as fiduciaries on behalf of their customers, some changes to the banks' balance sheets would have to be made.[15] The customers' sovereign money accounts would be subsidiary accounts of banks held at the central bank which the banks would manage on a fiduciary basis.[16] Thus, money would be entered in the books directly between the customers' accounts at the central bank which would lead to a clear separation of banks' equity capital in their balance sheets and abolish inter-banking transactions.[17] This system of sovereign money would also affect banks' lending business. Although banks would still be able to grant loans, the overall amount of granted loans would slowly diminish. This is due to the fact that banks lost the privilege of creating money and the seigniorage resulting from this, thus they would need to use alternative sources of funding such as borrowing money from central banks or issuing securities at the capital market.[18]

8.1.1.3 Interlinkage to Central Bank Digital Currency

Although there are few authors that directly point out that introducing central bank digital currency could facilitate a radical change to the current banking system towards sovereign money or narrow banking,[19] the actual interlinkage between central bank digital currency and the aforementioned banking or money systems seems difficult to encounter at first glance.

The topic of structural disintermediation can also be described as disintermediation risks in normal times. These risks are based on the high attractiveness of central bank digital currency. If central bank digital currency gains attractiveness, customers will tend do use it extraordinarily, especially as potential store of value. This customer behaviour could lead to a high-quantity withdrawal of deposits which would result in a severe reduction of funding sources for commercial banks.[20] According to a study, in a scenario with intense use as store of value, households

[13]Mancini-Griffoli et al. (2018), p. 13.

[14]Cf. Felber (2014), p. 64; Huber (2018), pp. 156 and 159.

[15]Cf. Felber (2014), pp. 65 and 66.

[16]Huber (2018), p. 163.

[17]Felber (2014), p. 65; Huber (2018), p. 163.

[18]Huber (2018), p. 163; Thiele (2019), p. 87; Brunnermeier and Niepelt (2019), p. 39; Mayer (2015), p. 54.

[19]See for example Utzig (2020), p. 20; Panetta (2018), p. 4.

[20]Bindseil (2020), p. 9; Mancini-Griffoli et al. (2018), p. 21; BIS (2021), p. 6; Broadbent (2016), p. 2; Sanches and Keister (2021), p. 24.

and NFCs[21] would replace about 50%, NBFIs[22] about 90% of their bank deposits with central bank digital currency.[23] This in turn would affect both commercial banks and central banks as well as the overall economy.

Banks would need to adapt to the potential loss of funding sources. This could happen in various ways.[24] To begin with, banks could raise their interest rates on deposits, making them more attractive to central bank digital currency.[25] But these raises will be limited. Raising the interest rates the banks pay to their customers increases banks' costs, reduces their profitability and the capability of building up capital buffers, thus reducing customers' trust in them and leading to even more shifts.[26] Nonetheless, banks will raise their interest rates to a certain percentage. As a consequence, in order to not lose profitability, the banks will have to refinance their increased costs. Refinancing can be done in two ways. A first approach would be deleveraging, i.e. the reduction of banks' liabilities.[27] Connected to this, banks would shrink their lending business or increase the loan rates, both reducing the demand for loans by the real economy and hampering overall economic activity.[28] A second approach for banks would be to look for alternative sources of funding. This could be done either via wholesale market funding or via central bank funding. Regarding wholesale funding, banks could issue bonds or equity or accept wholesale deposits.[29] But this contains a bunch of uncertainties and risks.[30] For example, this form of funding strongly depends on the demand at capital markets.[31] Furthermore, regulatory aspects need to be considered. A source of founding that depends on market forces is inherently subject to high volatility. In this case, banking regulation[32] requires to hold more liquid assets.[33] In addition, increasing the dependence on the non-bank finance sector could call for more regulation in this sector, raising

---

[21] Non-financial corporation.

[22] Non-bank financial intermediary.

[23] Adalid et al. (2022), p. 11.

[24] See for a compact overview Hanl and Michaelis (2019), p. 10.

[25] Sanches and Keister (2021), p. 22; Agur et al. (2022), p. 70; Bindseil (2020), p. 9; Mancini-Griffoli et al. (2018), p. 21.

[26] Bindseil et al. (2021), p. 7.

[27] ECB (2020), p. 17; BIS (2021), p. 6.

[28] Mancini-Griffoli et al. (2018), p. 21; Agur et al. (2022), p. 75; Broadbent (2016), p. 6; BIS (2021), p. 9.

[29] ECB (2020), p. 17; Mancini-Griffoli et al. (2018), p. 23.

[30] Cf. Broadbent (2016), p. 7; ECB (2020), p. 17.

[31] CPMI-MC (2018), p. 15 fn. 26.

[32] See Articles 411 ff. Regulation (EU) No 575/2013 of the European Parliament and of the Council of 26 June 2013 on prudential requirements for credit institutions and investment firms and amending Regulation (EU) No 648/2012 (27 June 2013) OJ L 176/1, lastly amended by Regulation (EU) 2022/2036 (25 October 2022) OJ L 275/1. Moreover, Adalid et al. (2022), p. 26 assume that banks would voluntarily hold a buffer above their regulatory requirement which is at least as high as half of their current liquidity buffer, see also Barrdear and Kumhof (2016), p. 14.

[33] Mancini-Griffoli et al. (2018), p. 23; CPMI-MC (2018), p. 15 fn. 26.

bureaucratic costs.[34] Connected to the risk of high volatility, banks' maturity transformation function could be negatively affected which could ultimately lead to an increased pro-cyclicality of the banks' lending business.[35] Moreover, to cover long term wholesale liabilities, banks would need to acquire high-value liquid assets.[36] As a consequence, funding costs increase in average and thus decrease the net interest margin[37] of banks.[38] This is also due to the fact that wholesale-investors strive for more financial security when shifting from government securities to private bonds and equity, hence demanding for higher interest rates of banks' bonds and equity and thus lowering banks' return on equity[39] (RoE).[40] However, to refinance their increased costs, banks could opt for central bank funding as well. In a first step, they would reduce their excess reserves held at the central banks' accounts.[41] If this would not be sufficient to compensate the deposit outflow, banks would then start to borrow central bank money in form of reserves from the central banks.[42] This in turn arouses slight associations with the narrow banking system presented above.[43] In conclusion, however banks react to the deposit outflow, their profitability compared to the status quo will significantly decrease and their core business for the real economy, i.e. the lending business, as well as other businesses cross-subsidised with deposit rates will be hampered.[44]

Regarding the central banks, special attention needs to be paid to banks' increased borrowing of central bank reserves. In the short-term, the increased demand for central bank money would lead to a raise of the marginal lending rates for overnight credits.[45] As this would still widen the commercial banks' funding gap caused by the deposit outflows, in order to counteract the central banks could lower the marginal lending rate, hereby making reserves more affordable for commercial banks, or increase the volume of reserves in circulation.[46] However, although this would increase central banks' seigniorage,[47] both measures would lengthen the central

[34] BIS (2021), p. 10.

[35] BIS (2021), p. 8.

[36] BIS (2021), p. 7.

[37] The net interest margin (NIM) is defined as the spread of the remuneration costs the bank pays for the deposits and the revenue of its lending business proportional to the balance sheet total and indicates banks' profitability, cf. Priewasser (2001), pp. 239 and 240.

[38] BIS (2021), p. 7.

[39] The return on equity (RoE) is defined as the ratio of the profit in a certain period to the shareholder capital, cf. Eilenberger (2012), p. 500.

[40] BIS (2021), p. 10.

[41] Bindseil et al. (2021), p. 8 fn. 8; Hanl and Michaelis (2019), p. 9.

[42] Hanl and Michaelis (2019), p. 9; Bindseil et al. (2021), p. 8 fn. 8.

[43] Cf. Panetta (2018), p. 4; CPMI-MC (2018), p. 16.

[44] Hanl and Michaelis (2019), p. 10; CPMI-MC (2018), p. 15.

[45] BIS (2021), p. 11.

[46] Bindseil (2020), p. 11; BIS (2021), p. 11.

[47] Bindseil (2020), p. 12.

banks' balance sheets.[48] To avoid this consequence, central banks could purchase government[49] or corporate bonds in the capital market and the governments or corporations use the money for acquiring bank bonds or equity, meaning that central banks refinance commercial banks only indirectly.[50] Furthermore, an increased demand for central bank reserves influences the quantity and the value of collateral eligible for Eurosystem credit operations. According to Article 18.1, second indent, ESCB Statute the ECB and national central banks may conduct credit operations with credit institutions and other market participants, with lending being based on adequate collateral. With an increased demand for reserves, the demand for high-quality collateral also increases and thus consolidates existing shortages of eligible collateral.[51] This would lead to a raise of collateral prices and central banks perhaps have to loosen or expand their collateral framework.[52] If central banks were to expand their collateral framework and accept government bonds or private assets on a much larger scale than they do now, this could endanger the classical credit allocation in the two-tiered banking system and point towards the system of sovereign money.[53] Hence, the fact of increasing demand for central bank reserves and the central banks purchasing government or corporate bonds or expanding their collateral framework to these assets points at the interlinkage between central bank digital currency and the above mentioned structural disintermediation risks.

8.1.2 Cyclical Disintermediation

In contrast to the structural disintermediation, the discussion on cyclical disintermediation does not circle around changing the banking or money system or the role of the financial intermediaries but rather discusses the effects of central bank digital currency on banks in times of a financial crisis.

The economic aspect of introducing central bank digital currency can serve as an excellent example on how to study the 'anatomy of a crisis'.[54] Crises always start with a sudden event that influences the investors' behaviour such as the introduction of an innovation, a new technology, a war, high inflation or other disasters.[55] If

---

[48] BIS (2021), p. 11; Bindseil (2020), p. 10.

[49] Purchasing government bonds at the capital market may circumvent the prohibition of monetary financing according to Article 123 (1) TFEU, cf. case C-62/14 *Gauweiler* ECLI:EU:C:2015:400, para. 93 ff.; Häde (2022a), para. 10 ff.; Tutsch (2015), para. 25 ff.

[50] Bindseil (2020), p. 10.

[51] Bindseil (2020), p. 11.

[52] ECB (2020), p. 16; Broadbent (2016), p. 5; Bindseil et al. (2021), p. 8.

[53] CPMI-MC (2018), p. 14; Bindseil (2020), p. 13.

[54] Lastra (2006), p. 111 with reference to Kindleberger, Manias, Panics and Crashes – A History of Financial Crises.

[55] Lastra (2006), p. 111.

investors assume that their profit outweighs the potential risks of that product, a boom of usage follows the event.[56] As this attracts more and more investors that want to benefit from the booming profits, this growing number of market participants leads to financial distress in other market segments.[57] In this regard, financial crises are often associated with liquidity crises.[58] The common form of a funding liquidity crisis can be described as a situation where the investor's behaviour leads to funding distress of economic agents who depend on external refinancing.[59] Especially banks and cashless fund transfers are exposed to financial distress by nature because of their volume.[60]

Having in mind this 'anatomy' when introducing an account-based central bank digital currency as an innovation in the financial sector, one has to take into consideration that shifting current digital savings in private money, such as on-demand deposits held at commercial banks, to the central bank digital currency would highly be facilitated. In the digital age, this can happen with only a few clicks with the computer mouse. Since central bank digital currency is by definition a liability item of the central bank, this form of public money will be considered as 'safe haven'.[61] In times of a financial crisis, people will follow Gresham's law[62] and withdraw their private money endangered by the banks' insolvency risks and shift more to safe (central bank) money.[63] When analysing possible deposit outflows in times of a crisis, customers can shift their deposits either to other banks, physical central bank money (cash) or now central bank digital currency.[64] This is nothing new as in past crises minor bank runs occurred as well.[65] Furthermore, there are measures to limit the possibility of deposit outflows. Shifting deposits to other banks will depend on the pricing by this other bank and on the trust of the customers in this bank's stability.[66] Especially the latter is strongly influenced by the banking regulatory framework as well as the existing Deposit Guarantee Scheme.[67] As in times of a wide spreading financial crisis even major banks could be affected, the customers will nonetheless opt for safe central bank money. But shifting to the existing retail

[56] Lastra (2006), p. 111.

[57] Lastra (2006), p. 112.

[58] Bindseil (2014), p. 145.

[59] Bindseil (2014), p. 145.

[60] Lastra (2006), pp. 138, 143.

[61] BIS (2021), p. 12.

[62] In the past people tried to return the coins with a silver content below value as soon as possible back to the money circulation while keeping valuable gold coins as long as possible, meaning the 'bad money' displaces the 'good money' in terms of payments while it is the other way around with regards to savings, Huber (2018), p. 224.

[63] Huber (2018), p. 27.

[64] Bindseil (2020), p. 14.

[65] Mancini-Griffoli et al. (2018), p. 24.

[66] Cf. Bindseil (2020), p. 15.

[67] BIS (2021), p. 12; see also for main arrangements to prevent financial distress Lastra (2006), pp. 113 ff.

central bank money, i.e. cash, is limited by its physicality. This physicality poses risks and costs.[68] Banks would need to hold enough banknotes in their ATMs and face holding costs. Customers would face long queues, possible ATM fees, a monthly/daily cash withdrawal limit and the risk of theft or loss.[69] This is fundamentally different for central bank digital currency as there would be zero or very low transaction and holding costs and shifting deposits would be fast and easy to handle for customers.[70] These technical conditions would facilitate the risk of runs which would not only emerge for banks but also for non-bank intermediaries that offer deposit-like financial services, for example money market fonds.[71] Lastly, in terms of accounting, a shift from deposits to central bank digital currency would be an asset swap for the households and possibly an exchange on the liability side for the financial intermediaries, but it would lengthen the central banks' balance sheet.[72] This once again raises the question of how the parties involved will react, raising concerns on the increased dependence of commercial banks on central banks or fostering price rises and the scarcity of collateral as described above.

8.1.3 Preliminary Conclusions

In conclusion, central bank digital currency has the potential to disrupt the existing banking or money system in general (sovereign money, narrow banking) or in times of a financial crisis (bank runs). Moreover, it could hamper the credit allocation to the real economy and thus hinder overall economic growth and wealth. However, the specific impact of central bank digital currency on financial stability is still not predictable to its fullest extent. The impact strongly depends on several circumstances, some of which can only be steered to a very limited extent. In particular, those—limitedly steerable—circumstances are the demand for the central bank digital currency by the population and the way the financial intermediaries will react to potential deposit outflows. But most important, the disruptive potential depends on how central bank digital currency is used by the public. Thus, special attention needs to be paid to the question of how the central bank digital currency can be designed and how to ensure its use as means of payment rather than as a storage of value.[73]

---

[68] Cf. Bindseil et al. (2021), p. 9.

[69] Adalid et al. (2022), p. 41.

[70] CPMI-MC (2018), p. 16; ECB (2020), p. 17; BIS (2021), p. 12; Hanl and Michaelis (2019), p. 11; Bindseil et al. (2021), p. 9.

[71] BIS (2021), p. 13.

[72] CPMI-MC (2018), pp. 24 and 25.

[73] Cf. Bindseil (2020), p. 8. See for the design options Sect. 8.3.

8.2 Legal Context

The economic problems identified above concern various legal aspects which shall be examined more closely. In particular, disintermediation risks may lead to legislative countermeasures that raise questions of fundamental rights (see Sect. 8.2.1), public interests (see Sect. 8.2.2) and the division of powers between EU institutions (see Sect. 8.2.3).

8.2.1 Fundamental Rights

To begin with, the economic disintermediation risks can be looked at under the perspective of individual rights. In this regard, the financial intermediaries' fundamental rights seem to be the first legal position affected.

Financial intermediaries such as commercial banks, credit providers and non-banks offering deposit-like financial services can refer to Article 16 of the Charter of Fundamental Rights of the European Union (CFR). According to this, the freedom to conduct a business in accordance with Union law and national laws and practices is recognised. Thus, Article 16 CFR '(. . .) covers the freedom to exercise an economic or commercial activity (. . .)'.[74] According to the explanations relating to the Charter,[75] this provision serves the principle of open market economy with free competition in the meaning of Article 119 (1), (3) TFEU. An economic or commercial activity is the provision of goods or services against payment.[76] Hence, the economic activities of the financial intermediaries, such as creating private money, i.e. lending and deposit intaking on a commercial basis, are covered under Article 16 CFR.

Following the classical dogmatic of fundamental rights, the introduction of central bank digital currency would need to impose restrictions on these activities. This might appear questionable at first glance because it will be the customers that directly trigger the discussed disintermediation risks by withdrawing their deposits and shifting them to central bank digital currency. According to a common definition, a restriction of fundamental rights needing justification is every provision that intends detriments for the fundamental rights subject or that is sufficiently connected to the detriment.[77] However, the introduction of central bank digital currency will not contain a legal act that prohibits financial intermediaries from taking deposits or granting credits. The detrimental behaviour pertinent to the intermediaries' fundamental rights is exercised by persons not bound by fundamental rights, cf. Article 51 (1), first sentence, CFR. Thus, one needs to enquire whether Article 16 CFR could

[74] Case C-283/11 *Sky Österreich* ECLI:EU:C:2013:28, para. 42.

[75] Explanations relating to the Charter of Fundamental Rights (14 December 2017) OJ C 303/17.

[76] Jarass (2021), para. 8.

[77] Frenz (2009), para. 2734.

also be restricted by indirect or de facto interferences. When interpreting Article 16 CFR it needs to be taken into consideration that in the past the ECJ understood the right to conduct a business as a manifestation of the freedom to choose an occupation.[78] Thus, ECJ case-law on Article 15 CFR can be used for the interpretation as well. Regarding Article 15 CFR, the ECJ states that a restriction, to be considered as such, needs to have a 'sufficiently direct and significant effect'.[79] To ensure full effectiveness of the Union law, for identifying a relevant restriction of fundamental rights it merely matters if there are detriments that are attributable to a public authority and that are not caused by the aggrieved party.[80] The introduction of central bank digital currency by the EU co-legislators without any restrictions to its store-of-value-function would create an environment in which the intermediaries are not able to conduct their business as they do now, facing a loss of profitability and rising costs. Even though increased costs due to increased competition of private money with central bank digital currency could not be seen as a restriction with regard to the objective of Article 16 CFR,[81] structurally changing the money and banking system in a way that the financial intermediaries lose their privilege to create private money and grant credits can be seen as to have a sufficient and significant effect on the intermediaries' fundamental rights. The same applies for the fact that CBDC facilitates major deposit outflows in times of a financial crisis.

However, it should be noted that any restriction of fundamental rights can be justified, cf. Article 52 (1) CFR. It is settled case-law of the ECJ that '(...) the freedom to conduct a business is not absolute, but must be viewed in relation to its social function [and it] may be subject to a broad range of interventions on the part of public authorities which may limit the exercise of economic activity in the public interest'.[82] In this regard the ECJ states that the freedom to conduct a business '(...) may be restricted, provided that any restrictions in fact correspond to objectives of general interest pursued by the European Community and do not constitute in relation to the aim pursued a disproportionate and intolerable interference, impairing the very substance of the rights guaranteed'.[83] As stated above, central bank digital currency could foster innovation, competition and the EU's strategic autonomy and monetary sovereignty.[84] These aims and objectives are without doubt of general interest. Nonetheless, central bank digital currency shall not impair the very

[78] Case C-4/73 *Nold* ECLI:EU:C:1974:51, para 14; case C-230/78 *Eridania* ECLI:EU:C:1979:216, para. 20 ff.; case C-210/03 *Swedish Match* ECLI:EU:C:2004:802, para. 72 and 73; Bernsdorff (2019), para. 1; Kotzur (2023), para. 1; Jarass (2021), para. 4.

[79] Case C-435/02 *Springer* ECLI:EU:C:2004:552, para. 49.

[80] Cf. case C-84/95 *Bosphorus* ECLI:EU:C:1996:312, para. 22; Penski and Elsner (2001), p. 267; Frenz (2009), para. 2604.

[81] Cf. Frenz (2009), para. 2745; Jarass (2021), para. 14.

[82] Case C-283/11 *Sky Österreich* ECLI:EU:C:2013:28, para. 45 and 46 (comments added).

[83] Case C-200/96 *Metronome* ECLI:EU:C:1998:172, para. 21. See also case C-544/10 *Deutsches Weintor* ECLI:EU:C:2012:526, para. 54 and joined cases C-184/02 and C-223/02 *Spain and Finland/Parliament and Council* ECLI:EU:C:2004:497, para. 52.

[84] See Sect. 1.2.

substance of the freedom to conduct a business. This means that central bank digital currency shall not lead to a situation where the intermediaries are not able to conduct their commercial or economic activity at all.[85] Thus, introducing central bank digital currency with the aim to establish a sovereign money or narrow banking system could be seen as an infringement of the very substance of the freedom of credit institutions to conduct their business. Accordingly, the EU co-legislators would have to respect the principle of proportionality and take into consideration measures to restrict central bank digital currency's store-of-value-function. These measures should mitigate the restrictions on financial intermediaries and ensure the functionality of central bank digital currency to its fullest extent at the same time.

8.2.2 *Public Interests*

Besides individual rights, the economic discussion on disintermediation risks also touches on public interests.

On the one hand, central bank digital currency can be looked at in the light of the principle of an open market economy with free competition, Article 119 (1) TFEU. According to this fundamental principle for the European economic constitution, all economic activities shall be in principle kept free from public restrictions.[86] They should be the outcome of consumer preferences and technological change.[87] Nonetheless, this provision does not aim at prohibiting every intervention in competition, especially increasing the competition.[88] As mentioned above, the introduction of central bank digital currency should foster innovation and competition. Due to the aforementioned economic risks, commercial banks would lose competitiveness and market shares to the benefit of other financial market participants such as non-bank intermediaries if they do not take countermeasures.[89] In this regard, increasing the attractiveness of central bank digital currency would force commercial banks to strive for innovation by way of raising the interest rates or by developing new complementary financial services that distinguish them from their public and private competitors.[90] They can also strengthen their complementary services such as payment services.[91] Moreover, they could strive for enhancing their market position and thus increase customers' trust which would make them less vulnerable to deposit outflows caused by the lack of customers' trust.[92] However, the principle of an open

[85] Cf. Frenz (2009), para. 2765.

[86] Kempen (2018), para. 15.

[87] Cœuré (2018).

[88] Kempen (2018), para. 16.

[89] Bindseil (2020), p. 11.

[90] BIS (2021), p. 11; ECB (2020), p. 16.

[91] Cf. Panetta (2018), p. 4.

[92] Cf. Sanches and Keister (2021), p. 24.

market economy implies the general rule that the state itself should appear as little as possible as an economic subject.[93] This rule would be disregarded if the introduction of CBDC would confer the role of an intermediary on the central bank or at least increase the role of the central bank as an market participant in the economy.[94]

On the other hand, central bank digital currency also impacts financial stability. Financial stability is not clearly defined in EU law. Nonetheless, it can be found several times in the EU primary law, for example in Article 127 (5) TFEU and Article 141 (2), fourth indent, TFEU. It is also mentioned in EU secondary law, for example in recital 44 and Article 1 of the SSMR[95] and recitals 10 and 15 of the ESRB-Regulation.[96] Under Article 3 (1) ESRB-Regulation, the European Systemic Risk Board (ESRB) has the task to prevent systemic risks to financial stability. These provisions show that protecting financial stability and preventing financial instability are key public interests in the European Union. As mentioned, financial stability is not defined in EU law. Thus, different approaches on how to define it can be found in the literature. On the one hand, financial stability can be defined from a functional angle. Accordingly, financial stability is a state in which the participants of the financial system—financial intermediaries, markets and infrastructures—are able to perform their specific tasks adequately.[97] On the other hand, the aspect of overall stability and resilience can be stressed. According to this approach, financial stability is a state of safety and soundness of the financial system in which it can withstand financial shocks, imbalances and crises due to increased overall resilience of the financial participants.[98] However, the EU secondary law can also be used for understanding the concept of financial stability. Article 2 lit. c, first sentence, ESRB-Regulation defines the aim that is pursued by protecting financial stability. According to this provision, 'systemic risk' means a risk of disruption in the financial system with the potential to have serious negative consequences for the real economy of the Union or of one or more of its Member States and for the functioning of the internal market. Although this is a provision from EU secondary law tailored to the tasks of the ESRB that cannot be used to define terms mentioned in EU primary law, the provision shows how a state of financial instability would look like. Hence, protecting financial stability aims at mitigating disruptions in the financial system with severe consequences for the real economy and the functioning

[93]Kempen (2018), para. 16.

[94]Cf. CPMI-MC (2018), p. 14; Lavayssière (2022), p. 15.

[95]Council Regulation (EU) No 1024/2013 of 15 October 2013 conferring specific tasks on the European Central Bank concerning policies relating to the prudential supervision of credit institutions (29 October 2013) OJ L 287/63.

[96]Regulation (EU) No 1092/2010 of the European Parliament and of the Council of 24 November 2010 on European Union macro-prudential oversight of the financial system and establishing a European Systemic Risk Board (15 December 2010) OJ L 331/1, lastly amended by Regulation (EU) 2019/2176 (27 December 2019) OJ L 334/146.

[97]Cf. Ohler (2015), para. 42; Gianviti (2010), para. 22.93.

[98]Cf. Selmayr (2015), para. 60; Lastra (2006), p. 92. See also the understanding of the ECB, https://www.ecb.europa.eu/ecb/tasks/stability/html/index.en.html (Accessed 31.07.2023).

of the internal market. For protecting the real economy, supplying money, i.e. the lending business, is of utmost importance.[99] Furthermore according to Article 2 lit. c, second sentence, ESRB-Regulation, all types of financial intermediaries may be potentially systemically important to some degree. This is complemented by recital 16 of the SSMR which states that the safety and soundness of large credit institutions is essential to ensure the stability of the financial system and that smaller credit institutions can also pose a threat to financial stability. Hence, the safety and soundness of financial intermediaries are crucial for protecting financial stability. Although these factors are mostly ensured by prudential supervision, the economic discussion above demonstrates potential disintermediation risks that pose a threat to financial stability if central bank digital currency is introduced. Apart from that, it should be noted that central bank digital currency could also contribute to stabilising the financial system. According to economic studies, observing the flow of funds into central bank digital currency may provide additional information to the supervisory authorities at the forefront of a run and enable them to intervene more timely.[100]

In conclusion, there is a tension between ensuring the free competition and align with an open market economy on the one hand and protecting the safety and soundness of financial intermediaries to prevent risks for financial stability on the other hand. Easing this tension calls for restrictive measures taken by the EU co-legislators who must respect thereby the principle of proportionality.

8.2.3 Division of Powers

As set out before, both perspectives require measures that restrict the store-of-value-function in order to prevent possible financial stability risks caused by the usage of central bank digital currency as an investment. Since this task concerns fundamental rights as well as crucial public interests, it is first of all the EU co-legislators who are responsible to consider these measures. However, since the digital euro will be a direct liability item of the ECB and the ECB will decide about specific choices of the technical design, the questions arises as to how to divide the powers of these EU institutions and what role each of them will have.

8.2.3.1 Scope of Powers

As mentioned above, the measures to be taken shall aim at mitigating possible risks for financial stability caused by the introduction of central bank digital currency. If the EU co-legislators empower the ECB to implement specific measures in order to

[99] Cf. Ohler (2015), para. 42; Selmayr (2015), para. 60.

[100] Keister and Monnet (2022), pp. 20 ff.

safeguard financial stability, this then raises the question whether this can be seen as an extension to the scope of ECB's powers to the detriment of other authorities.

When it comes to safeguarding financial stability, the allocation of competences is not clearly expressed in EU law and thus, legal dispute can arise. The only provision in EU primary law that confers competences regarding financial stability is Article 127 (5) TFEU. According to this provision, the ESCB shall contribute to the smooth conduct of policies pursued by the competent authorities relating to the prudential supervision of credit institutions and the stability of the financial system. Starting with the wording of this provision it becomes clear that the ESCB is not assigned any exclusive power in the field of financial stability but rather contributes to the measures taken by the competent authorities.[101] That means that financial stability cannot be considered as the ESCB's primary objective.[102] Nonetheless, it could be argued that financial stability and monetary policy are correlated because increasing the volume of money in circulation also increases the risk of financial distress.[103] Hence, financial stability could be seen as a prerequisite for monetary policy which is a primary objective of the ESCB, Article 127 (1), (2), first indent, TFEU.[104] Moreover it could be argued that 'financial stability is a precondition for the real economy to provide jobs, credit and growth'[105] and thus is part of the general economic policy, cf. Article 127 (1), second sentence, TFEU.[106] In both ways, financial stability would be given a higher significance in ESCB's objectives. However, although financial stability may provide the background for monetary policy, it is conceptually and practically not identical.[107] Furthermore, the wording of Article 127 (5) TFEU appears to be clear, thus these interpretations cannot be used to inadmissibly circumvent the conferral of merely contributory powers and establish financial stability as a primary objective of the ESCB.[108] Due to the lack of a clear allocation in the Treaties, financial stability cannot be seen as an exclusive Union competence, but rather as a concern of various authorities at the Union and Member State level.[109] For example, it can be derived from Article 136 (3) TFEU that Member States adopt measures to maintain financial stability.[110] Moreover, with respect to the principle of conferral, cf. Article 5 (1), first sentence, (2) TEU, all competences not expressively conferred on the Union remain competences of the Member States. Thus, it could be questionable why the EU co-legislators shall now be entitled to adopt measures protecting financial stability. The need for pursuing

[101] Friebel (2022), para. 86 and 137; Lastra and Psaroudakis (2020), para. 26.43.

[102] Albertazzi et al. (2021), p. 7; Ioannidis et al. (2021), p. 20.

[103] Gianviti (2010), para. 22.108.

[104] Ohler (2015), para. 39 ff.; Friebel (2022), para. 136; Lastra and Psaroudakis (2020), para. 26.39.

[105] Recital 1 of the ESRB-Regulation.

[106] Selmayr (2015), para. 63.

[107] Lastra and Psaroudakis (2020), para. 26.44.

[108] Albertazzi et al. (2021), p. 8; Friebel (2022), para. 145; Ioannidis et al. (2021), p. 20.

[109] Friebel (2022), para. 138.

[110] Ohler (2015), para. 38.

this objective arises from the possible side effects of establishing central bank digital currency. If the task to adopt corresponding measures were on the Member States, the use of the digital euro as the single currency would be endangered. Thus, regulating aspects of financial stability directly linked to the introduction of the digital euro is subject to the EU co-legislators' competence under Article 133 TFEU.

Regarding the institutional competence, one needs to take into consideration the existence of the European System of Financial Supervision (ESFS) consisting of the EBA, the EIOPA, the ESMA and the ESRB.[111] Looking at the tasks conferred on the ESRB and the ESCB, safeguarding financial stability is a rather contributary task for the ESCB, cf. Article 127 (5) TFEU, whereas it is a primary objective for the ESRB, cf. Article 3 (1) ESRB-Regulation.[112] This leads to the fact that the ESRB has a broader range of tools in the field of financial stability whereas the ESCB can only choose from a limited, non-binding set of tools, cf. Articles 15 to 18 ESRB-Regulation on the one hand and Article 25.1 ESCB Statute on the other hand.[113] From a legal policy standpoint, having such a system to protect financial stability raises the question of why the EU co-legislators shall confer the power to implement the measures to restrict central bank digital currency's store-of-value-function on the E(S)CB. To begin with, as already mentioned, the ESCB/ECB issues the digital euro and thus is the body closest to the subject. In addition, the ESCB/ECB has had experience in the field of supervision and thus contributed to financial stability long before the ESRB was established, which is also recognised by the EU co-legislators.[114] Hence, it appears consequent to use the ESCB's experience. Furthermore, competences conferred on the ESRB under EU secondary law do not prevent the EU co-legislators to confer powers in the field of financial stability on other bodies.

8.2.3.2 Independence of the European Central Bank

The section above focused on the question of whether the EU co-legislators are competent under Article 133 TFEU to confer the task of implementing the measures for protecting financial stability on the ESCB and de facto the ECB, cf. Article 129 (1) TFEU. In addition, it is also questionable how detailed these provisions can be. This is due to the independence of the ECB which is guaranteed under EU primary law, cf. Articles 130, 282 (3), third and fourth sentence, TFEU. Pursuant to Article 130, first sentence, TFEU, when exercising the powers and carrying out the tasks and duties conferred upon them by the Treaties and the Statute of the ESCB and of the ECB, neither the European Central Bank, nor a national central bank, nor any member of their decision-making bodies shall seek or take instructions from

[111] Hartig (2012), p. 775.

[112] Hartig (2012), p. 777.

[113] Cf. Friebel (2022), para. 149.

[114] See for example recital 24 of the ESRB-Regulation and recital 13 of the SSMR.

Union institutions, bodies, offices or agencies, from any government of a Member State or from any other body. Since the duty to implement measures safeguarding financial stability does not arise from the Treaties but rather from a regulation adopted in accordance with Article 133 TFEU, the core legal question is to what extent the ECB is bound by EU secondary law.

In this regard, there are two views that are diametrically opposed. On the one hand, EU secondary law is solely legally binding if there is an exclusive provision in the Treaties allowing for conferral on the ECB.[115] On the other hand, EU secondary law is always binding because of the democratic legitimacy of the EU co-legislators.[116] However, besides these rather academic views, the judgement of the ECJ in the *OLAF*-case[117] is of utmost importance in practice. According to this decision, Article 130 TFEU seeks to enable the ECB to effectively pursue its objectives attributed by the TFEU and the ESCB Statute.[118] However, provisions like Article 127 (1), second sentence, TFEU and Article 127 (6) TFEU show that the Treaties do not aim at completely excluding the ECB from Union law.[119] The ECJ consequently states '(. . .) that there are no grounds which prima facie preclude the Community legislature from adopting, by virtue of the powers conferred on it by the EC Treaty and under the conditions laid down therein, legislative measures capable of applying to the ECB'.[120] From this statement a first condition for enacting secondary law by the EU co-legislators with effect for the ECB can be derived. This is, as clarified in Article 13 (2), first sentence, TEU, that there needs to be a legal basis in the Treaties conferring (any)[121] legislative powers upon the EU co-legislators.[122] Furthermore, the ECB needs to establish that the secondary law act in question undermines its ability to perform independently the specific tasks conferred on it by the Treaties.[123] Hence, Article 130, first sentence, TFEU needs to be reduced teleologically in the sense that it only prohibits legislative acts that impair the fulfilment of ECB's objective of price stability.[124]

The legal basis for a regulation that empowers the ECB to implement measures safeguarding financial stability is Article 133 TFEU. The main purpose of these measures is to prevent risks for financial stability if central bank digital currency is massively to be used as an investment. Restricting central bank digital currency's

---

[115]Zilioli and Selmayr (2001), p. 39.

[116]Dutzler (2001), pp. 9 and 15; Editorial Comments (1996), p. 626; Lavranos (2003), p. 886; Amtenbrink and de Haan (2002), p. 70; Torrent (1999), p. 1234.

[117]Case C-11/00 *OLAF* ECLI:EU:C:2003:395.

[118]Case C-11/00 *OLAF* ECLI:EU:C:2003:395, para. 134.

[119]Case C-11/00 *OLAF* ECLI:EU:C:2003:395, para. 135.

[120]Case C-11/00 *OLAF* ECLI:EU:C:2003:395, para. 136.

[121]Häde (2022b), para. 71.

[122]Selmayr (2015), para. 90.

[123]Case C-11/00 *OLAF* ECLI:EU:C:2003:395, para. 137.

[124]Griller (2023), para. 31; Häde (2022b), para. 73; Opinion of Advocate General Jacobs, C-11/00, ECLI:EU:C:2002:556, para. 155; Selmayr (2015), para. 91.

store-of-value-function would be done by narrowing the amount each end-user could hold or transfer.[125] However, this will also influence the quantity of central bank digital currency in circulation. Regulating the quantity of public money in circulation is first of all a task of monetary policy.[126] Thus, possible measures to be taken will have a dual nature. On the one hand, they will serve to maintain financial stability. On the other hand, they can be used within ECB's monetary policy mandate, cf. Article 127 (2), first indent, TFEU. Although the restrictive measures could be used for monetary policy objectives, this is not the intention of the EU co-legislators.[127] The measures are not intended to regulate the quantity of central bank digital currency after its issuance, but to prevent risks for financial stability if the issuance leads to a massive change in customer behaviour. This primary focus on financial stability can be demonstrated by including a variety of measures in the regulation of which the ECB can choose to implement in a way that suits best the expected economic behaviour of customers. Hence, despite the measures' dual nature, conferring their implementation upon the ECB does not impact the ECB's ability to fulfil its primary objective of maintaining price stability. However, since the customer behaviour strongly depends on the overall economic situation, there would need to be a margin of appreciation left to the ECB because it is closer to the markets and its participants. The EU co-legislators would need to list and define the measures, but when and to what extent they will be implemented (e.g. remuneration rate, specific level of holding or transaction cap etc.), should be on the ECB to decide. Regarding the latter, the ECB should be obliged to report periodically on what measures have been taken or not taken and the (economic) reasons for its decision. This accountability is not alien to the Treaties, cf. Article 284 (3), subparagraph 1, TFEU nor to areas where EU secondary law has conferred powers upon the ECB, cf. Article 20 SSMR.

8.2.3.3 Banking Supervision

Next to ECB's scope of competences related to other Union bodies, it should also be taken into consideration how to distinguish ECB's competences in the areas of monetary policy and banking supervision. According to the aim of the EU co-legislators, the ECB shall use the measures to prevent bank runs and thus a financial crisis caused by commercial banks' liquidity shortages and reduced lending operations. However, this objective can also be connected to banking supervision and the ECB's macroprudential powers. As already mentioned, the SSMR confers specific prudential supervision tasks on the ECB. According to Article 4 (3), first sentence, SSMR, for the purpose of carrying out the tasks conferred on it by this

---

[125] For more details see Sect. 8.3.

[126] Waldhoff (2022), para. 39 and 45; Ohler (2021), pp. 42 and 81.

[127] Cf. also case C-370/12 *Pringle* ECLI:EU:C:2012:756, para. 56; case C-62/14 *Gauweiler* ECLI:EU:C:2015:400, para. 52.

Regulation the ECB shall apply all relevant Union law, and where this Union law is composed of Directives, the national legislation transposing those Directives. Hence, in case of a banking crisis due to banks' liquidity shortages the ECB could apply the relevant supervisory Union law and their national implementation acts.[128] For this purpose, especially the early intervention measures of Article 27 BRRD[129] could be used, which apply in situations of rapidly deteriorating financial conditions, including deteriorating liquidity situations and increasing levels of leverage. Furthermore, ECB's supervisory powers under Article 16 SSMR should be considered. With these two provisions combined the ECB could also address the potential systemic risks of central bank digital currency. This could be done by either varying the standards for institutions' own funds[130] (cf. Articles 25 to 386 CRR[131]) to battle the credit risk and operational risk[132] and improve the institution's resilience in the long term.[133] Or it could be done by varying the standards for the liquidity management (cf. Articles 411 to 428 CRR in conjunction with Regulation (EU) 2015/61[134]) to address short-term liquidity shortages caused by deposit outflows due to a loss of customers' trust.[135] However, it should be noted that the aforementioned competences only apply in the case that a singular credit institution is in distress or failed. Thus, ECB's competences under the SSMR only apply to particular financial market participants while the measures safeguarding financial stability are of general application to prevent the financial intermediaries in total from being in distress. Hence, when restricting central bank digital currency's store-of-value-function the ECB cannot act as a banking supervisory body under the SSMR. Similar thoughts apply to the unwritten Emergency Liquidity Assistance (ELA) programmes of the ECB in their role as lender of last resort.[136] ELA provides specially collateralized central bank

[128] Cf. Glos and Benzig (2018), para. 50.

[129] Directive 2014/59/EU of the European Parliament and of the Council of 15 May 2014 establishing a framework for the recovery and resolution of credit institutions and investment firms and amending Council Directive 82/891/EEC, and Directives 2001/24/EC, 2002/47/EC, 2004/25/EC, 2005/56/EC, 2007/36/EC, 2011/35/EU, 2012/30/EU and 2013/36/EU, and Regulations (EU) No 1093/2010 and (EU) No 648/2012, of the European Parliament and of the Council (12 June 2014) OJ L 173/190, lastly amended by Regulation (EU) 2022/2036 (25 October 2022) OJ L 275/1.

[130] See the definition in Article 4 No. 118 CRR.

[131] Regulation (EU) No 575/2013 of the European Parliament and of the Council of 26 June 2013 on prudential requirements for credit institutions and investment firms and amending Regulation (EU) No 648/2012 (27 June 2013) OJ L 176/1, lastly amended by Regulation (EU) 2022/2036 (25 October 2022) OJ L 275/1.

[132] See the definition in Article 4 No. 52 CRR.

[133] Cf. Laufenberg (2018), para. 2.

[134] Commission Delegated Regulation (EU) 2015/61 of 10 October 2014 to supplement Regulation (EU) No 575/2013 of the European Parliament and the Council with regard to liquidity coverage requirement for Credit Institutions (17 January 2015) OJ L 11/1, lastly amended by Commission Delegated Regulation (EU) 2022/786 (20 May 2022) OJ L 141/1.

[135] Cf. Laufenberg (2018), para. 2.

[136] Bindseil (2014), pp. 242 and 243.

credits at higher interest rates. Since these are provided to individual banks in distress only, ELA is not suitable to address systemic risks as a whole.[137]

8.3 Design Options

Now that the economic dimension and its legal context have become clear, the following section focuses on possible measure to restrict the use of central bank digital currency as an investment. To do so, several measures are discussed in the literature.[138]

8.3.1 Remuneration

To begin with, a system of remuneration of central bank digital currency holdings is discussed.[139] Remunerating holdings could be done either with fixed or variable interest rates.[140] The latter would be linked via a spread to other central bank rates such as the main refinancing operation rate (MRO) or the standing facility rate.[141] While applying variable remuneration rates to the account-based digital euro would be easy to execute, this would not be the case for the digital euro as a bearer-instrument that is used for several consecutive offline-payments.[142] However, different remuneration rates for both functionalities of the digital euro would hamper the convertibility between these forms.[143]

Predominantly, a tiered remuneration system is advocated in the discussion so far.[144] For this, *Bindseil*[145] invented an often-cited system which should be presented in the following part. The reasoning behind using a (multi-)tier remuneration system is that even with a negative interest rate in a one-tier system there will still be users that would convert their deposits into central bank digital currency, accepting a constant reduction of their holdings.[146] The basic concept of a multi-tier remuneration system appears to be simple as there will be a certain holding threshold with a positive or neutral remuneration below that figure and an unattractive and

[137] Bindseil (2014), pp. 242 and 243.

[138] For an overview see BIS (2021), p. 2; Panetta (2021); ECB (2020), p. 17.

[139] Cf. Hanl and Michaelis (2019), p. 9; Bindseil et al. (2021), p. 12.

[140] ECB (2020), p. 32.

[141] ECB (2020), p. 32.

[142] ECB (2020), p. 34.

[143] ECB (2020), p. 34 fn. 60.

[144] Cf. ECB (2020), pp. 28 and 32; CPMI-MC (2018), p. 11.

[145] Bindseil (2020), pp. 22 ff.

[146] CPMI-MC (2018), p. 17; Bindseil (2020), p. 22.

possibly negative remuneration above that threshold.[147] This technique is already known for the remuneration of government deposits held at the central banks, cf. Article 4 (1) DALM-Guide.[148] However, the difficulty of this system is to identify the adequate threshold and calibrate the remuneration rate. Regarding the threshold, *Bindseil* argues in favour of EUR 3000 for individuals because this represents the average monthly net income of households in the EU.[149] *Panetta* joins this threshold with the reasoning that this would be the same amount citizens would not exceed when holding cash.[150] The threshold for corporations should be different and aligned to the corporations' size and their presumed need for payment means.[151] Others favour a general threshold that amounts to the same sum which is covered by the Deposit Guarantee Scheme.[152] Regarding the remuneration rate, *Bindseil* uses the ECB's deposit facility rate for calibrating, which is currently[153] 3.50%. Accordingly, remuneration for tier 1 (below threshold) should equal the deposit facility rate with a zero-lower-bound while remuneration for tier 2 (above threshold) should be 2% below the deposit facility rate with a zero-upper-bound.[154] This link to the deposit facility rate could be varied flexibly, according to the economic surroundings, ranging up to 10% below the deposit facility rate for tier-two holdings in situations of financial crises.[155]

Nevertheless, a (multi-tier) remuneration system also raises concerns. To begin with, it could be argued that preventing the use of central bank digital currency as an investment could also be achieved by implementing a one-tier system and temporarily adjusting the remuneration.[156] However, agreeing with *Bindseil*, a multi-tier system would offer some economic and political benefits. From an economic perspective, the different tiers would represent the functions of money more closely, especially the function as means of payment (below threshold) and the function as storage of value (above threshold).[157] From a political point of view, a multi-tier system would ensure overall attractiveness of central bank digital currency as there would be no need to remunerate every holding negatively.[158] Next to this, the

[147] Bindseil (2020), p. 22.

[148] Guideline (EU) 2019/671 of the European Central Bank of 9 April 2019 on domestic asset and liability management operations by the national central banks (recast) (ECB/2019/7) (29 April 2019) OJ L 113/11.

[149] Bindseil (2020), p. 24.

[150] Panetta (2021).

[151] Bindseil (2020), p. 24.

[152] CPMI-MC (2018), p. 11.

[153] Rate for July 2023, https://www.bundesbank.de/dynamic/action/de/statistiken/zeitreihen-datenbanken/zeitreihen-datenbank/723452/723452?tsId=BBK01.SU0200&dateSelect=2022.

[154] Bindseil (2020), p. 25.

[155] Bindseil (2020), p. 26.

[156] Bindseil (2020), p. 23.

[157] Bindseil (2020), p. 23.

[158] Bindseil (2020), p. 24.

remuneration rate for tier-2-holdings raises further critics. First of all, the effectiveness in practice could be doubted because end-users could still shift to the non-remunerated cash in high volume.[159] Moreover, using negative interest rates could affect the public opinion and general acceptance.[160] Furthermore, it seems questionable whether a variable interest rate could be implemented to the digital euro as a bearer-instrument used for offline-payments with a higher degree of privacy or anonymity.[161] And lastly, one needs to consider the arbitrage-effect on secondary markets, meaning the lending of excessive holdings to other end-users and taking advantage of the spread between the lending interest rate and the penalty interest rate.[162] This could circumvent the tiered remuneration's aim to prevent the usage as an investment. These critical aspects could hamper the overall effectiveness of a remuneration system as a tool to prevent financial disintermediation risks.

8.3.2 Holding and Transaction Limits

A second approach would be to limit the amount of central bank digital currency accessible by end-users for holdings. This could be done by either setting an individual or general limit the users can hold or by limiting the volume of the wallets and restricting the number of wallets in circulation.[163] Here as well as for the remuneration threshold most authors favour a cap of EUR 3000 for individual holdings.[164] According to an economic study, this specific holding limit, interpreted as a hard cap,[165] would not amplify the scale and speed of bank runs[166] whereas each increase by EUR 1000 would raise the deposit substitution rate by 2%.[167] The key aspect when using holding limits is the function of central bank digital currency as means of payment. What happens if a transaction would exceed the payee's holding limit? Would the exceeding amount only or the transaction as a whole be rejected? How could the payer know beforehand if his transaction will prevail? Would he therefore always need to know the payee's current holding balance before initiating and authorising the transaction? To answer parts of these questions, most authors

[159] BIS (2021), p. 15.

[160] BIS (2021), p. 16.

[161] Cf. Bindseil et al. (2021), p. 12.

[162] BIS (2021), p. 16.

[163] ECB (2019), p. 8.

[164] Cf. Panetta (2021); Adalid et al. (2022), p. 12. See BIS (2021), p. 15 which argues for holding limits tailored to households and corporates. See in this regard also Bindseil et al. (2021), pp. 10 ff.

[165] With a soft limit holding units above the threshold would be possible but excess holdings would be subject to unattractive remuneration, cf. Adalid et al. (2022), p. 38.

[166] Adalid et al. (2022), p. 38 (see p. 40 chart 14a for the link between increased limits and speed and scale of bank runs).

[167] Adalid et al. (2022), p. 13.

favour a so-called 'waterfall-solution'.[168] With this tool, the exceeding transfer amount would automatically be shifted to private scriptural money in the payee's account held with the payee's financial intermediary.[169] Thus, the payee would not need to disclose his holding balance to the payer before the transaction. However, this requires all end-users to have access to an account held with a financial intermediary.[170] This could raise concerns regarding the question of financial inclusion, cf. Article 16 PAD.[171] Furthermore, as there would be no network-connectivity for offline-payments, exceeding transactions would possibly be rejected as a whole.[172] This would hamper the payment function of the digital euro as a bearer-instrument. Lastly, to ensure effectiveness of the holding limit, it would need to be implemented for every end-user individually and by design which would require the disclosure of the end-user's identity at least during onboarding to prevent the use of strawmen.[173]

These holding limits can also be complemented by measures limiting the transfer amount. This could be done by either directly limiting the amount that the payer can transact in a certain period (a day/a month etc.) or by charging fees for transactions that are exceeding specific volumes or numbers of transactions.[174]

8.3.3 Miscellaneous Measures

In addition to the frequently mentioned measures above there are other suggestions to limit the usage of central bank digital currency as an investment.

First, the fungibility of central bank digital currency can be restricted. This refers to the convertibility to other non-bank-assets such as cash and central bank reserves or to bank deposits.[175] Both restrictions would lower the overall attractiveness of central bank digital currency and reduce the deposit outflows. However, the suggestion to impose limits on convertibility is predominantly rejected because the convertibility of money to other forms of money at par is not only a key user demand but also a core principle in central banking.[176] Furthermore, it is questionable how

[168] See for example CPMI-MC (2018), p. 11; BIS (2021), p. 16; Bindseil et al. (2021), p. 11.

[169] ECB (2020), p. 28; Bindseil (2020), p. 22.

[170] ECB (2020), p. 28; Bindseil (2020), p. 22.

[171] Directive 2014/92/EU of the European Parliament and of the Council of 23 July 2014 on the comparability of fees related to payment accounts, payment account switching and access to payment accounts with basic features (28 August 2014) *OJ L 257/214.*

[172] ECB (2020), p. 34 fn. 59.

[173] Panetta (2021); ECB (2020), p. 28.

[174] BIS (2021), pp. 14 and 16.

[175] Adalid et al. (2022), p. 39; Mancini-Griffoli et al. (2018), p. 23; Wierts and Boven (2020), p. 35; Juks (2018), p. 96; Kiff et al. (2020), p. 16.

[176] Kiff et al. (2020), p. 32; Bindseil (2020), p. 19; Grünewald et al. (2021), p. 1047; Meaning et al. (2018), p. 14; Bindseil et al. (2021), p. 11.

plausible limits on convertibility between central bank liabilities are in practice because this would raise the question of what would be the economy's unit of account?[177]

Second, some authors suggest to amend the existing banking supervision and regulatory framework.[178] This could be done by adjusting the liquidity standards which consist of the Liquidity Coverage Ratio (LCR) and the Net Stable Funding Ratio (NSFR), cf. Articles 411 to 428 CRR. Since the LCR is the ratio of the liquidity buffer and the net liquidity outflows over a period of 30 days,[179] the currently calculated LCRs do not take into account the possibility of a simplified deposit shifting under central bank digital currency. Hence, there would be room for adjustment by way of requiring more liquid assets to counter deposit outflows. Furthermore, the central banks could adjust their regulatory framework on collateral and access to central bank reserves in order to provide more liquidity.[180] But, as already discussed above, this would lead to a shortage of high-quality liquid assets and undesirably increase the dependence of commercial banks on central banks.

Third, the above-mentioned measures can also be combined. For this, the Sand Dollar of the Bahamas could be seen as a leading case. The Central Bank of the Bahamas uses a tiered system with holding and transaction limits for individual holdings.[181] Individuals can choose between two wallets. The tier-1-wallet has a holding limit of B$ 500 with a monthly transaction limit of B$ 1500. The digital units can be accessed either by mobile phone applications or by a physical payment card. For both, government-issued identification is not required, allowing for more privacy. Thus, tier-1-wallets can be considered as close to cash as possible. However, since this tier-1-wallet cannot be linked to a bank account, there is no waterfall-solution. This means that any exceeding payment would be rejected as a whole. The tier-2-wallet allows for a holding limit of B$ 8000 with a monthly transaction limit of B$ 10,000. Here, government-issued identification is required and since it can be linked to a bank account, the waterfall-solution is implemented. For corporations and merchants, the Central Bank of the Bahamas chooses a different approach.[182] The Sand Dollar can be accessed through a mobile phone or smart point of sale terminals. The wallets have a holding limit of B$ 8000 to B$ 1,000,000 and unlimited annual transactions. They must be linked to a bank account for incoming transactions that exceed the holding limit. However, it should be noted that sole proprietors with low volumes of transactions can also choose the individual wallets.[183]

Lastly, a model of *Kumhof and Noone* presents four core design principles which should minimise the likelihood of bank disintermediation. These four

---

[177] Meaning et al. (2018), p. 5.

[178] Juks (2018), pp. 95 and 96; BIS (2021), p. 16; cf. also Bindseil (2014), p. 269.

[179] For the calculation see Laufenberg (2018), para. 29 and Bindseil (2014), p. 268.

[180] BIS (2021), p. 17.

[181] For this and the following see https://www.sanddollar.bs/individual (Accessed 31.07.2023).

[182] For this and the following see https://www.sanddollar.bs/merchants (Accessed 31.07.2023).

[183] Cf. https://www.sanddollar.bs/individual (Accessed 31.07.2023).

principles are:[184] Central bank digital currency pays an adjustable interest rate; it is not convertible into reserves and vice versa; there is no guaranteed, on-demand convertibility of bank deposits into central bank digital currency; the central bank issues the digital units only against eligible securities. This model is subject to critique as well as approval.[185] The first principle should be used to regulate the quantity of central bank digital currency, especially in the case of an oversupply by increasing demand.[186] However, it should be noted that this theoretical concept of oversupply would be dissolved in other ways in practice.[187] The second and third principles can be identified as the core of *Kumhof and Noone's* model and circle around limiting the convertibility between various forms of money. However, as mentioned above,[188] this convertibility is a key user demand and a core principle of money and central banking. Furthermore, the reasoning for the third principle (convertibility of deposits) does not fully convince. According to *Kumhof and Noone*, banks should not be obliged to convert deposits into central bank digital currency because this was also not the case for cash[189] and the fulfilment of such an obligation in times of crises was not credible.[190] However, the former argument raises concerns on the consistency with the principle of freedom of contract because most customers are in a contractual relation with their financial intermediaries from which a claim for paying out the deposit balance can be derived.[191] Moreover, the latter argument is in contrast to the idea of public money. To deny any obligation for an on-demand convertibility just because it is not credible that banks could fulfil it in times of crises rules out the guarantee that the central bank supplies public money to the economy, which is its core task. Instead, it should be tried to design the central bank digital currency in a way that the demand for it remains moderate. Or the regulatory framework should be adjusted so that banks could fulfil the demand for convertibility. The fourth principle (issuing only against eligible securities) is indeed not an innovation caused by central bank digital currency because the ESCB already conducts credit operations based on adequate collateral, cf. Art. 18.1, second indent, ESCB Statute. What appears inconsistent to this principle, which *Bindseil* rightly pointed out,[192] is the fact that securities created by unknown third-parties but not reserves created by the central banks should be accepted against the issue of central bank digital currency. If the fourth principle aims at allowing the central banks to

---

[184] Kumhof and Noone (2018), p. 5.

[185] Bjerg (2018); Juks (2018), p. 96 fn. 35; Bindseil (2020), pp. 17 ff.

[186] Kumhof and Noone (2018), p. 8.

[187] See for that Bindseil (2020), pp. 17 and 18.

[188] See footnote 176 with further references.

[189] According to the authors, the current practice of cash's convertibility should result to be a historical practice, at least in the United Kingdom, see Kumhof and Noone (2018), p. 14.

[190] Kumhof and Noone (2018), p. 14.

[191] Cf. Sect. 7.1.2.

[192] Bindseil (2020), p. 21.

manage their balance sheet risks,[193] then accepting safe and sound collateral such as reserves would be the logical consequence. In essence, the model of *Kumhof and Noone* results to be a combination of various measures mentioned above with a core focus on limiting the convertibility of CBDC.

8.4 Opinion

The economic discussion on disintermediation risks, its legal context and possible countermeasures have now been presented.

In this regard, it does not seem realistic that CBDC will cause structural disintermediation. The concept of sovereign money would need to be introduced by a legislative act because it strongly affects fundamental rights. However, there has been no official statement of EU organs relating to that context or signalising such radical change. The same accounts for the narrow banking system. Central bank digital currency will exist complementarily to the private money of commercial banks whereas in a system of narrow banking private scriptural money would be eliminated.[194] Nonetheless, if commercial banks were to become too dependent on central banks' funding, attention should be paid that this shall not covertly circumvent the current system of private and public money.

Furthermore, one needs to acknowledge that capital runs into low-risk capital markets assets are still possible even today. Hence, a deposit shift during normal times as well as in times of financial crises is no innovation caused by central bank digital currency. But nowadays' shifts to capital market assets face constraints, which are set by the pricing mechanism, the volume of overall assets that can be shifted and the financial education of the population.[195] These limits would not apply to central bank digital currency in the same way. Thus, the risk for a run is inherently higher compared to alternative forms of digital money that are accessible nowadays.[196] Nevertheless, risks sometimes pose chances. This inherent risk of deposit shifts puts pressure on banks to become more innovative. They could focus more on enhancing their complementary services and thus increase the competition in the banking sector.[197] Moreover, the possible effects on banks' lending business strongly depend on the competition with non-bank-lending businesses as well.[198] Thus, disintermediation effects will also depend on banks' market shares and their ability to develop new business models that enable them to pull ahead in

[193] Kumhof and Noone (2018), p. 17.

[194] CPMI-MC (2018), p. 16 fn. 29.

[195] Bindseil et al. (2021), p. 9.

[196] Bindseil et al. (2021), p. 9.

[197] Panetta (2018), p. 4; BIS (2021), p. 6.

[198] BIS (2021), p. 6.

competition.[199] In addition, albeit speculative, central bank digital currency could have a stabilising effect for the financial system because customers could refrain from banks engaged in high-risk investments by shifting their deposits and thus discipline the banks.[200]

Despite the positive effects of central bank digital currency for competition, its introduction touches on fundamental rights of the financial intermediaries. Thus, preventing its use as an investment seems necessary to meet the principle of proportionality. Restricting central bank digital currency's store-of-value-function would be best done by design.[201] The CBDC will need to be designed in a way that allows the ECB to control its quantity in circulation.[202] Insofar, a number of measures has been presented above. To respect the ECB's margin of appreciation and its experience in questions of financial stability, the EU co-legislators should predefine possible measure in the regulation and leave the specific calibration to the ECB.

Regarding a possible remuneration of holdings, the respective interest rate environment needs to be considered. A non-remunerated central bank digital currency in an environment with negative interest rates[203] would face high demand and would lead to undesired substitution effects with deposits.[204] In an environment with positive interest rates, a non-remunerated central bank digital currency would not be attractive in normal times.[205] In times of a crisis, customers would only shift their deposits to CBDC if the financial system was affected as whole, otherwise they would just shift to other financial service providers to maximize their yields. Thus, the non-remuneration of public money in an environment with high interest rates prevents bank runs caused by central bank digital currency by itself.[206] If the ECB decides to use positive remuneration, this could also influence the investment choices of professional and institutional investors as central bank digital currency would compete with other capital market products.[207] Furthermore, this could lead to a lower hard cap for the money market interest rate.[208] For these reasons, a positive remuneration of central bank digital currency standing alone without further restrictions does not appear to be suitable and appropriate.

Therefore, the usage of limits seems to be recommendable. Limits are also not alien to the European legislation, as there are, for example, different due-diligence obligations for transactions (EUR 10,000 for cash, cf. Article 11 lit. c AMLD) or

---

[199] Sanches and Keister (2021), p. 24.

[200] Mancini-Griffoli et al. (2018), p. 23; Hanl and Michaelis (2019), p. 10.

[201] Panetta (2021); Adalid et al. (2022), p. 7; ECB (2022a), p. 9; Meaning et al. (2018), p. 12.

[202] Bindseil (2020), p. 13.

[203] Meaning a negative deposit facility rate and a rate for the MRO of zero.

[204] Adalid et al. (2022), p. 8; CPMI-MC (2018), p. 11.

[205] Adalid et al. (2022), p. 7.

[206] Bindseil (2020), p. 16.

[207] CPMI-MC (2018), p. 11.

[208] CPMI-MC (2018), p. 11.

holdings (EUR 150, cf. Article 12 (1) AMLD) above a certain limit.[209] By definition, transaction limits restrict the means-of-payment-function of CBDC as money. Hence, their implementation should be proportionate with respect to other public and private interests. Convertibility limits put into question fundamental principles of public money and central banking. If their use were to be considered as inevitably necessary, the usage should be restricted to a predefined short period.[210]

Furthermore, holding limits will be *the* instrument to restrict the store-of-value-function. However, when using holding limits two main aspects should be borne in mind. What happens to payments exceeding the limit?[211] Furthermore, the holding limits should be calibrated to fit the specific user type (individuals, corporations, merchants etc.).[212] A 'one-size-fits-all' holding limit does not seem appropriate.[213] Hence, in any case a waterfall-solution should be implemented to underline central bank digital currency's primary function as means of payment.[214] For this, special attention needs to be paid to the possibility of linking central bank digital currency holdings to a bank account and the right to open a bank account guaranteed under Article 16 PAD. However, for the digital euro as a bearer-instrument, some restrictions to this right would need to be accepted. As by definition there will be no network-connectivity, exceeding payments cannot be transferred automatically to the payee's bank account. In order to still guarantee its usage as means of payment, there could be a specific low-volume holding limit which would make it easier for the owner to track the transactions made and thus allow him to determine the resulting buffer to the hard cap.[215] For calibrating the cap, a careful economic analysis needs to be done. This analysis should be complemented by policy objectives as well. Even though a holding limit should prevent central bank digital currency from becoming too attractive, it should not discourage the economic actors from using central bank digital currency as a whole. Hence, a cap should not be set too low, leaving room for its practical use in daily life of consumers and businesses. For calibration, relying on proven parameters can be useful. Some arguments for the EUR 3000 limit for individuals refer to similarities with cash.[216] However, it should be noted that although central bank digital currency can be designed to be as close to cash as possible, it will not actually be cash. The physicality of cash sets limits to its storage by nature[217] which is not the case for an account-based digital euro. Hence, using comparisons with cash is convincing to a limited extent only. Alternatively,

---

[209] Cf. Manger-Nestler (2021), p. 7.

[210] Cf. ECB (2022b), slide 7.

[211] ECB (2022b), slide 8.

[212] ECB (2022b), slide 8; Bindseil et al. (2021), pp. 10 and 11.

[213] ECB (2022b), slide 8.

[214] This is also the view of ECB (2022a), p. 10.

[215] In this direction also ECB (2022a), p. 10.

[216] Panetta (2021): amount citizens would not exceed when holding cash; Panetta (2022): aggregated amount would be comparable with the current holdings of banknotes in circulation.

[217] E.g. storage space and costs.

using the amount covered by the Deposit Guarantee Scheme[218] would make central bank digital currency become closer to deposits. This would facilitate rather than prevent users from shifting their deposits to CBDC. Thus, using the average monthly net income appears reasonable. In this way, consumers could use central bank digital currency primarily as means of payment for their monthly expenses rather than building up an investment. From the EU co-legislators' point of view, it should be noted that prescribing a fixed cap in the regulation is not suitable.[219] In this way, later economic developments such as inflation and increased wages would not be covered adequately. Similar arguments can be established for holding limits for corporations and merchants. Their limits should be calibrated according to individual needs. However, this approach appears to be too detailed to be regulated in a European regulation. But, the EU co-legislators could at least outline different groups (e.g. sole proprietors, SMEs, larger capital or trading companies) for which specific limits could then be determined by the ECB, based on market researchs. Hence, the co-legislators would at least set some boundaries in an area which is sensitive to fundamental rights.

To conclude, both remuneration as well as limits for holdings and transactions are suitable tools to prevent the usage of central bank digital currency as an investment rather than as means of payment. Hence, a combination of these tools would be worth to consider.[220] The specific calibration should be left to the ECB. For this, the particular economic environment at the time of the anticipated issuance should be respected.[221] Furthermore, the tools must be designed in a way that enables the ECB to adapt them flexibly according to changing economic circumstances. In the end, one thing should not be forgotten: The aim is to design an innovative means of payment that is easy to understand and simple to use.[222] Too many different limits pursuing different purposes[223] can therefore pose risks to the practicability and the general acceptance of CBDC.

References

Adalid R et al (2022) Central bank digital currency and bank intermediation. ECB Occasional Paper Series No. 293. https://www.ecb.europa.eu/pub/pdf/scpops/ecb.op293~652cf2b1aa.en.pdf. Accessed 31 July 2023

[218] In this direction CPMI-MC (2018), p. 11.

[219] Cf. ECB (2022a), p. 9.

[220] Cf. Panetta (2022); ECB (2022a), p. 9.

[221] Adalid et al. (2022), p. 26; ECB (2022a), p. 9.

[222] Panetta (2022).

[223] Limits for financial stability, AML and CFT, each subdivided in account based and bearer-instrument.

Adrian T, Mancini-Griffoli T (2019) The rise of digital money. IMF FinTech Notes No. 19/01. https://www.imf.org/-/media/Files/Publications/FTN063/2019/English/FTNEA2019001.ashx. Accessed 31 July 2023

Agur I, Ari A, Dell'Ariccia G (2022) Designing central bank digital currencies. J Monet Econ 125: 62–79

Albertazzi U et al (2021) The role of financial stability considerations in monetary policy and the interaction with macroprudential policy in the euro area. ECB Occasional Paper Series No. 272. https://www.ecb.europa.eu/pub/pdf/scpops/ecb.op272~dd8168a8cc.en.pdf. Accessed 31 July 2023

Amtenbrink F, de Haan J (2002) The European Central Bank: an independent specialized organization of Community law. CMLRev 39:65–76

Barrdear J, Kumhof M (2016) The macroeconomics of central bank issued digital currencies. Bank of England Staff Working Paper No. 605. https://www.bankofengland.co.uk/working-paper/2016/the-macroeconomics-of-central-bank-issued-digital-currencies. Accessed 31 July 2023

Bernsdorff (2019) Art. 16 GRC. In: Meyer J, Höhlscheidt S (eds) Charta der Grundrechte der Europäischen Union, 5th edn. Nomos, Baden-Baden

Bindseil U (2014) Monetary policy operations and the financial system. Oxford

Bindseil U (2020) Tiered CBDC and the financial system. ECB Working Paper Series No. 2351. https://www.ecb.europa.eu/pub/pdf/scpwps/ecb.wp2351~c8c18bbd60.en.pdf. Accessed 31 July 2023

Bindseil U, Panetta F, Terol I (2021) Central bank digital currency: functional scope, pricing and controls. Occasional Paper Series No. 286. https://www.ecb.europa.eu/pub/pdf/scpops/ecb.op286~9d472374ea.en.pdf. Accessed 31 July 2023

BIS (2021) Central bank digital currencies: financial stability implications. https://www.bis.org/publ/othp42_fin_stab.pdf. Accessed 31 July 2023

Bjerg O (2018) Breaking the Gilt Standard – the problem of parity in Kumhof and Noone's design principles for central bank digital currencies. CBS Working Paper. https://research-api.cbs.dk/ws/portalfiles/portal/58519458/WP_Breaking_the_Gilt_Standard.pdf. Accessed 31 July 2023

Broadbent B (2016) Central banks and digital currencies. Speech at the London School of Economics, 02.03.2016. https://www.bis.org/review/r160303e.pdf. Accessed 31 July 2023

Brunnermeier M, Niepelt D (2019) On the equivalence of private and public money. J Monet Econ 106:27–41

Cœuré B (2018) The future of central bank money. Speech at the International Center for Monetary and Banking Studies Geneva, 14.05.2018. https://www.ecb.europa.eu/press/key/date/2018/html/ecb.sp180514_4.en.html. Accessed 31 July 2023

CPMI-MC (2018) Central bank digital currencies. https://www.bis.org/cpmi/publ/d174.pdf. Accessed 31 July 2023

Dutzler B (2001) OLAF or the question of applicability of secondary community law to the ECB. European Integration online papers, vol 5. http://eiop.or.at/eiop/pdf/2001-001.pdf. Accessed 31 July 2023

ECB (2019) Exploring anonymity in central bank digital currencies. In Focus Series No. 4. https://www.ecb.europa.eu/paym/intro/publications/pdf/ecb.mipinfocus191217.en.pdf. Accessed 31 July 2023

ECB (2020) Report on a digital euro. https://www.ecb.europa.eu/pub/pdf/other/Report_on_a_digital_euro~4d7268b458.en.pdf. Accessed 31 July 2023

ECB (2022a) Progress on the investigation phase of a digital euro. https://www.ecb.europa.eu/paym/digital_euro/investigation/governance/shared/files/ecb.degov220929.en.pdf?8eec0678b57e98372a7ae6b59047604b. Accessed 31 July 2023

ECB (2022b) Eurogroup – potential impact of a digital euro on the financial system and the use of cash. https://www.ecb.europa.eu/paym/digital_euro/investigation/governance/shared/files/ecb.degov220711_tools.en.pdf?fb2430528d8f964513dd66ffcd8cbaf7. Accessed 31 July 2023

Editorial Comments (1996) Executive agencies within the EC: The European Central Bank – a model? CMLRev 33:623–631
Eilenberger G (2012) Bankbetriebswirtschaftslehre, 8th edn. Oldenbourg, München
Felber C (2014) Geld. Deuticke Verlag, Wien
Frenz W (2009) Handbuch Europarecht, vol 4. Springer, Berlin and Heidelberg. https://doi.org/10.1007/978-3-540-31117-1
Friebel (2022) Art. 127 TFEU. In: Siekmann H (ed) The European Monetary Union – a commentary on the legal foundations. Bloomsbury Publishing, London
Gianviti (2010) The objectives of central banks. In: Giovanoli M, Devos D (eds) International monetary and financial law – the global crisis. Oxford
Gischer H, Herz B, Menkhoff L (2020) Geld, Kredit und Banken, 4th edn. Springer, Berlin
Glos, Benzig (2018) § 2. In: Binder J, Glos A, Riepe J (eds) Handbuch Bankaufsichtsrecht. RWS, Köln
Griller (2023) Art. 130 AEUV. In: Grabitz E, Hilf M, Nettesheim M (eds) Das Recht der Europäischen Union, 78th edn. Beck, München
Grünewald S et al (2021) Digital euro and ECB powers. CMLRev 58:1029–1056. https://doi.org/10.2139/ssrn.3807855
Häde (2022a) Art. 123 AEUV. In: Calliess C, Ruffert M (eds) EUV/AEUV Kommentar, 6th edn. Beck, München
Häde (2022b) Art. 127 AEUV. In: Calliess C, Ruffert M (eds) EUV/AEUV Kommentar, 6th edn. Beck, München
Hanl A, Michaelis J (2019) Digitales Zentralbankgeld als neues Instrument der Geldpolitik, MAGKS Joint Discussion Paper Series in Economics, No. 09-2019
Hartig H (2012) Die Befugnisse von EZB und ESRB auf dem Gebiet der Finanzsystemstabilität. EuZW 2012:775–779
Huber J (2018) Monetäre Souveränität. Metropolis-Verlag, Marburg
Ioannidis M, Murphy Hlásková S, Zilioli C (2021) The mandate of the ECB: legal considerations in the ECB's monetary policy strategy review. ECB Occasional Paper Series No. 276. https://www.ecb.europa.eu/pub/pdf/scpops/ecb.op276~3c53a6755d.en.pdf. Accessed 31 July 2023
Jarass (2021) Art. 16 GRC. In: Jarass H (ed) Charta der Grundrechte der EU, 4th edn. Beck, München
Juks R (2018) When a central bank digital currency meets private money: effects of an e-krona on banks. Sveriges Riksbank Economic Review: special issue on the e-krona 2018(3):79–99. https://www.riksbank.se/globalassets/media/rapporter/pov/engelska/2018/economic-review-3-2018.pdf. Accessed 31 July 2023
Keister T, Monnet C (2022) Central bank digital currency: stability and information. Office of Financial Research Working Paper No. 22-04. https://www.financialresearch.gov/working-papers/files/OFRwp-22-04_central-bank-digital-currency.pdf. Accessed 31 July 2023
Kempen (2018) Art. 119 AEUV. In: Streinz R (ed) Beck'scher Kurzkommentar EUV/AEUV, 3rd edn. Beck, München
Kiff J et al (2020) A survey of research on retail central bank digital currency. IMF Working Papers WP/20/104. https://www.imf.org/-/media/Files/Publications/WP/2020/English/wpiea2020104-print-pdf.ashx. Accessed 31 July 2023
Kotzur (2023) Art. 16 GRC. In: Geiger R, Khan D, Kotzur M, Kirchmair L (eds) EUV/AEUV, 7th edn. Beck, München
Kumhof M, Noone C (2018) Central bank digital currencies – design principles and balance sheet implications. Bank of England Staff Working Paper No. 275. https://www.bankofengland.co.uk/working-paper/2018/central-bank-digital-currencies%2D%2D-design-principles-and-balance-sheet-implications. Accessed 31 July 2023
Lastra R (2006) Legal foundations of international monetary stability. Oxford
Lastra, Psaroudakis (2020) Prudential supervisory tasks. In: Amtenbrink F, Herrmann C (eds) The EU law of economic and monetary union. Oxford

Laufenberg (2018) § 9. In: Binder J, Glos A, Riepe J (eds) Handbuch Bankaufsichtsrecht. RWS, Köln

Lavayssière X (2022) Central bank digital currencies – the quest for public digital payment infrastructures. https://www.blockchain-polytechnique.com/wp-content/uploads/2022/12/Outlook-Central-Bank-Digital-Currencies-Publuc-Digital-Payment-infrastructure-Blockchain-at-Polytechnique.pdf. Accessed 31 July 2023

Lavranos N (2003) Die begrenzte, funktionelle Unabhängigkeit der Europäischen Zentralbank – Anmerkung zum Urteil des Gerichtshofs vom 10.7.2003, EUGH 10.07.2003 Aktenzeichen Rs. C-11/00 (Kommission gegen EZB). EuR 2003:878–887

Mancini-Griffoli T et al (2018) Casting light on central bank digital currency. Staff Discussion Note No. 18/08. https://www.imf.org/en/Publications/Staff-Discussion-Notes/Issues/2018/11/13/Casting-Light-on-Central-Bank-Digital-Currencies-46233. Accessed 31 July 2023

Manger-Nestler C (2021) Digitales Zentralbankgeld aus währungsrechtlicher Sicht. RdZ 2021:4–11

Mayer T (2015) Die neue Ordnung des Geldes, 2nd edn. FBV, München

Meaning J et al (2018) Broadening narrow money: monetary policy with a central bank digital currency. Bank of England Staff Working Paper No. 724. https://www.bankofengland.co.uk/working-paper/2018/broadening-narrow-money-monetary-policy-with-a-central-bank-digital-currency. Accessed 31 July 2023

Ohler C (2015) Bankenaufsicht und Geldpolitik in der Währungsunion, § 3. Beck, München

Ohler C (2021) Unkonventionelle Geldpolitik. Mohr Siebeck, Tübingen

Panetta F (2018) 21st century cash: central banking, technological innovation and digital currencies. SUERF Policy Note No. 40. https://www.suerf.org/policynotes/3251/21st-century-cash-central-banking-technological-innovation-and-digital-currencies. Accessed 31 July 2023

Panetta F (2021) Evolution or revolution? The impact of a digital euro on the financial system. Speech at a Bruegel online seminar, 10.02.2021. https://www.ecb.europa.eu/press/key/date/2021/html/ecb.sp210210~a1665d3188.en.html. Accessed 31 July 2023

Panetta F (2022) The digital euro and the evolution of the financial system. Introductory statement at the Committee on Economic and Monetary Affairs of the European Parliament, 15.06.2022. https://www.ecb.europa.eu/press/key/date/2022/html/ecb.sp220615~0b859eb8bc.en.html. Accessed 31 July 2023

Penski U, Elsner R (2001) Eigentumsgewährleistung und Berufsfreiheit als Gemeinschaftsgrundrechte in der Rechtsprechung des Europäischen Gerichtshofs. DÖV 2001: 265–275

Priewasser E (2001) Bankbetriebslehre, 7th edn. Oldenbourg, München

Sanches D, Keister T (2021) Should central banks issue digital currency? Federal Reserve Bank of Philadelphia Working Paper 21-37. https://www.philadelphiafed.org/-/media/frbp/assets/working-papers/2021/wp21-37.pdf. Accessed 31 July 2023

Selmayr (2015) Art. 282 AEUV. In: Groeben H, Schwarze J, Hatje A (eds) Europäisches Unionsrecht, 7th edn. Nomos, Baden-Baden

Thiele A (2019) Die europäische Zentralbank. Mohr Siebeck, Tübingen

Torrent R (1999) Who is the European Central Bank the Central Bank of? CMLRev 36:1229–1241

Tutsch (2015) Art. 123 AEUV. In: Groeben H, Schwarze J, Hatje A (eds) Europäisches Unionsrecht, 7th edn. Nomos, Baden-Baden

Utzig S (2020) Redaktionsgespräch. Kreditwesen 73(24):20–22

Waldhoff (2022) Art. 127 TFEU. In: Siekmann H (ed) The European Monetary Union – a commentary on the legal foundations. Bloomsbury Publishing, London

Wierts P, Boven H (2020) Central bank digital currency: objectives, preconditions and design choices. De Nederlandsche Bank Occasional Studies vol 20-01. https://www.dnb.nl/en/publications/publicatieoverzicht/research-publications/occasional-studies/nr-1-2020-central-bank-digital-currency-objectives-preconditions-and-design-choices/. Accessed 31 July 2023

Zilioli C, Selmayr M (2001) The law of the European Central Bank. Hart Publishing, Oxford and Portland

Chapter 9
Monetary Policy

Abstract This chapter enquires the relation of central bank digital currency and monetary policy. First, it presents how monetary policy normally functions. Then, it examines how central bank digital currency can be linked to that. Here, the chapter pays special attention to the impact of CBDC on the monetary policy transmission. In addition, it focuses on the highly debated topic of remunerating holdings, in particular using negative interest rates. The chapter links that to the fundamental right to property under Article 17 of the European Charta of Fundamental Rights. Furthermore, the chapter examines whether CBDC can be seen as a new tool of monetary policy.

9.1 Monetary Policy's Mode of Action

According to Article 127 (2), second indent, TFEU, the ESCB defines and implements the monetary policy of the Union. The process through which monetary policy decisions of the ECB (cf. Article 282 (2), first sentence, TFEU) affect the economy in general is called monetary policy transmission mechanism.[1] In simple terms, this transmission mechanism is the link between an operational target that the ECB can influence directly and an ultimate objective.[2] This ultimate objective is to maintain price stability, Article 127 (1), first sentence, TFEU.[3] To achieve the operational target the ECB conventionally[4] uses three different tools, the so-called monetary policy instruments.[5] These are open market operations,[6] standing facilities[7] and

[1] Tuori (2020), para. 22.25; ECB (2011), p. 58; Holtemöller (2008), p. 185; Ohler (2021), p. 213.

[2] Bindseil (2014), p. 9.

[3] Lastra and Psaroudakis (2020), para. 26.36; Görgens et al. (2013), p. 119.

[4] For unconventional tools see Ohler (2021).

[5] Bindseil (2014), p. 9.

[6] For more details see Bindseil (2014), p. 9 and Tuori (2020), para. 22.44.

[7] For more details see Tuori (2020), para. 22.51 ff.

L. Kriese, *Central Bank Digital Currency*,
https://doi.org/10.1007/978-3-031-44738-9_9

reserve requirements.[8] These monetary policy instruments impact the real economy through so-called transmission channels.[9] The most important channels in the euro area are the interest rate channel and the credit channel.[10] The operational target the ECB aims to influence is the short-term money market[11] interest rate.[12] To do so, at the very beginning of every monetary policy operation the ECB changes the official interest rates[13] either directly or by the amount of funds provided to commercial banks.[14] Changing the official interest rates also changes the funding conditions for credit institutions as central bank liquidity becomes more or less expensive.[15] These increased or decreased funding costs are then expected to be passed on from the credit institutions to their customers, i.e. the real economy.

In the interest rate channel, this pass-on happens when the short-term money market interest rates affect other interest rates.[16] Other short-term interest rates, such as short-term lending rates and bank deposit rates are affected immediately.[17] However, changing short-term interest rates does not immediately lead to a change of long-term interest rates. Those long-term rates on capital markets are influenced by so-called arbitrage effects.[18] These arbitrage effects ground on the market participants' expectations on the profitability of certain financial products and their correct anticipation of a future change in interest rates.[19] However, a change of the interest rates for financial products available to households and firms also changes their behaviour on spending, saving and investing.[20] Higher interest rates lead to more saving while lower interest rates make households and firms consume and invest more.[21] This increased or lowered demand by households and firms in turn affects the price level for goods and services.[22]

---

[8]For more details see Bindseil (2014), p. 10.

[9]ECB (2011), p. 59; Tuori (2020), para. 22.26; Ohler (2021), p. 214.

[10]ECB (2011), p. 62. For more details on the various other channels see Görgens et al. (2013), p. 274.

[11]Money markets are that part of the financial markets on which short-term financial instruments (maturity up to 1 year) are traded, cf. Ohler (2015), para. 45.

[12]Cf. Bank of England (1999), p. 162; Ohler (2021), p. 219; Deutsche Bundesbank (2019), p. 52.

[13]The three key interest rates are the deposit facility rate, the marginal lending facility rate and the main refinancing operation rate.

[14]Tuori (2020), para. 22.26; ECB (2011), p. 59.

[15]ECB (2011), p. 59.

[16]Cf. Tuori (2020), para. 22.26.

[17]Holtemöller (2008), p. 185; Bank of England (1999), pp. 161 and 162; ECB (2011), p. 59.

[18]ECB (2011), p. 60; Görgens et al. (2013), pp. 138, 276; Bank of England (1999), p. 162.

[19]Cf. ECB (2011), p. 60; Görgens et al. (2013), pp. 138, 276; Bank of England (1999), p. 162. For more details on arbitrage and the so-called Expectations Theory see Holtemöller (2008), pp. 260 ff. and Görgens et al. (2013), pp. 145 ff.

[20]Bank of England (1999), p. 162; ECB (2011), p. 60.

[21]Ohler (2021), p. 237; Bank of England (1999), p. 164.

[22]Bank of England (1999), p. 162; ECB (2011), p. 60.

In the credit channel, passing on increased funding costs by credit institutions works differently. In simple terms, the credit channel affects the credit supply by banks.[23] This can be done by three different subtypes. First, the bank lending channel. In this channel, higher official interest rates raise the banks' funding costs and forces the banks to increase their credit interest rates which will increase the credit default risk[24] for individuals which means that banks will not grant a credit to these individuals.[25] Second, there is the balance sheet channel. Here, increased official interest rates reduce the households' and firms' net worth which lowers the value of their assets that can be used as collateral and hence reduces their ability to borrow money.[26] And lastly, there is the risk-taking channel. This channel affects the banks' willingness to accept certain risks when granting credits and leads to amendments of the banks' internal credit standards.[27]

To conclude, the monetary policy transmission mechanism is a complex and nested process. It consists of two interlaced levels: the relation of central banks and credit institutions and the relation of credit institutions and their customers. Since bank-based funding is still predominant in continental Europe, credit institutions play a key role for the monetary policy transmission.[28] This leads to the following important features of the current practice of monetary policy. First, the effectiveness of monetary policy transmission strongly depends on sound credit institutions and their compliant behaviour.[29] Second, central banks cannot directly influence the subjects of the real economy, i.e. households and firms.[30] Third, since several economic agents are involved at different levels, monetary policy instruments take a considerable time[31] to affect the ultimate objective and the central banks' overall steering ability is limited.[32]

9.2 Central Bank Digital Currency's Impact

Bearing in mind these characteristics of monetary policy, the following section will now examine the possible impact of central bank digital currency on monetary policy. For that, it shall be enquired how central bank digital currency could affect

[23] Ohler (2021), p. 214.

[24] For the calculation see Bindseil (2014), p. 147.

[25] ECB (2011), p. 60; Görgens et al. (2013), p. 274.

[26] ECB (2011), p. 60; Görgens et al. (2013), p. 297.

[27] See for more detail Görgens et al. (2013), pp. 303 ff.; ECB (2011), p. 61.

[28] Deutsche Bundesbank (2019), p. 46; Görgens et al. (2013), p. 187.

[29] Ohler (2021), pp. 227 and 231; Holtemöller (2008), p. 187; Görgens et al. (2013), p. 321; Deutsche Bundesbank (2019), p. 46; Ohler (2015), para. 43.

[30] Ohler (2015), para. 43; Ohler (2021), p. 226.

[31] The ECB estimates between one and two years, cf. ECB (2011), p. 62.

[32] ECB (2011), p. 58; Ohler (2021), p. 229; Ohler (2015), para. 43.

the monetary policy transmission and whether it could be seen as a new monetary policy instrument (see Sect. 9.2.1). Then, the legal issues of applying (negative) remuneration rates will be analysed (see Sect. 9.2.2).

9.2.1 Central Bank Digital Currency and Monetary Policy Transmission

The introduction of central bank digital currency can affect monetary policy in various ways. The following section presents an overview:

9.2.1.1 Strengthening the Pass-Through of Monetary Policy

As showed above, the monetary policy transmission depends on the compliant behaviour of banks, which transmit the central banks' monetary policy signals to the real economy. In the negative interest economic environment of the past years, many banks, for several reasons, have not passed on these negative interest rates (completely) to their customers.[33] This non-compliant bank behaviour hampers the monetary policy transmission. Hence, in the economic literature it is discussed whether central bank digital currency can strengthen the pass-through of monetary policy rates and lead to a more direct transmission. The crucial starting point for these considerations is the banks' respondence to the introduction of an interest-bearing central bank digital currency.[34] Remunerated central bank digital currency would compete with bank deposits. As the shift of deposits to central bank digital currency is facilitated, an increase of central bank digital currency's interest rate would lead to an outflow of deposits towards central bank digital currency.[35] This puts upward pressure on banks' deposit rates to avoid deposit shifts.[36] The same accounts for a reduction of central bank digital currency's interest rate which allows banks to reduce their deposit rates as well.[37] This banks' reaction to the varying central bank digital currency's interest rates allows for a more direct transmission of monetary policy rates.[38] However, central bank digital currency's impact on monetary policy in this regard is opaque. First, this pass-through strongly depends on the banks' adjustments. If they decide to focus more on term funding or to apply artificial frictions on the convertibility of deposits and central bank digital currency (e.g. withdrawal fees or increasing benefits for depositors), this pass-through would

[33]Cœuré (2018).

[34]Meaning et al. (2018), p. 12; Cœuré (2018).

[35]Meaning et al. (2018), p. 21.

[36]Nessén et al. (2018), p. 35; CPMI-MC (2018), p. 11.

[37]Panetta (2018), p. 6.

[38]CPMI-MC (2018), p. 12; Cœuré (2018); Panetta (2018), p. 6; Armelius et al. (2018), p. 53.

not work.[39] Second, from a microeconomic view, a simultaneous pass-through is often not wanted because the spread sometimes represents compensations for certain risks and costs related to cross-subsidised services.[40] And lastly, with a view to stimulating the short-term money market interest rates, there are other liquidity-absorbing instruments that could be supplied to non-bank money market participants in order to achieve the same objective.[41]

9.2.1.2 Entrenching the Zero Lower Bound

Traditionally, monetary policy faces a zero lower bound (ZLB), which means that any policy rate below zero is not effective.[42] This is due to the fact that cash does not bear any interest and thus, when applying negative policy rates, market participants will simply shift to cash.[43] However, holding cash is accompanied with particular costs (e.g. transport, storage, insurance etc.), thus some market participants would accept interest rates below zero to a certain point before shifting to cash.[44] This point is called the effective lower bound (ELB), which can be below zero. Since there will be no or fewer costs for central bank digital currency, some authors argue that now the effective lower bound strongly depends on the remuneration of central bank digital currency.[45] The effectiveness of this new ELB varies, depending on how attractive central bank digital currency is in relation to other assets.[46] Accordingly, for central bank reserves it has been shown that when issuing a non-interest-bearing CBDC, the interest rates for central bank reserves cannot be below zero.[47] As a consequence, negative monetary policy interest rates would not be possible any longer.[48] Furthermore, a non-remunerated central bank digital currency is likely to set an ELB constraint that is more closely to zero on all market rates, risking that monetary policy tools are not working effectively.[49] If central bank digital currency would be remunerated, the ELB would be the highest of either the cash-related ZLB or the interest rate for central bank digital currency.[50] However, it should be noted

[39] Meaning et al. (2018), p. 21; Armelius et al. (2018), p. 53.

[40] CPMI-MC (2018), p. 12.

[41] CPMI-MC (2018), p. 12.

[42] Armelius et al. (2018), p. 45.

[43] Armelius et al. (2018), p. 45.

[44] Nessén et al. (2018), p. 36; Armelius et al. (2018), p. 45; Hanl and Michaelis (2019), p. 12.

[45] Meaning et al. (2018), p. 17; Hanl and Michaelis (2019), p. 12; Nessén et al. (2018), p. 36.

[46] Armelius et al. (2018), p. 45.

[47] Armelius et al. (2018), p. 47.

[48] Nessén et al. (2018), p. 36; Bindseil et al. (2021), p. 9; Hanl and Michaelis (2019), p. 12; Bindseil and Panetta (2020).

[49] Armelius et al. (2018), pp. 49 and 52.

[50] Nessén et al. (2018), p. 36.

that applying negative remuneration rates to central bank digital currency could be limited if cash is still in use because the cash-related ZLB will still exist.[51]

9.2.1.3 Impacting the Transmission Channels

When it comes to conducting and implementing monetary policy, broad agreement in the literature exists that central bank digital currency will not significantly alter the monetary policy implementation.[52] Nonetheless, some impacts for the bank lending channel in particular will be noticeable. Since shifting deposits to central bank digital currency and vice versa can be done easily, the banks' funding costs will significantly change.[53] This is ambivalent because on the one hand it strengthens the bank lending channel as banks become more sensitive to policy rate changes (pass-through, cf. above).[54] On the other hand, increased funding costs curtail the net interest margin and will ultimately result in a lower bank lending capability.[55] This in turn could weaken the bank lending channel.[56] Furthermore, if banks lose central bank reserves that can be used to fulfil the deposit-to-central-bank-digital-currency request of their customers because of minimum reserve requirements, central banks could be pushed to inject more liquidity by open market operations or to alter the interest rates on central bank reserves.[57] Especially the latter would then influence the interest rate channel as well because the central bank reserves rates are used to steer the short-term interest rates.

9.2.1.4 Usage as a New Monetary Policy Tool

However, the key economic discussion circles around the question whether central bank digital currency is or can be used as a new monetary policy tool. This is a highly debated topic which shall not be presented exhaustively here. Some authors advocate the use as a new monetary policy tool, varying in notion and reasoning. The

---

[51] CPMI-MC (2018), p. 12; Hanl and Michaelis (2019), p. 12; Armelius et al. (2018), p. 45.

[52] Mancini-Griffoli et al. (2018), pp. 25 and 26; CPMI-MC (2018), p. 13; Meaning et al. (2018), p. 22; Armelius et al. (2018), p. 55; Bindseil (2020), p. 6.

[53] Meaning et al. (2018), p. 22.

[54] Meaning et al. (2018), p. 22.

[55] Armelius et al. (2018), p. 55; Meaning et al. (2018), p. 23; Hanl and Michaelis (2019), pp. 12 and 13.

[56] Other opinion is Panetta (2022b) according to whom the banks' lending capability will increase due to the so-called crowd-in effect.

[57] Mancini-Griffoli et al. (2018), p. 26 fn. 44.

most comprehensive models on this were conducted by *Barrdear and Kumhof*[58] and *Meaning et al.*[59]

Barrdear and Kumhof favour the use of central bank digital currency as a 'second monetary policy instrument' in addition to the existing monetary policy interest rates.[60] Accordingly, central bank digital currency could be used in two ways for monetary policy. First, quantity rules could apply, i.e. adjusting the quantity of central bank digital currency in relation to the gross domestic product (GDP), perhaps with countercyclical variations.[61] In a recession, the central bank should withdraw liquidity through buying government bonds for central bank digital currency.[62] Second, price rules could apply, i.e. using a spread between the interest rates paid on central bank digital currency and the monetary policy interest rates.[63] In a recession, central banks should withdraw liquidity by lowering the interest rate on central bank digital currency and thus make it less attractive in relation to other assets, e.g. government bonds.[64] Furthermore, according to *Barrdear and Kumhof*, central bank digital currency could be used to provide additional monetary stimulus in a zero-lower-bound-economy without the need for negative interest rates.[65] This should be done via discretionary and perhaps countercyclical injections of a certain amount of central bank digital currency in relation to the GDP.[66]

Meaning et al. agree that quantity or price rules could apply to central bank digital currency as a new monetary policy tool.[67] However, when applying price rules, they propose different remuneration rates on central bank digital currency relative to the specific holder.[68] Accordingly, to prevent net interest margin losses, the interest rate paid on central bank digital currency held by MFIs[69] should be higher than those rates paid on the one held by non-MFIs (i.e. households and firms).[70] Moreover, the spread between both interest rates could be used as an additional dimension of monetary policy transmission.[71]

[58] Barrdear and Kumhof (2016).

[59] Meaning et al. (2018).

[60] Barrdear and Kumhof (2016), p. 12.

[61] Barrdear and Kumhof (2016), p. 39.

[62] Barrdear and Kumhof (2016), p. 40.

[63] Barrdear and Kumhof (2016), p. 40.

[64] Barrdear and Kumhof (2016), p. 40.

[65] Barrdear and Kumhof (2016), p. 63.

[66] Barrdear and Kumhof (2016), p. 64.

[67] Barrdear and Kumhof (2016), pp. 17 and 18.

[68] Meaning et al. (2018), p. 25.

[69] Monetary financial institution, i.e. financial institutions whose business is to receive deposits, grant credit and/or invest in securities, cf. ECB Glossary https://www.ecb.europa.eu/services/glossary/html/glossm.en.html (Accessed 31.07.2023).

[70] Meaning et al. (2018), p. 25.

[71] Meaning et al. (2018), p. 26.

Other authors also agree that the decision on remunerating central bank digital currency could be seen as a new and second monetary policy tool.[72] *Berentsen and Schär* state that this decision should even be used as the 'main policy tool'.[73] However, it should be noted that this statement is not backed by economic but rather by political reasoning. Accordingly, it should prevent political upheavals due to the fact that only the public money held by MFIs is paid but not the one held by the broader population.[74]

However, the views in favour of using central bank digital currency as a (new) monetary policy tool ground on basic assumptions that can be challenged. The model of *Barrdear and Kumhof* is based on the theoretic assumption that central bank digital currency is only imperfectly substitutable for other financial assets such as bank deposits and reserves.[75] This tends to be in the same direction as applying limits on the convertibility to prevent financial instability (see above). As already mentioned, this limited substitutionability would contrast basic principles of (central) banking and would reduce the public trust in the new currency format. The model of *Meaning et al.* grounds on the assumption that central bank digital currency as defined in this paper and central bank reserves are not distinct, i.e. there is only one central bank digital currency. In the case that central bank digital currency and reserves are distinct, *Meaning et al.* apply a different approach. Accordingly, the interest rate paid on central bank digital currency held by MFIs should be the monetary policy tool equivalent to today's interest rates on reserves, whereas the interest rate paid on central bank digital currency held by non-MFIs should be used for financial stability reasons, i.e. controlling the demand relative to bank deposits.[76] Lastly, and most important, all theories are based on the assumption that central bank digital currency is to be remunerated. Mostly this is due to the pre-assumption that remuneration will be used for financial stability reasons anyway. Thus, in order to not circumvent monetary policy rates, the remuneration needs to be integrated into the central banks' monetary policy tool set.[77] However, besides financial stability aspects, remunerating central bank digital currency would only be needed from a monetary policy's point of view if central bank reserves disappear.[78] Because in the current conventional monetary policy system only the interest rates connected to central bank reserves such as overnight deposit rates are relevant to steer the

---

[72] Kumhof and Noone (2018), p. 11; Hanl and Michaelis (2019), p. 11; Nessén et al. (2018), p. 35; Armelius et al. (2018), p. 44; Hua Jiang and Zhu (2021).

[73] Berentsen and Schär (2018), p. 102.

[74] Berentsen and Schär (2018), p. 102. See also the concerns expressed by Meaning et al. (2018), p. 26.

[75] See for e.g. Barrdear and Kumhof (2016), pp. 12, 39, 64.

[76] Meaning et al. (2018), pp. 7 and 8, 26.

[77] Cf. in this regard Nessén et al. (2018), p. 35; Armelius et al. (2018), p. 58.

[78] Mancini-Griffoli et al. (2018), p. 26.

short-term interest rates.[79] Hence, from a monetary policy's point of view, remunerating central bank digital currency would not add any additional value.[80]

Furthermore, all economic models presented so far, studied central bank digital currency in its design as account based or the online functionality. What has not been considered is the bearer-instrument or the offline functionality. Since this does not involve financial intermediaries, one could speak of a new opportunity for monetary policy. In the current monetary policy practice, central banks cannot directly influence the actors of the real economy. This could change if end-users directly access central bank digital currency without third-party intermediation.[81] In this regard, central banks could set the interest rate for the central bank digital currency accessible by the real economy and thus steer the saving or consuming and investing behaviour more directly. It would not be necessary to use the banks as a middle level of monetary policy transmission. This is comparable to applying interest rates on cash and could significantly alter the key characteristics of monetary policy conducted so far. The effectiveness of monetary policy transmission would not depend on the financial intermediaries' compliance any longer. Furthermore, since the middle level in the transmission mechanism is left aside, the time it takes for monetary policy instruments to affect the ultimate objective of price stability would be reduced. Hence, one could even speak about a less limited steering ability of the central banks. Thus, one could consider this as an innovation in monetary policy. However, it could probably not be considered as a new tool because the usage of remuneration is still a conventional price rule. But it could be worth naming it a new transmission channel.

However, this innovation also poses difficulties. To be effectively used as a monetary policy tool, a wide-spread use of central bank digital currency as a bearer-instrument would be a compelling pre-condition.[82] But a central bank digital currency that is too successful and attractive is also not desirable for financial stability reasons (see above).[83] If holding limits were to apply and if these were to be calibrated in a way that ultimately leads to an amount of central bank digital currency in circulation that is as close to the current number of banknotes in circulation as possible,[84] then private scriptural money would still be the predominant form of money. Nonetheless, this bears the potential to impact a large number of actors of the real economy, but the actual monetary policy influence of the central banks would be limited.[85] Due to the holding limits for safeguarding financial stability and also the limits for safeguarding privacy, only smaller amounts of public

[79] Bindseil (2020), p. 19.

[80] CPMI-MC (2018), p. 13; Bindseil (2020), p. 18; Bindseil and Panetta (2020); Panetta (2022b).

[81] Cf. Cœuré (2018).

[82] Cf. CPMI-MC (2018), p. 10.

[83] Panetta (2022b) speaks about striking the right balance between 'not too successful' and 'successful enough'.

[84] Cf. Panetta (2022a).

[85] Cf. CPMI-MC (2018), p. 11.

money could be used for monetary policy incentives and central banks would still largely depend on the middle level of the transmission mechanism, especially for larger holdings of money. Furthermore, the offline functionality poses some technical difficulties for applying remuneration.[86] This would lead to the fact that the central bank could not act flexibly in applying varying interest rates but rather has to set a fixed rate that needs to be updated when the end-user connects the HBI to a network. This in turn would not enable the central bank to react adequately to rapid but severe changes in the overall economic environment. To conclude, applying interest rates on central bank digital currency as a bearer-instrument could lead to a more direct monetary policy transmission but still faces constraints that have to be examined more closely.

9.2.2 Legal Considerations

If the central bank digital currency were nonetheless to be remunerated, some legal concerns arise.

The first concern refers to the question of whether the ECB is empowered to decide on remunerating the digital euro as part of its monetary policy mandate. In this regard, it is settled case-law of the ECJ that the ECB enjoys broad discretion because monetary policy decisions are of technical and complex nature.[87] Furthermore, the ECJ stresses the importance of the monetary policy transmission mechanism for the primary objective of the ESCB under Article 127 (1) TFEU and that safeguarding an appropriate transmission mechanism is a key competence of the E(S)CB.[88] Hence, from this case-law one can derive that the ECB's monetary policy competence encompasses the decision on the use of instruments needed to prevent disturbances in the monetary policy transmission and to implement the identified measures to make monetary policy work credible.[89] Thus, if the ECB concludes—after careful and impartial examination and with adequate reasoning[90]—that remunerating central bank digital currency is likely to contribute to safeguarding an appropriate transmission mechanism, then this decision would fall within ECB's monetary policy competence.

Secondly, since price rules such as remuneration aim at triggering financial incentives and disincentives, the usage of positive as well as negative interest rates appears necessary. In particular, using negative interest rates (so-called negative

[86] Cf. above Sect. 8.3.1; ECB (2020), p. 34; Bindseil et al. (2021), p. 12.

[87] Case C-62/14 *Gauweiler* ECLI:EU:C:2015:400, para. 68, 75; case C-493/17 *Weiss* ECLI:EU:C:2018:1000, para. 74, 91.

[88] Case C-62/14 *Gauweiler* ECLI:EU:C:2015:400, para. 49, 50.

[89] Lastra and Psaroudakis (2020), para 26.40.

[90] Case C-493/17 *Weiss* ECLI:EU:C:2018:1000, para. 30; case C-62/14 *Gauweiler* ECLI:EU:C:2015:400, para. 69.

interest rate policy, NIRP) draws attention. The NIRP in general is a comparably young monetary policy instrument and arose as a necessity out of the lower-zero bound that has been dominating the economic environment in the past years.[91] However, applying negative interest rates on central bank digital currency holdings may face some legal concerns. When conducting monetary policy, the Eurosystem is legally bound by the Treaties and especially the European Charta of Fundamental Rights.[92] Therefore, some authors argue that applying negative interest rates on central bank digital currency can be seen as a deprivation of property, violating Article 17 CFR.[93] This, however, requires closer legal examination.

9.2.2.1 Scope of Protection

According to Article 17 (1) CFR, everyone has the right to own, use, dispose of and bequeath his or her lawfully acquired possessions. No one may be deprived of his or her possessions, except in the public interest and in the cases and under the conditions provided for by law, subject to fair compensation being paid in good time for their loss. The use of property may be regulated by law in so far as is necessary for the general interest. According to the ECJ's settled case-law, Article 17 CFR 'applies to rights with an asset value creating an established legal position under the legal system, enabling the holder to exercise those rights autonomously and for his benefit'.[94] In this sense and in conjunction with Article 345 TFEU, Article 17 CFR is a fundamental right whose object of protection is shaped by the legal systems of the Member States and the Union.[95] Furthermore, Article 17 CFR does not protect the assets of a person as a whole.[96]

For central bank digital currency two aspects seem questionable in this regard. First, central bank digital currency needs to be considered as a right with an asset value that creates an established legal position under the legal system. The central bank digital currency is by definition a liability item of the issuing central bank. However, this does not lead to an established legal position in that sense because it is not clear whether accounting as a liability in the central bank's balance sheet results in a legal claim of the owner.[97] However, from the two manifestations or functionalities of central bank digital currency one can derive, if necessary with the help of

[91] Deutsche Bundesbank (2019), p. 47; Ohler (2021), p. 219.

[92] Ohler (2015), para. 43.

[93] Strobel (2021), p. 558; Huber (2018), p. 231.

[94] Case C-283/11 *Sky Österreich* ECLI:EU:C:2013:28, para. 34; case C-398/13 P *Inuit Tapiriit Kanatami/Commission* ECLI:EU:C:2015:535, para. 60; case C-235/17 *Commission/Hungary* ECLI:EU:C:2019:432, para. 69.

[95] Jarass (2021), para. 6; Calliess (2022), para. 4.

[96] Jarass (2021), para. 6; Calliess (2022), para. 8. Cf. also joint cases C-143/88 and 92/89 *Zuckerfabrik Süderdithmarschen* ECLI:EU:C:1991:65, para. 74. See further Frenz (2009), para. 2856 ff.

[97] See the remarks in Sect. 7.1.1.1 under 'Claim'.

amending the civil law,[98] that the (civil) law recognises the ownership of the currency units as an established legal position. But one can question whether remunerating central bank digital currency would perhaps cover the assets of a person as a whole. Traditionally, taxes are not recognised as a violation of the right to property under national law because they address the assets of a person as a whole rather than a clear distinctive and single asset position.[99] Although negative interest rates may seem tax-alike,[100] they are limited to the specific amount of central bank digital currency holdings, not the (financial) assets of a person in general.[101] Hence, the ownership of central bank digital currency units falls within the scope of protection under Article 17 (1), first sentence, CFR.

9.2.2.2 Violation

Next, applying negative interest rates on central bank digital currency by the ECB needs to be regarded as a violation of Article 17 (1) CFR. The right to property can be violated by an unjustified deprivation or regulation of the use of property, Article 17 (1), second and third sentence, CFR. To be justified, the deprivation or regulation needs to comply with the respective requirements laid out in Article 17 (1), second and third sentence, CFR. Furthermore, the principle of proportionality must be ensured, cf. Article 52 (1) CFR.[102]

However, before assessing a violation of the right to property, the NIRP of the ECB must be justiciable in the meaning that it can be ascribed to the ECB as a Union body that is bound to fundamental rights.[103] Traditionally, decisions of monetary policy were regarded as not justiciable in the meaning that they do not violate fundamental rights.[104] This is based on the fact that in the traditional monetary policy transmission mechanism the ECB's steering ability is only limited.[105] The way its decision impacts the bearers of fundamental rights, strongly depends on how the financial intermediaries, especially banks, react to the monetary policy signals.[106] However, this will not be the case for remunerating central bank digital currency. The interest rates would be set for a form of money that can be accessed

[98] See Sect. 7.4.

[99] Cf. BVerfG, 09.03.1971 – 2 BvR 326/69, juris para. 61; BVerfG, 19.10.1983 – 2 BvR 298/81, juris para. 47; BVerfG, 08.04.1997 – 1 BvR 48/94, juris para. 130.

[100] Kirchhof (2021), p. 177.

[101] Cf. in that sense also ECtHR No. 13378/05, para. 59 – *Burden/United Kingdom*; ECtHR No. 14902/04, para. 552 ff. – *OAO Neftyanaya Kompaniya Yukos/Russia*; Kirchhof (2021), pp. 166 and 167.

[102] Case C-235/17 *Commission/Hungary* ECLI:EU:C:2019:432, para. 89.

[103] Cf. Frenz (2009), para. 2893.

[104] Cf. BVerfG, 24.09.1965 – 1 BvR 228/65; BVerfG, 09.03.1971 – 2 BvR 326/69, juris para. 61.

[105] Cf. BVerwG, 29.01.1973 – I C 38.68, juris para. 38; Ohler (2015), para. 22, 43.

[106] Ohler (2015), para. 46.

directly by the broad public. Other than in the current practice, the ECB would not set interest rates for money that is only accessible by certain financial institutions, i.e. central bank reserves. Rather, it is comparable to remunerating cash which is accessible by everyone. Hence, central banks do not steer indirectly but rather directly the behaviour of the end-users. Thus, applying the NIRP to central bank digital currency is a measure that can be ascribed directly to the ECB as a Union body and therefore is justiciable.

The deprivation in the sense of Article 17 (1), second sentence, CFR is to be understood as the formal concept of expropriation, meaning the permanent and complete deprivation of specific possessions for the benefit of the state or third parties.[107] In this regard, the deprivation must be the aim and purpose of the measure in question in the sense of finality.[108] Some authors suggest that applying negative interest rates to central bank digital currency is to be regarded as a deprivation in this sense.[109] However, when the central bank applies negative interest rates on the central bank digital currency, it is not aiming at depriving the currency units that are covered from the interest rate. It aims at setting financial incentives to spend or invest the money. In the formal understanding of expropriation, applying the NIRP on central bank digital currency cannot be classified as a deprivation. However, it can be categorised as a regulation of the use of property. This includes all regulations that prohibit or permit a certain usage of the possessions.[110] As said, the NIRP sanctions the saving of central bank digital currency and sets the incentive to spend and invest the money.

To justify this regulation of the use of property it must pursue a legitimate public interest and be proportionate to the public interest concerned, Article 17 (1), third sentence, Article 52 (1) CFR.[111] As a legitimate interest one can consider the safeguarding of the effectiveness of monetary policy in order to achieve the ultimate objective of price stability. This is a valid public interest of the Union, cf. Article 127 (2), second indent, TFEU.[112] According to the settled case-law of the ECJ, the principle of proportionality requires that the acts in question are appropriate for attaining the legitimate objectives pursued and do not go beyond what is necessary in order to achieve those objectives.[113] In this regard, one could argue that applying the NIRP on central bank digital currency is appropriate for safeguarding the effectiveness of monetary policy because the current monetary policy strongly depends on the compliance of the financial intermediaries involved. With the NIRP, the central bank could directly influence the households and firms and thus achieve a stronger

---

107 Ziniel (2019), para. 40; Heselhaus (2020), para. 60; Frenz (2009), para. 2897.

108 Joint cases C-402/05 P and C-415/05 P *Kadi* ECLI:EU:C:2008:461, para. 358; Frenz (2009), para. 2905.

109 Strobel (2021), p. 558; Huber (2018), p. 231; Kirchhof (2021), pp. 176, 189.

110 Ziniel (2019), para. 42; Heselhaus (2020), para. 70.

111 Cf. case C-235/17 *Commission/Hungary* ECLI:EU:C:2019:432, para. 89.

112 Cf. also Eibl (2020), pp. 400 ff.

113 Case C-62/14 *Gauweiler* ECLI:EU:C:2015:400, para. 67.

pass-through of monetary policy impulses. However, it appears questionable whether applying the NIRP on central bank digital currency is necessary to safeguard the effectiveness of monetary policy. As already mentioned, due to several limits, the NIRP could only apply to a limited amount of central bank digital currency in circulation. The central banks would still need to rely on the bank-intermediated pass-through. For the remaining amount of central bank digital currency, the measure in questions does not weigh very heavily because it is possible for end-users to avoid negative interest rates and shift their currency units to cash.[114]

Furthermore, to be justified, the regulation of the use of property must be established by law.[115] On could consider to use Article 12.1 (1), second sentence, ESCB Statute. In this regard, the remuneration rate for central bank digital currency could be seen as a key interest rate next to the deposit facility rate, the marginal lending facility rate, the main refinancing operations rate and the (zero-per-cent) rate on banknotes. However, when the provision of the ESCB Statute in question was drafted, the contracting parties did not have in mind that such a key interest rate could be directly applied to the general public. From a point of view of a theory of democracy, one could also argue that a regulation or directive would be necessary to enable the ECB to use negative interest rates on the broad public.[116]

Although applying the NIRP on central bank digital currency appears legally possible, one should take into account the following. Applying a negative interest rate on an official currency that is broadly accessible by the public and aims at a wide-spread use can be counterproductive. Furthermore, the image of the central bank could be affected if the general public perceives the central bank as 'depriving' it of their money, especially in times of rapid changes in the economy.[117] Hence, from a policy point of view, it should be carefully considered whether applying (negative) interest rates on central bank digital currency really appears necessary for monetary policy objectives.[118]

9.2.2.3 Follow-up: Remuneration for Financial Stability

These considerations regarding the use of remuneration for monetary policy objectives also force to consider the usage of remuneration for preventing financial instability. As explained above, one could apply a tiered remuneration system with possibly negative interest rates for large holdings above a certain threshold. Again, this can be considered as a regulation of the use of property in the meaning of Article 17 (1), third sentence, CFR. Preserving the financial stability would be a key general interest. However, here the principle of proportionality seems to set stricter limits

[114]Cf. Strobel (2021), p. 558.

[115]Ziniel (2019), para. 43.

[116]Cf. Frenz (2009), para. 2913.

[117]Bindseil and Panetta (2020).

[118]Cf. in this direction Bindseil and Panetta (2020); Panetta (2022b).

than for monetary policy. First, as already discussed,[119] it can be doubted whether a (negative) remuneration of central bank digital currency is appropriate to achieve financial stability. Second, there are other means such as (holding, transaction, convertibility) limits to achieve the object of financial stability as well.[120] Hence, applying (negative) interest rates does not seem necessary to achieve the objective pursued and could be regarded as a violation of the principle of proportionality. Besides this legal issue, the policy aspect of negative interest rates also comes into play here. The general public opinion would not distinguish between negative interest rates for monetary policy or financial stability reasons. In both cases the central bank would be regarded as 'depriving' the owners of their money. This could hamper the confidence of the public and the overall acceptance of the central bank.

9.3 Summary

As set out in this section, the impact of central bank digital currency on monetary policy is manifold. One the one hand, it could both strengthen and weaken the monetary policy transmission pass-through. On the other hand, although central bank digital currency would perhaps not alter the implementation of monetary policy in general, applying price rules to it as part of ECB's monetary policy competence raises economic, legal and political concerns and needs to be carefully considered. Lastly, the additional benefits of using remuneration for central bank digital currency as a new key interest rate are too opaque to finally proclaim central bank digital currency as a new monetary policy instrument.

References

Armelius H et al (2018) The e-krona and the macroeconomy. Sveriges Riksbank Economic Review. special issue on the e-krona 2018(3):43–65. https://www.riksbank.se/globalassets/media/rapporter/pov/engelska/2018/economic-review-3-2018.pdf. Accessed 31 July 2023

Bank of England (1999) The transmission mechanism of monetary policy. Quarterly Bulletin June. https://www.bankofengland.co.uk/quarterly-bulletin/1999/q2/the-transmission-mechanism-of-monetary-policy. Accessed 31 July 2023

Barrdear J, Kumhof M (2016) The macroeconomics of central bank issued digital currencies. Bank of England Staff Working Paper No. 605. https://www.bankofengland.co.uk/working-paper/2016/the-macroeconomics-of-central-bank-issued-digital-currencies. Accessed 31 July 2023

Berentsen A, Schär F (2018) The case for central bank electronic money and the non-case for central bank cryptocurrencies. Federal Reserve Bank of St. Louis Review, Second Quarter 2018, 100(2):97–106. https://doi.org/10.20955/r.2018.97-106

[119] See Sect. 8.3.1.

[120] Cf. also Bindseil and Panetta (2020).

Bindseil U (2014) Monetary policy operations and the financial system. Oxford
Bindseil U (2020) Tiered CBDC and the financial system. ECB Working Paper Series No. 2351. https://www.ecb.europa.eu/pub/pdf/scpwps/ecb.wp2351~c8c18bbd60.en.pdf. Accessed 31 July 2023
Bindseil U, Panetta F (2020) Central bank digital currency remuneration in a world with low or negative nominal interest rates. VoxEU, 5 October 2020. https://cepr.org/voxeu/columns/central-bank-digital-currency-remuneration-world-low-or-negative-nominal-interest. Accessed 31 July 2023
Bindseil U, Panetta F, Terol I (2021) Central bank digital currency: functional scope, pricing and controls. Occasional Paper Series No. 286. https://www.ecb.europa.eu/pub/pdf/scpops/ecb.op286~9d472374ea.en.pdf. Accessed 31 July 2023
Calliess (2022) Art. 17 GRC. In: Calliess C, Ruffert M (eds) EUV/AEUV Kommentar, 6th edn. Beck, München
Cœuré B (2018) The future of central bank money. Speech at the International Center for Monetary and Banking Studies Geneva, 14.05.2018. https://www.ecb.europa.eu/press/key/date/2018/html/ecb.sp180514_4.en.html. Accessed 31 July 2023
CPMI-MC (2018) Central bank digital currencies. https://www.bis.org/cpmi/publ/d174.pdf. Accessed 31 July 2023
Deutsche Bundesbank (2019) Monatsbericht April. https://www.bundesbank.de/de/publikationen/berichte/monatsberichte/monatsbericht-april-2019-793790. Accessed 31 July 2023
ECB (2011) The monetary policy of the ECB. https://www.ecb.europa.eu/pub/pdf/other/monetarypolicy2011en.pdf. Accessed 31 July 2023
ECB (2020) Report on a digital euro. https://www.ecb.europa.eu/pub/pdf/other/Report_on_a_digital_euro~4d7268b458.en.pdf. Accessed 31 July 2023
Eibl J (2020) Privatheit durch Bargeld? Mohr Siebeck, Tübingen
Frenz W (2009) Handbuch Europarecht, vol 4. Springer, Berlin and Heidelberg. https://doi.org/10.1007/978-3-540-31117-1
Görgens E et al (2013) Europäische Geldpolitik, 6th edn. UTB, München
Hanl A, Michaelis J (2019) Digitales Zentralbankgeld als neues Instrument der Geldpolitik, MAGKS Joint Discussion Paper Series in Economics, No. 09-2019
Heselhaus (2020) § 36. In: Heselhaus S, Nowak C (eds) Handbuch der Europäischen Grundrechte, 2nd edn. Beck, München
Holtemöller O (2008) Geldtheorie und Geldpolitik. Mohr Siebeck, Tübingen
Hua Jiang J, Zhu Y (2021) Monetary policy pass-through with central bank digital currency. Bank of Canada Staff Working Paper 2021-10. https://www.bankofcanada.ca/2021/03/staff-working-paper-2021-10/. Accessed 31 July 2023
Huber J (2018) Monetäre Souveränität. Metropolis-Verlag, Marburg
Jarass (2021) Art. 17 GRC. In: Jarass H (ed) Charta der Grundrechte der EU, 4th edn. Beck, München
Kirchhof P (2021) Geld im Sog der Negativzinsen. Beck, München
Kumhof M, Noone C (2018) Central bank digital currencies – design principles and balance sheet implications. Bank of England Staff Working Paper No. 275. https://www.bankofengland.co.uk/working-paper/2018/central-bank-digital-currencies%2D%2D-design-principles-and-balance-sheet-implications. Accessed 31 July 2023
Lastra, Psaroudakis (2020) Prudential supervisory tasks. In: Amtenbrink F, Herrmann C (eds) The EU law of economic and monetary union. Oxford
Mancini-Griffoli T et al (2018) Casting light on central bank digital currency. Staff Discussion Note No. 18/08. https://www.imf.org/en/Publications/Staff-Discussion-Notes/Issues/2018/11/13/Casting-Light-on-Central-Bank-Digital-Currencies-46233. Accessed 31 July 2023
Meaning J et al (2018) Broadening narrow money: monetary policy with a central bank digital currency. Bank of England Staff Working Paper No. 724. https://www.bankofengland.co.uk/working-paper/2018/broadening-narrow-money-monetary-policy-with-a-central-bank-digital-currency. Accessed 31 July 2023

Nessén M, Sellin P, Åsberg Sommar P (2018) The implications of an E-krona for the Riksbank's operational framework for implementing monetary policy. Sveriges Riksbank Economic Review: special issue on the e-krona 2018(3):29–42. https://www.riksbank.se/globalassets/media/rapporter/pov/engelska/2018/economic-review-3-2018.pdf. Accessed 31 July 2023

Ohler C (2015) Bankenaufsicht und Geldpolitik in der Währungsunion, § 3. Beck, München

Ohler C (2021) Unkonventionelle Geldpolitik. Mohr Siebeck, Tübingen

Panetta F (2018) 21st century cash: central banking, technological innovation and digital currencies. SUERF Policy Note No. 40. https://www.suerf.org/policynotes/3251/21st-century-cash-central-banking-technological-innovation-and-digital-currencies. Accessed 31 July 2023

Panetta F (2022a) The digital euro and the evolution of the financial system. Introductory statement at the Committee on Economic and Monetary Affairs of the European Parliament, 15.06.2022. https://www.ecb.europa.eu/press/key/date/2022/html/ecb.sp220615~0b859eb8bc.en.html. Accessed 31 July 2023

Panetta F (2022b) More than an intellectual game: exploring the monetary policy and financial stability implications of central bank digital currencies. Opening speech at the IESE Business School Banking Initiative Conference on Technology and Finance, 08.04.2022. https://www.ecb.europa.eu/press/key/date/2022/html/ecb.sp220408~980e39957b.en.html. Accessed 31 July 2023

Strobel B (2021) Digitaler Euro? – Ein Überblick über die rechtlichen und wirtschaftlichen Fragen. BKR 2021:556–561

Tuori (2020) Monetary policy. In: Amtenbrink F, Herrmann C (eds) The EU law of economic and monetary union. Oxford

Ziniel (2019) Art. 17 GRC. In: Holoubek M, Lienbacher G (eds) GRC-Kommentar, 2nd edn. Manz, Wien

Part IV
Conclusion

Chapter 10
A Milestone in the History of Means of Payment

Abstract This chapter summarises the main findings of the book and provides concise answers to the key questions related to central bank digital currency. With the international dimension of the digital euro in particular and CBDC in general, the chapter shows an area that has not been discussed in the book and leaves room for further academic research.

The discussion on establishing central bank digital currency arose in a time where the current system of (public) money was put under pressure by the emergence of private and foreign innovative means of payment. To face this danger to the monetary and political sovereignty, numerous central banks across several jurisdictions worked on a solution to push ahead full speed. However, the depth of the associated technical, legal, economic and political problems is becoming apparent only gradually. And still, there is great uncertainty. Central bank digital currency is a moving target with a lot of ongoing work. Various actors stemming from the private and the public sector are involved in the development. Several concerns were expressed: Will CBDC lead to public surveillance of the citizens? Will it impair the business model of the financial intermediaries? Will it even work? But the most important question is: What will be the additional value of CBDC?

This book aimed at answering some of these questions by providing background information as well as in-depth analyses. Over the course of the book, it has become clear that the final use case of CBDC in practice will largely depend on its design and whether it is inclusive and easy to handle. In this regard, the book concluded that it seems likely to issue and distribute the CBDC using both the central banks as well as the financial intermediaries, who will form a public-private-partnership. Furthermore, the technology underlying CBDC can be a combination of traditional technologies and innovative technologies, such as the distributed ledger technology. In this regard, the innovation CBDC poses is to further examine whether settlement systems based on the distributed ledger technology can be developed as well. Moreover, CBDC is likely to have at least two functionalities that enable the end-users to use it for online and offline payments.

It has been shown that CBDC and the digital euro in particular poses a variety of fundamental legal and economic questions. To fully grasp the dimension, the book

L. Kriese, *Central Bank Digital Currency*,
https://doi.org/10.1007/978-3-031-44738-9_10

often distinguished between the two manifestations of the digital euro. While the account-based manifestation of CBDC faces less uncertainties, the manifestation as a bearer-instrument challenges the current technical and legal order. The digital euro as a bearer-instrument faces numerous difficulties such as the double-spending problem for consecutive offline payments, the treatment under civil law and the anti-money laundering framework and the application of limits for safeguarding financial stability. When enquiring these problematic issues, the book followed an inductive method and partly used the existing academic and legislative treatment of crypto-assets. However, it has been shown that the topic results to be too complex to be covered by the existing legal and technical order. To adequately tackle these challenges, it is necessary that the public and private parties involved combine their knowledge and jointly work together. However, due to the fact that the digital euro poses fairly new questions of widespread reach, the book concluded that the basic decisions need to be taken by the EU co-legislators whereas the European Central Bank uses mostly its technical expertise to foster the development of a digital euro. In some cases, this requires comprehensive legislative action by amending the current legal framework or even introducing new legal provisions. Furthermore, establishing the digital euro also touches upon existing areas which need to be looked at as well for consistency, such as the legal tender of euro cash.

An area that has not been discussed in this book is the international dimension of the digital euro. The international dimension poses new challenges and adds an additional layer to the existing challenges. Should the digital euro be used in the non-euro area as well? Shall visitors to the euro area be granted access to the digital euro? How will this impact the economy and financial stability of the countries in and outside the euro area? What impact will an international use have on the balance sheet of the Eurosystem and the ability to conduct monetary policy? How can one make sure that the requirements set for data protection and financial stability are respected abroad? How will an international use change the role of the (digital) euro compared to other major currencies? Could the factual 'euroisation' in non-euro area countries circumvent the convergence criteria laid down in Article 140 TFEU? Furthermore, how can different CBDCs across different jurisdictions be used without friction (so-called interoperability)? In this regard, the book leaves room for further academic research.[1]

Hence, central bank digital currency is a sophisticated topic in many areas. To fully grasp it in every detail proves to be a mammoth task. However, many experts with high expertise are tasked with examining the optimal choice for the technical, legal and economic challenges. This also contains to vividly explain the additional value CBDC has for the public and to clear up the prejudices à la Orwellian dystopia. If the right course is set here, CBDC and the digital euro have the potential to become a milestone in the history of means of payment.

[1]See for e.g. Ferrari Minesso et al. (2022), pp. 54 ff.; Pfister (2020), p. 41; Papaschalis (2022), pp. 117 ff.; Grünewald (2022), pp. 127 ff.

References

Ferrari Minesso M, Mehl A, Stracca L (2022) Central bank digital currency in an open economy. J Monet Econ 127:54–68. https://doi.org/10.1016/j.jmoneco.2022.02.001

Grünewald S (2022) Legal interoperability of the digital euro: prospects and challenges. In: ESCB Legal Conference 2022. https://www.ecb.europa.eu/pub/pdf/other/ecb.escblegalconferenceproceedings2022~1646d63f3e.en.pdf?08c4311f6b5f39ecf6e6a188cc55c06d. Accessed 31 July 2023

Papaschalis (2022) Legal interoperability of retail CBDCs: initial considerations. In: ESCB Legal Conference 2022. https://www.ecb.europa.eu/pub/pdf/other/ecb.escblegalconferenceproceedings2022~1646d63f3e.en.pdf?08c4311f6b5f39ecf6e6a188cc55c06d. Accessed 31 July 2023

Pfister C (2020) Central bank digital currency. https://publications.banque-france.fr/en/central-bank-digital-currency. Accessed 31 July 2023

Appendix: Draft Proposal for a Regulation on the Digital Euro

REGULATION OF THE EUROPEAN PARLIAMENT AND OF THE COUNCIL
on establishing and regulating a digital euro

(Text with EEA relevance)

THE EUROPEAN PARLIAMENT AND THE COUNCIL OF THE EUROPEAN UNION –
Having regard to the Treaty on the Functioning of the European Union, and in particular Article 133 thereof,

Having regard to the proposal from the European Commission,

After transmission of the draft legislative act to the national parliaments,

Having regard to the opinion of the European Central Bank,

Having regard to the opinion of the European Economic and Social Committee,

Acting in accordance with the ordinary legislative procedure,

HAVE ADOPTED THIS REGULATION:

TITLE I
General provisions

Article 1
Subject matter

This Regulation establishes the digital euro and regulates its essential aspects within the competence of the European Union for monetary policy.

L. Kriese, *Central Bank Digital Currency*,
https://doi.org/10.1007/978-3-031-44738-9

Article 2
Scope

(1) This Regulation regulates the following essential aspects:
    (a) The role of financial intermediaries in distributing the digital euro
    (b) The legal tender status of the digital euro
    (c) The position of the digital euro in civil law
    (d) Data-protection and anti-money laundering requirements governing the digital euro
    (e) The tools that may be implemented for limiting the use of the digital euro as a store of value
(2) Within the framework of this Regulation, the European Central Bank may decide within in its own competences in the field of monetary policy on the following:
    (a) The specific technical design of the digital euro
    (b) The implementation of tools limiting the use of the digital euro as a store of value
    (c) The implementation of instruments applying to the digital euro for conducting monetary policy

Article 3
Definitions

For the purposes of this Regulation, the following definitions apply:

1. 'digital euro' means a digital representation of currency units denominated in euro that can be transferred or stored with the use of the distributed ledger technology or a similar technology and is issued by the European Central Bank or the national central banks when acting in their capacity as monetary authority or other public authorities;
2. 'distributed ledger technology' or 'DLT' means a type of technology that supports the distributed recording of encrypted data;
3. 'digital euro as a bearer-instrument' means a functionality that, using a hardware-based bearer instrument, allows a number of near-field transactions to be carried out directly between the parties to the transaction without the need for an intermediating third party to validate the transaction, and which does not require connection to a network;
4. 'hardware-based bearer instrument' means a physical medium for the use of and access to the units of the digital euro, such as a payment card, a mobile phone or any other technical device equipped with a counterfeit-proof software recognised by a central bank of the European System of Central Banks;
5. 'account-based digital euro' means a functionality that allows for transactions to be carried out without the parties to the transaction being physically present by using third-party financial intermediaries and a connection to a network;
6. 'financial intermediary' means an entity that provides financial services and acts between a central bank and the end-user of the digital euro

Article 4
Issuance

The European Central Bank shall have the exclusive right to decide on the amount and the timing of the issuance of the digital euro and to authorise the issuance within the European Union.

TITLE II
Distribution and Functionalities

Article 5
Functionalities

The digital euro shall be usable both as a bearer-instrument and as account-based.

Article 6
Distribution

(1) The digital euro shall be distributed by all payment service providers authorised and supervised under Directive 2015/2366 and by all crypto-asset service providers authorised and supervised under the Regulation on Markets in Crypto assets.
(2) The distribution consists of the following services:
  (a) Enabling users to get access to digital euro holdings
  (b) Enabling users to transfer and receive the digital euro as means of payment
  (c) Providing users with the necessary payment instruments
  (d) Maintaining the payment instruments
  (e) Linking the digital euro holding of the user with another payment account in the meaning of Article 2 (3) of Directive 2014/92/EU of the user at the request of the user

Article 7
Legal framework

The digital euro shall be regarded as 'fund' within the meaning of Article 4 No. 25 of Directive 2015/2366 and Article 2 (22) of Directive 2014/92/EU.

TITLE III
Usability

Chapter 1
Legal tender

Article 8
Legal tender status

(1) The digital euro shall have the status as legal tender within the Union.
(2) A payment with a digital euro that has legal tender status cannot be refused in the settlement of a debt denominated in euro at its full face-value and has the effect of discharging the debt.

Article 9
Exemptions from mandatory acceptance

(1) By derogation from the second paragraph of Article 8 of this Regulation, the following persons and entities are not obliged to accept a payment made with a digital euro:
  (a) Natural persons that interact on a private basis;
  (b) Legal entities that generally do not accept digital or electronic means of payment;
  (c) Public authorities of the Member States if the law of the respective Member State explicitly allows the authority to refuse payments made in euro-denominated banknotes and coins;
  (d) Legal entities designated by the Commission after an assessment of the digital euro carried out in accordance with Article 21 of this Regulation.
(2) [1]The exemptions from mandatory acceptance made in paragraph one of this Article shall last three years, beginning from the first issuance of the digital euro. [2]This duration can be prolonged by the Commission at any time for another period of three years.
(3) Excluding the obligation to accept a payment made in digital euro in general terms and conditions is prohibited for persons and entities that are not listed in paragraph one of this Article.

Chapter 2
Civil law

Article 10
Legal nature

The digital euro shall confer on its holder the exclusive right to use it and to prevent any third party not having his consent from using it.

Article 11
Change of ownership

(1) [1]The right to a digital euro may be transferred to others. [2]For a digital euro as a bearer-instrument this shall be done by transferring the digital euro or by transferring the hardware-based bearer-instrument. [3]The right to a digital euro

cannot be transferred by disclosing the technical access requirements for it to the recipient.

(2) The transfer of the digital euro shall require that the holder and the acquirer agree on the change of ownership and that a transcription is made in favour of the acquirer in the technical medium of record in which the issuer makes a technical note of the issue.

(3) The transfer of the hardware-based bearer-instrument shall be governed by the rules of the Member States applicable to the transfer of tangible movable goods.

Article 12

Bona fide acquisition and expiration of third party's rights

(1) [1]By virtue of a transfer effected in accordance with Article 11 using the digital euro as a bearer-instrument, the transferee shall become the new owner even if the transferor is not the owner of the digital euro or of the hardware-based bearer-instrument, unless he is not in good faith at the time when he would acquire ownership under those provisions. [2]The acquirer shall not be in good faith if he knows or is unaware as a result of gross negligence that the transferor is not the owner of the digital euro or the hardware-based bearer-instrument.

(2) [1]The acquisition of ownership on the basis of the first paragraph of this Article shall also occur if the digital euro or the hardware-based bearer-instrument had been stolen from the owner, had been lost or had otherwise gone astray. [2]This shall be without prejudice to claims for restitution arising from other provisions of the law of the Member States. [3]Member States shall be free to enact further claims for restitution within the meaning of sentence 2 in the cases referred to in sentence 1.

(3) [1]If a digital euro or the hardware-based bearer-instrument transferred in accordance with Article 11 of this Article is encumbered with the right of a third party, the right shall expire upon the acquisition of ownership. [2]This shall not apply if the acquirer is not in good faith with respect to the right at the relevant time in accordance with sentence 1.

Article 13

Rights in rem

(1) The right to a digital euro may be the subject of rights *in rem*, in particular a lien.

(2) The creation of a right *in rem* shall be governed by the applicable rules of the Member States.

Article 14

Compulsory enforcement

(1) [1]The right to a digital euro may be levied in execution. [2]The admissibility of the compulsory enforcement against this right shall be governed by the general rules of the Member States.
(2) The compulsory enforcement for monetary claims shall take place against the digital euro or against the hardware-based bearer-instrument.
(3) [1]The compulsory enforcement of the digital euro shall be governed by the rules of the Member States applicable to the attachment of claims. [2]In order to ensure the feasibility of the compulsory enforcement, the official organ competent for the compulsory enforcement under the national rules is entitled to obtain the factual power of disposal over the seized units of the digital euro for realisation. [3]The debtor is obliged to cooperate in this. [4]The provisions of the Member States applicable to the enforcement of obligations to cooperate in the compulsory enforcement proceedings shall apply to the debtor's duty to cooperate under sentence 3.
(4) The compulsory enforcement against the hardware-based bearer-instrument shall be governed by the rules of the Member States applicable to the compulsory enforcement against movable tangible property.

Article 15
Protection

[1]The owner of the right to a digital euro shall be entitled to the rights of protection applicable to an owner of property under the rules of the Member States. [2]The claims for restitution shall be limited to a sum-based restitution unless the owner proves a special interest in the specific units of the digital euro.

Chapter 3
Limits to the use as store of value

Article 16
Limits

(1) Under the conditions set out in Article 17 of this Regulation, the European Central Bank may decide to apply the following instruments to limit the use of the digital euro as store of value:
    (a) Remunerating digital euro holdings
    (b) Limiting the amount held by a user of the digital euro
    (c) Limiting the amount of digital euro that can be transferred by a user in a period
    (d) Limiting the convertibility from the digital euro to other means of payment
(2) The European Central Bank may also decide to combine the instruments laid down in the first paragraph of this Article.

Article 17
Conditions

(1) The use of the instruments set out in Article 16 shall aim at the safeguarding of financial stability and financial intermediation and shall respect the principle of proportionality.
(2) The instruments shall be implemented in a preventive manner.
(3) The implementation and application of the instruments shall take place in accordance with the respective economic environment.
(4) Without prejudice to the competences of the European Central Bank in monetary policy, remunerating digital euro holdings shall exclude the use of negative interest rates with the aim to safeguard financial stability and financial intermediation.
(5) The European Central Bank shall calibrate the instruments laid out in (b), (c) and (d) of paragraph one of Article 16 with respect to the economic needs of the following groups:
   (a) Individuals
   (b) Legal entities that trade goods and services
(6) The instrument laid down in (d) of paragraph one of Article 16 shall only be applied for a pre-defined period of time.

TITLE IV
Data protection and Anti-money laundering

Article 18
Legal framework

(1) The processing of data related to the use of the digital euro conferred on the European Central Bank and the financial intermediaries mentioned in paragraph one of Article 6 of this Regulation is necessary to prevent money laundering and terrorist financing.
(2) In accordance with Article 5 of the Regulation 2016/679 the European Central Bank and the financial intermediaries mentioned in paragraph one of Article 6 of this Regulation shall only process the personal data that is necessary to fulfil the tasks conferred up on by this Regulation or other Union or national law.
(3) To ensure the condition laid down in paragraph 2 of this Article, the European Central Bank shall apply privacy-enhancing techniques in the technical design of the digital euro.

Article 19
Low-value payments

(1) [1]Low-value payments with an account-based digital euro shall be identified as area of low risk to money laundering and terrorist financing in the meaning

of Article 15 (1) of Directive (EU) 2015/849. [2]A low-value payment within the meaning of sentence one is a payment that does not exceed the amount of EUR 1.000.

(2) No due diligence measures within the meaning of Article 13 of Directive (EU) 2015/849 shall apply to a payment that is made with a digital euro as a bearer-instrument and that does not exceed the amount of EUR 150.

TITLE V
Reporting and Assessment

Article 20
Reporting obligation

Every three years, beginning from the first issuance of the digital euro, the European Central Bank shall submit to the European Parliament, to the Council and to the Commission a report on:

(a) The selection and use of any instruments to limit the use of the digital euro as store of value pursuant to Article 16 and how the criteria laid down in Article 17 are met
(b) The use and development of privacy-enhancing techniques pursuant to Article 18

Article 21
Review and Assessment

(1) By three years from the date of application of this Regulation, and every three years thereafter, the Commission shall present a report to the European Parliament and to the Council on the application of this Regulation, accompanied where appropriate by proposals for a revision of this Regulation.
(2) The report shall pay special attention to the following:
    (a) The exemptions from mandatory acceptance made in paragraph one of Article 9
    (b) The decision to prolong the exemptions from mandatory acceptance pursuant to paragraph two of Article 9
    (c) The classification of low-value payments as low-risk areas pursuant to paragraph one of Article 19 and the limit for low-value payments set therein
    (d) The potential risks the treatment of the digital euro as a bearer-instrument under paragraph two of Article 19 poses for money laundering and terrorist financing

GPSR Compliance

The European Union's (EU) General Product Safety Regulation (GPSR) is a set of rules that requires consumer products to be safe and our obligations to ensure this.

If you have any concerns about our products, you can contact us on ProductSafety@springernature.com

In case Publisher is established outside the EU, the EU authorized representative is:

Springer Nature Customer Service Center GmbH
Europaplatz 3
69115 Heidelberg, Germany

Batch number: 10726135

Printed by Printforce, the Netherlands